Domine Deus
Amazing Grace

The Jew in the Lotus

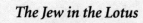

The Jew in the Lotus

A Poet's Rediscovery of Jewish Identity in Buddhist India

Rodger Kamenetz

HarperOne
An Imprint of HarperCollinsPublishers

HarperOne

HarperCollins books may be purchased for educational, business, or sales promotional use. For information, please e-mail the Special Markets Department at SPsales@harpercollins.com.

HarperCollins Web site: http://www.harpercollins.com

HarperCollins®, 📖®, and HarperOne™ are trademarks of HarperCollins Publishers.

FIRST HARPERCOLLINS PAPERBACK EDITION PUBLISHED IN 1995
ISBN: 978–0–06–136739–7

Library of Congress Cataloging-in-Publication Data is available.

An Earlier Edition of This Book Was Cataloged As Follows:
Kamenetz, Rodger.
　The Jew in the lotus : a poet's rediscovery of Jewish identity in Buddhist India / Rodger Kamenetz.
　　p. cm.
　ISBN: 0–06–064576–8 (cloth : alk. paper)
　　　1. Buddhism—Relations—Judaism.　　2. Judaism—Relations—Buddhism.
　3. Dialogue—Religious aspects—Buddhism. 4. Dialogue—Religious Aspects—Judaism. 5. Buddhist converts from Judaism. 6. Kamenetz, Rodger—Religion.
　7. Kamenetz, Rodger—Journeys—India—Dharmsala. 8. Dharmsala (India)—Religious life and customs. I. Title.
BQ4610.J8K36 1994
296.3'872—dc20　　　　　　　　　　　　　　　　　　　　　93–34477

18 19 20 LSC(H) 10 9

For Mo, kindness on her tongue
For Anya and for Kezia, my daughters and my joy

Contents

Acknowledgments

My deep thanks to Dr. Marc Lieberman, for bringing the dialogue together, and for asking me along. His intelligence, energy, innate kindness, and deep fund of knowledge are valuable in themselves, but I especially treasure them in my longtime friend.

Thanks too to all the participants who were generous with their time and themselves, both in Dharamsala and since. Dr. Nathan Katz, Rabbi Joy Levitt, Dr. Marc Lieberman, Dr. Blu Greenberg, Dr. Moshe Waldoks, Rabbi Jonathan Omer-Man, and Rabbi Zalman Schachter-Shalomi gave generous postdialogue interviews and shared with me photographs, documents, tape recordings, and videotapes. Special thanks to my fellow reporter, Shoshana Edelberg. I am also grateful for interviews and conversations with Rabbi Irving Greenberg, Michael Sautman, Marc Lieberman, Joseph Goldstein, Rabbi David Wolfe-Blank, Rabbi Leah Novick, Joseph Mark Cohen, Greg Burton, Robert Esformes, Andy Gold, Nancy Garfield, Rabbi Paul Caplan, and Dr. Arthur Waskow. Elie Wiesel was kind enough to share a few anecdotes with me that were of great help.

Several Western Buddhists were very generous with their time, Ven. Thubten Pemo, Dr. Alex Birzen, Ruth Sonam. I want to particularly thank Ven. Thubten Chodron for a lengthy interview at my home.

Also gracious in providing time for an interview was David Rome. I want to thank Allen Ginsberg for taking time from his busy schedule for our interview sessions. I also want to thank Ram Dass for a very generous and stimulating interview.

While working on this book I've had the opportunity to consult informally with a number of Buddhist scholars and practitioners on the computer net—thank you denizens of Buddha-L and BUDDHIST for your generosity, especially Dr. Richard Hayes and Dr. Robin Kornman, for your clarifications. Any errors in either Jewish or Buddhist doctrines are all my responsibility.

Of my Tibetan friends, I want to thank Laktor, our able translator; Karma Gelek, our official host in Dharamsala; and Rinchen Choegyal and Tenzin Choegyal, our hosts at Kashmir Cottage for their many kindnesses. Getting to know Tibetan people has been a wonderful bonus of this work. I want to remember as well the late Geshe Khenrab of Montreal for his insights and generosity. I am immensely grateful for the opportunity and privilege of having met with His Holiness the Dalai Lama.

Most of all I owe a debt of gratitude to Mr. Charles Halpern, who urged this project upon me with gentle persistence.

During the time I worked on this book, I received generous financial assistance from the Nathan Cummings Foundation, from the National Endowment for the Arts, from the Louisiana State Arts Council, and from the College of Arts and Sciences of Louisiana State University. I thank all of these institutions. I especially acknowledge the assistance of Patricia Cummings and the Nama Rupa Foundation for the use of a transcript of all the Jewish dialogues with the Dalai Lama.

My warm thanks to Luann Rouff, who shepherded me through the transformation of manuscript to book and answered my many questions, and to Laurie McGee and Dahlia Armon, whose copyediting and proofreading were extremely helpful. Thanks too to Rachel Lehmann-Haupt for her time and energy. And to my agent, Katinka Matson; my editor, Amy Hertz; and all the professional staff at Harper San Francisco who have helped in so many ways—thank-you so much.

Introduction

In late October 1990, I traveled to Dharamsala, a remote hill town in northern India. I came to write about a religious dialogue between a group of Jewish delegates and the XIV Dalai Lama of Tibet.

I was looking forward to this trip. I'd never been to India and the idea of shlepping mezuzahs and matzahs through remote corners of the Punjab appealed to me. I also thought I would learn a lot. I'd written about Jewish life before, but I had little knowledge of Buddhism. And though in recent years I'd become increasingly aware of the Dalai Lama's activities, as a personage in my consciousness, he seemed as fabulous as the Unicorn.

Before I left the United States, I studied the modern history of Tibet. Her great national tragedy began with the Chinese Army occupation in 1950, which overturned centuries of mutual nonbelligerence. Years of empty negotiations followed between Tibetan and Chinese officials. Finally in March 1959 a dramatic uprising against Chinese rule broke out in Lhasa, the capital. Feeling the Dalai Lama's life was in danger, ordinary Tibetans surrounded his palace. Hoping to avert bloodshed, he fled to India. He has been joined in exile by more than 115,000 refugees. In that terrible month alone, Chinese soldiers killed 87,000 Tibetans in Lhasa. Since then the Chinese have continued a systematic effort to destroy Tibetan resistance. One out of ten Tibetans has been held in prisons or forced labor camps for ten years or more. The Chinese People's Liberation Army (PLA) has repeatedly fired on unarmed Tibetan demonstrators. All told, an estimated 1.2 million Tibetans have died as a result of the occupation.

Destroying Tibet's religion has been a key Chinese policy. Public teaching of Buddhism is forbidden. Monks and nuns have been singled out for public humiliation and torture. Temples have been used for granaries and monasteries for machine shops. The huge Ganden monastery in Lhasa, once the world's third largest, has been reduced to a heap of rubble. The Chinese forces have systematically pillaged and then razed more than 6,000 Buddhist monasteries.

The Tibetans have lost their land, their temples, their leading religious teachers. And now they risk losing their identity as a people altogether. The Beijing government, by encouraging a massive influx into Tibet of Han Chinese settlers, is perpetrating a slow-motion genocide that escapes the notice of most of the planet. Today, in Lhasa, the ethnic Chinese outnumber the native Tibetans.

To anyone conscious of Jewish history, parallels to the Tibetan situation leap to mind. As Rabbi Irving "Yitz" Greenberg, a member of our delegation to Dharamsala, wrote, "This is what the destruction of the Temple must have been like in Jewish history." He referred to events two thousand years ago, when the Romans destroyed Jerusalem and expelled the Jewish people from their spiritual homeland, beginning nineteen centuries of exile and dispersion. Rabbi Lawrence Kushner made a different parallel when he told the Dalai Lama in 1989, "The Chinese came to your people as the Germans came to ours."

Faced with the destruction of his people and their tradition of Buddhism, the Dalai Lama has been tireless in his efforts to bring freedom to Tibet. Restricted in travel by his Indian hosts and by difficulties obtaining a visa, he was not able to come to the United States until 1979. But since then, through personal appearances, and dialogue with religious and political leaders, he has gained increasing respect and notice for the Tibetan cause. In 1989, the same year he was awarded the Nobel Peace Prize for his nonviolent efforts, the Dalai Lama turned for the first time to the Jewish people for help. "Tell me your secret," he said, "the secret of Jewish spiritual survival in exile."

As my grandfather might have said, Who would have thought to ask?

Jews have survived twenty centuries of exile and dispersion, persecution and vilification, economic hardship, expulsion, forced conversion, Crusades, Inquisition, blood libel, pogrom—you name it, Jews survived it. But up until now few outsiders have ever looked upon this as much of an accomplishment.

In the Dalai Lama's eyes, and to many of the Tibetans, Jews are survival experts. The idea that Jewish history, with all its traumas, is relevant to another exiled people was inspiring.

But another attraction to Dharamsala was equally important. This dialogue would be an unprecedented meeting of two ancient religious traditions, an opportunity for leading religious Jews to immerse themselves in a living Buddhist community—that had never happened, as far as we knew, in thousands of years of Jewish and Buddhist history.

The Dalai Lama is not only the head of the leading sect of Tibetan Buddhism, but its most innovative thinker. In exile, he has carefully directed the preservation of the spiritual treasures of the Tibetan people. Dharamsala itself, though a small town, has an extraordinary number of learned monks, abbots, and Buddhist sages and is a worldwide center for Buddhist study. The Dalai Lama is considered a spiritual master by most of the world's Buddhists.

Another important feature of the dialogue was the Dalai Lama's request for teaching about kabbalah and Jewish meditation. And he in turn would respond to questions about Buddhist esoteric teachings and practices. This exchange of secrets proved to be even more powerful and fascinating than I could have imagined when I set out. The exploration of Buddhist tantra and Jewish kabbalah opened me to whole new ways of thinking and feeling.

The main organizers of the encounter in Dharamsala were two American Buddhists from Jewish backgrounds. And they in turn represented another important aspect of this dialogue. Over the past twenty years, many spiritually curious Jews have explored Buddhist teachings, and some have left Judaism altogether. A surprising number have become spiritual leaders, teachers, and organizers in the Western Buddhist community. Among them are Joseph Goldstein, Jack Kornfield, Sharon Salzberg, Bernard Glassman Sensei (a Zen roshi), Stephen Levine, and Jeffrey Miller (Surya Das), the first Jew to become a Tibetan lama.

I was also aware that the Jewish community views with a mixture of fear, alarm, and regret the loss of such Jews to other religions. This dialogue would address that concern as well.

These were the prospects I had in mind as I made my way to Frankfurt for the first leg of our journey together.

But I could not have imagined then how the actual experience would be much more radical and transforming, not only for me as an observer, but also for the Jewish delegates.

What follows, then, is the story of a historic dialogue between Jews and Buddhists. It is also the story of the movement of some Jews toward Buddhism over the past twenty years, and what this has to tell us about the problems in Jewish religious life today. But most of all, it is a story of the possibilities for Jewish renewal as I first encountered them in Dharamsala.

1

Sparks

I joined the stream of disembarking passengers in the Frankfurt airport, bumping and jostling in the narrow corridor to the main concourse. I was nervous, nothing new in itself. Nervous is my religion.

On previous visits to Europe I had always avoided touching down on German soil. Now I knew why. Seeing German on posters put me on edge. So did the voices of German citizens around me. This was nothing I could help, an involuntary reaction, a stubborn prejudice.

The mass of travelers surged into the main concourse and split up in all directions. I wandered around, hoping to bump into other members of my party, who were arriving from New York, Boston, London, and Israel. We were all to meet at the New Delhi departure gate. Near a ticket counter, a man with a briefcase was berating a clerk. My ears pricked up at the sound of his voice. A few syllables of German spoken in anger and already the grainy newsreel was unwinding: Hitler at a podium, the crowds at Munich, goose-stepping soldiers, the crowd responding with a massive Heil Hitler salute. And then, inevitably, the stacks and stacks of bodies . . .

But these businessmen and tourists hurrying through the concourse were not storm troopers, and it would have been a stretch to imagine myself as a Jewish victim in striped pajamas. I am a grandchild of immigrants, Jews with the luck to get to America soon after the pogroms opened the long twentieth-century European Jew-killing season.

So I had no rational reason to feel uncomfortable in the Frankfurt airport. Surely these good German citizens would wish me no harm. Why hold a grudge with ghosts?

Yet, despite my ongoing turbulence about my Jewish identity, my discomfort was visceral. German posters, German language, German people made me nervous, and I wanted very much to find the other members of my group. I wanted to be with other Jews.

That's when I saw the Torah.

In a crowd of German students, a tall man held it to his chest like a father clutching a chubby toddler. He was balding, with a fringe of wild hair and a thin goatee. With his wire-rimmed glasses and blue serge jacket, he looked like a café revolutionary. He was, in fact, Paul Mendes-Flohr, a distinguished professor of Modern Hebrew Thought at the Hebrew University in Jerusalem.

What surprised me was my surge of joy upon seeing Paul's Torah. It wasn't particularly pretty. It wasn't even familiar-looking. This was a Torah in a tin case, used by the Sephardi Jews of southern Europe, Asia, and the Middle East and meant to be read standing upright on a table. The case was decorated with an uninspired orange floral pattern. Yet it drew me and not just me. From all corners of that vast waiting room, our entire party gathered around it.

A Jewish mystic would have understood the Torah's magnetism. For the kabbalah teaches that the Jewish soul is composed of many brilliant sparks. I like the idea of a sparkling, multifaceted soul, with bright bits of reincarnated rabbinic sages jostling around with earthier types, nightclub owners, and peasants. In a way, the Jewish soul is like an airport concourse, crowded with competing sparks of life. And in that German concourse, even for a rather secular jumble of sparks like me, a Torah still has strong powers of attraction.

As Paul explained later, the Torah had been purchased in Tel Aviv that morning as a gift for the Dalai Lama. It was a printed replica, actually, not a real scroll, but that didn't matter. From the start of our journey it served many purposes. Symbolically, of course, we Jews were bringing our Torah—our wisdom—to Dharamsala. But at a far more visceral level, during a sometimes difficult journey through India, the Torah acted as a magnet, keeping the sparks of our Jewish souls aligned and, some believed, keeping our Jewish bodies safe.

That morning in Frankfurt, as we gathered around the Torah, I felt myself to be an unlikely candidate for this journey. I had hardly ever been what one could call a spiritual seeker. I was deeply interested in Jewishness—as culture and history. But I wasn't looking to Judaism—the religion—for answers to the deepest problems in my life.

I presumed that the participants in this dialogue would have strong religious commitments. I would be standing outside of that.

As for Tibetan Buddhism, I considered myself too stubbornly loyal a Jew to go shopping. I'd never been much for gurus. Were it not for the efforts of an old friend, Dr. Marc Lieberman, it would never have occurred to me to seek spiritual wisdom from a Dalai Lama.

Marc, a San Francisco ophthalmologist, was the first person to ever describe himself to me as a JUBU—a Jewish Buddhist. I've since learned that he is one among many, in a long line that goes back at least one hundred years.

The history of the spread of Buddhism to the West is complex and includes many different strands and influences, ranging from the impact of early translations of Buddhist texts on Emerson and the Transcendentalists to the nineteenth- and twentieth-century immigration of Japanese, Chinese, and other Asian Buddhists. Charles Prebish, a scholar and JUBU himself, has written of two distinct American Buddhisms. One consists primarily of traditional, conservative Asian-American Buddhist groups, which, like other ethnic groups, have brought their religion from the old country. The other, distinctively Western, Buddhism is both more innovative and less stable and draws primarily on non-Asian Americans.

In the past twenty years, JUBUs have played a significant and disproportionate role in the development of this second form of American Buddhism. Various surveys show Jewish participation in such groups ranging from 6 percent to 30 percent. This is up to twelve times the Jewish proportion of the American population, which is 2½ percent. In these same twenty years, American Jews have founded Buddhist meditation centers and acted as administrators, publishers, translators, and interpreters. They have been particularly prominent teachers and publicizers.

The very first Westerner to take refuge in the Buddha on American soil was a Jew, Charles Strauss. He dramatically proclaimed himself a Buddhist at a public lecture that followed the World Conference on Religions in 1893. Strauss set a pattern for American JUBUs by becoming an author and leading expositor of Buddhism in the West.

Similarly, a more recent phase of American Buddhism owes much of its impetus to the beat generation of writers in the 1950s, who were led by a self-proclaimed "Buddhist Jew."

Allen Ginsberg's openness, and his role as a very public personality, made his personal quest for wisdom influential, even paradigmatic, for a generation. Buddhist references are sprinkled throughout his poetry, but he did not become a serious practitioner until the 1970s. He remains a committed Buddhist, as the title of his most recent biography, *Dharma Lion,* indicates.

In a much more quiet, but perhaps deeper way, other Jews have been very important Buddhist teachers. In the early 1970s, four Jewish practitioners of Vipassana meditation—Joseph Goldstein, Jack Kornfield, Jacqueline Schwartz, and Sharon Salzberg—returned from their studies in India and Thailand to found the Insight Meditation Society in Barre, Massachusetts, which is today one of the most successful Buddhist teaching institutions in America. Goldstein and Kornfield have also collaborated on very popular books on basic meditation technique.

When a big surge began in the mid-1970s, Joseph Goldstein told me, "a strong predominance of Jewish people took an active, leading role. I came back from India in 1974 and that year Naropa Institute first started a big summer program—like a spiritual Woodstock. That's when I first started teaching. That was a seminal year."

The Naropa Institute in Boulder, Colorado, was founded by the late Chogyam Trungpa, a Tibetan teacher from the *kagyu* tradition. That tradition is not strictly monastic, and Trungpa became controversial for teaching a "crazy wisdom" that allegedly justified his own public drunkenness, sexual promiscuity, and violence. But perhaps in part because of his wildness, Trungpa could reach large numbers of disaffected young people who were, as Allen Ginsberg told me, "coming off the flower power accumulation of trips of the sixties." Many were Jews, and Trungpa used to joke that his students formed the Oy Vay school of Buddhism.

A number of Trungpa's intimates were Jews who moved high up in the hierarchy of Vajradhatu, the Buddhist community in Boulder. David Rome served as his personal secretary. Robin Kornman, now a professor of Buddhist studies and a translator, was also in the inner circle. Sam Bercholz founded Shambhala Books, the first major publisher of Tibetan Buddhist works in this country. Others, like Nathan Katz, who came to Naropa to study Tibetan language, became scholars of Buddhism and translators of Tibetan texts. Today in American universities there is an impressive roster of Buddhist scholars with Jewish backgrounds, perhaps up to 30 percent of the total faculty in Buddhist Studies. Among them are Anne Klein of Rice University, Stanley Weinstein at Yale, Alex Wayman and Matthew Kapstein at Columbia, Charles Prebish and Steve Heine of Penn State, and many more.

The big star at Naropa that Woodstock summer of 1974 was a teacher of Hinduism, Ram Dass, a.k.a. Richard Alpert, yet another Jew. He told me in an interview that the percentage of Jews involved in the early boom phase of Buddhism was "inordinate" and "outlandish." He said, "I can give you nine explanations that are glib, but I don't think I can get hold of it."

I could think of a number of reasons myself, none entirely satisfying. Where I came from, leaving Judaism for another religion seemed like a big betrayal.

That's why I related very personally to Marc Lieberman's change of direction. We have been close friends since I was fifteen. We met in the Sunday School of a Reform synagogue in Baltimore. After college, he went to Israel and studied briefly in a yeshiva. Living in Jerusalem he had picked up a much greater depth of Jewish learning and a much more Orthodox practice than we'd been raised with. He married a lovely Israeli woman and returned with her to our hometown. During that period in the late seventies, Marc was a very observant Jew and he taught me a great deal. We had long discussions about Talmud, midrash, and Hasidism. We often prayed together at an ancient run-down shul near Corned Beef Row in East Baltimore.

In the early eighties he moved to San Francisco, and shortly after that his marriage broke up. Meanwhile, I'd moved to Baton Rouge to teach at LSU. We stayed in touch. Soon I noticed that Marc was talking more and more enthusiastically about Buddhism.

At first I figured that, postdivorce, he was hungry for new answers. If he wanted to be a Jew in a lotus for a while and meditate, that was fine with me. Just a phase, I figured. But then a few years later, he married a fellow Buddhist practitioner, Nancy Garfield, in a Vietnamese Buddhist temple in San Francisco. Not just a phase anymore. Still, when I visited them in San Francisco, I noted that he made kiddush on Friday night and sent his son from his first marriage to Hebrew school. Even as a Buddhist he seemed a better Jew than I was, certainly more knowledgeable and observant than most I knew.

Then some interesting things began to happen. Marc spent three months on a Buddhist retreat in total silence. Marc met with the Dalai Lama. Marc and Nancy started a Buddhist foundation and began holding meditation sessions in their home. They made trips to Tibetan Buddhist monasteries in India.

Finally, in the fall of 1989 Marc told me he was organizing a dialogue session between rabbis and the Dalai Lama in New Jersey.

This remarkable project began with a visit from David Phillips, who is active in the American Jewish World Service, a relief agency helping Tibetan refugees in southern India. The Dalai Lama was very grateful to AJWS and told Phillips he wanted to learn more about Jews and Judaism. The Buddhist leader had also noticed that an impressive number of his followers in the West were from Jewish backgrounds.

In the spring of 1988, Phillips was Dr. Lieberman's guest for Shabbat dinner. Phillips must have observed the unusual combination in Lieberman's San Francisco home: at the table, Shabbat candles; in the living room, incense; at the doorway, a mezuzah; in the meditation room, a five-foot-high Buddha. If he glanced at the bookshelves, he would have seen dharma and kabbalah competing for space, and one was as likely to find Pali as Hebrew.

So Phillips asked Marc Lieberman for a list of books on Judaism for the Buddhist leader to read. Marc responded with a far more ambitious plan. Jews needed to learn about Buddhism, too. Why not have a dialogue with the Dalai Lama? Better yet, why not immerse rabbis and Jewish scholars in the life of a Buddhist community? They could bring the Torah to Dharamsala, the seat of the Tibetan exile, and they could return—he hoped—impressed by Buddhist wisdom. In the glow of Shabbat candles, it sounded like a marvelous idea.

Phillips agreed to get word back to the Dalai Lama. Marc set out to work on the Jewish side. Over the past decade, the Dalai Lama had had extensive dialogue with Christians, but none formally with Jews. Such a meeting seemed long overdue to Dr. Lieberman, but that wasn't a perception shared by the organized Jewish community.

Some work was being done with interfaith dialogue, mainly with Catholics, and with intergroup dialogue, mainly with Blacks. But at the time, Jewish philanthropies were preoccupied with Soviet emigration to Israel. And to most Jews the Dalai Lama was too exotic. They couldn't see the value in meeting with him. After sixty-five turndowns, Lieberman knew he had to find a way to break the ice.

Along the way, he had teamed up with Michael Sautman, another Bay Area Jew with strong Buddhist ties. A pilot active in relief work with the Tibetans, Sautman is also a personal student of the Dalai Lama.

With the Buddhist leader coming to New York in the fall of 1989, Lieberman hit on the idea of organizing a preliminary meeting in the United States. Sautman brought word from the Tibetans that the Dalai Lama would grant a few hours' time. Lieberman, with the help of Dr. Moshe Waldoks, a Jewish scholar and editor, arranged the rest. They invited rabbis and scholars representing all four branches of organized Judaism in the United States: Orthodox, Conservative, Reform, and Reconstructionist. Lieberman hoped the historic nature of the event could attract publicity and, eventually, funding for the more ambitious dialogue he had in mind.

They met at a Tibetan Buddhist monastery in Washington, New Jersey. After lunch and a tour of the grounds, the Jewish visitors entered the Buddhist temple and sat down with the Dalai Lama and his senior monks and translators. A Torah scroll was unwrapped and the Dalai Lama was photographed by the *New York Times* peering respectfully at its long lines of script.

In the animated discussion, the Dalai Lama expressed his admiration for the Jewish people and showed a particular interest in Jewish mysticism. But his request for details about kabbalah went largely unanswered. And the whole subject of the survival of exile peoples needed much more elaboration. These would have to wait for a full-length dialogue.

What did emerge into view was the warmth and energy between these two groups. Tibetans and Jews shared a similar sense of humor. When the Dalai Lama was presented with a tallis, in return he handed his guests the traditional gift of a silk *katak*. "I give you a scarf and you give me a scarf," he joked, and as the session ended, he walked away with another gift, a shofar, tucked into his robes. Though Marc later referred to it as a "crash course in Judaism 101," the initial encounter got great press, especially when, just a week after, the Dalai Lama received the Nobel Peace Prize for 1989. Now the Nathan Cummings Foundation offered to support the major dialogue in Dharamsala that Lieberman had been dreaming of for two years.

Not everyone in the Jewish community applauded the news. An influential New York Jewish newspaper ran a sarcastic headline about the session, "Dillying with the Dalai." In the article, the two Orthodox participants, Rabbi Yitz Greenberg and his wife, Dr. Blu Greenberg, were attacked for consorting with idol worshipers.

But even in liberal denominations the received idea is that all Eastern religions are "cults." Many assimilated Jews were horrified in the late sixties and seventies when charismatic leaders such as Ram Dass, a Jewish Hindu, or Allen Ginsberg, a Jewish Buddhist, led many other Jews out of the fold. Moonie, Hare Krishna, or Buddhist—what's the difference? They all ran together into every Jewish mother's nightmare—walking into a shopping mall and finding her *boychik*—or daughter—with a shaved head and a saffron robe, shaking a tambourine and chanting.

To some in the Jewish community, Dr. Marc Lieberman personified the danger. His mother was active in Baltimore's Jewish affairs, his late uncle Morris had been a prominent Reform rabbi, and his brother Elias had followed in his uncle's footsteps. What had happened to this quintessential "nice Jewish boy," and a doctor yet?

When the question of his background came up in the Jewish press after the first session with the Dalai Lama, Marc described himself with a mixed metaphor. "I have Jewish roots and Buddhist wings."

I knew what Marc meant by wings: Buddhism had gotten him somewhere spiritually in a way Judaism never had. In the years since he'd begun meditating, he seemed to have become calmer, less neurotic, more at ease.

I also knew what he meant by roots. We both came from very intense, extended Jewish families—with all the obligations and neuroses that implies. I knew we shared some of the same Jewish finicks, the same paranoias. We'd been raised in the era after the Holocaust with an intense consciousness of Jewish suffering. We both knew the long history of anti-Semitism. Yet in our lives we had met few signs of discrimination. We'd gone to the finest schools; all doors had been opened to us. With that freedom, we had chosen our own career paths, and they had moved us far from our families and childhood friends. I'd relocated to the deep *galut* of Louisiana and he'd settled in San Francisco. If the first generation of Jews in America were a people broken loose, we had broken even looser. In part, old guilt—fear of disappointing my family—had kept me tied to Judaism. But I could understand why, for Marc, that wasn't enough.

My big question was—could he maintain loyalty in both directions? Roots and wings? For the time being, at least, he had gotten all of us off the ground. He'd worked tirelessly for two years writing grant proposals and in the months preceding the trip had handled all the niggling details involved in transporting scholars, journalists, and a few extra family members to Dharamsala, in the state of Himachal Pradesh three hundred miles north of Delhi.

Given my basic orientation, I was surprised when he sent me a preliminary announcement. He'd scribbled on the cover letter, "Join me for yak butter tea in Dharamsala?" I called him immediately. He was serious and invited me to come along as an observer and to write about the results. I promised to be annoyingly accurate.

Now, four months later, while I tested my first Hindu dinner of the trip somewhere over the Kush, Marc stood in the aisle halfway between the flight attendant and Rabbi Greenberg. The stewardess was holding a tray of food, but the rabbi wasn't having any.

The flight kitchen, based in Delhi, had translated the kosher meal the Greenbergs had requested as Brahmin vegetarian. The meal was rice, peas, potatoes, dal, and an excruciatingly sour Indian pickle chutney. Conceivably kosher—if only one knew how it was cooked, what oils and vessels were used. But of course there was no way for the Greenbergs to be certain. Kosher? Not Kosher? Brahmin? Chutney? Who knew? Dr. Lieberman tried to reassure Rabbi Greenberg that Brahmin vegetarian was glatter than glatt kosher. But in the end, the rabbi and his wife left their meals uneaten. I saw Lieberman stretched between two worlds, Orthodox Jewish and Hindu, his kosher roots straining and his Eastern wings flapping.

I waved him over. My friend looked tired. He was suffering from culture lag. He'd spent the weekend with Nancy in a vihara, or Buddhist monastery, north of London. The contrast between the two worlds was strong. Monks are inclined to silence. Jews like to yak. Like it or not, and mostly not, Marc Lieberman had become a tour guide for a traveling bundle of Jewish anxieties, handling everything from money changing to hotel room shuffling.

But he hadn't lost his visionary gleam. When he first pitched the dialogue to me, it was always in very lofty terms, a dream of Buddhist monks and Jewish rabbis, lamas and sages, meeting with mutual respect and sharing their wisdom. Clearly it meant much to him personally as well. The unthinking Jewish reaction—the received idea—about Jews like Marc is powerfully negative. Apostates. Converts. The words were ugly.

But he had never cut his roots to Judaism. And for just that reason, they still fed back a strong current of pain. Unlike some JUBUs, Marc kept a foot in both worlds. That impressed me. He mentioned that when he discussed the dialogue in the vihara, his Buddhist teacher in England remarked that of all his students, those from a Jewish background had the most difficulty letting go of their previous attachments.

I wondered too about this persistence of Jewish interest among people who had spent years in a lotus posture scouring their consciousness with Buddhist meditation. (I wondered about the persistence of my own interest sometimes.) JUBUs like Marc could not be done with their Jewishness even though their contacts with the Jewish world, and particularly family, were sometimes difficult emotionally.

Maybe a Jewish Buddhist dialogue could help heal the division between Jews and JUBUs. Maybe it could heal a division within JUBUs themselves.

Now, somewhere over Pakistan, I teased him the way we always teased each other, saying that in Dharamsala, his lofty dreams would be realized. At the appointed moment, he would cross his eyes and have a vision. Rabbi Greenberg and the Dalai Lama would merge together on the same meditation cushion—as the Dalai Greenberg.

EARLY MORNING, MONDAY, OCTOBER 22, DELHI

First sight of Delhi from the air: strings of lights, amber, and snow. Wood smoke and solitary fires. The flight crew sprayed the cabin sporadically with little white bottles of bug repellent, a ritual fumigation.

Then the long descent, into the last portion of the night.

We wound down some ramps and stairs, into a huge white box: marble walls, marble floors. Through windows on the other side we could see the busy baggage area. After a while, we could even see our bags. But before we could retrieve them, we had to wait in line for two more hours, presenting our papers to bulky men in brown turbans, Gurkhas who sat stolidly behind ancient computer consoles.

The airport looked deserted, and the architecture was brute modern and anonymous—we could have been in Cleveland. The fluorescent glare on the glass made it hard to see outside. But a closer look revealed that every square inch was filled with human bodies—hands, faces pressed against the glass. It was a shock, like a massive wave breaking over the psyche, the collective power of all those eyes.

We walked out into the crowd. Four thirty in the morning. A dead heat and stillness, as if we were breathing the previous day's used air. Each of us was surrounded, by beggars and children in rags, by tour guides in white shirts and drivers' caps. Taxi drivers grabbed our elbows—other lithe men snatched at the handles of our luggage. I tightened my grip. In a moment we might be scattered, plucked off one by one into separate cabs.

A hearty man with Mongolian features rushed forward. Tsangpo, a Tibetan exile, directed Middle Path travel agency. He herded us together, driving off some of the more insistent beggars with a hoarse shout and rapid handwaving. The mass of bodies that had engulfed us now dispersed and regrouped around the next batch of arrivals. Meanwhile, Tsangpo and two women from the Office of Tibet draped white silk *kataks* around our necks, a traditional Tibetan greeting. I bowed to them and was led a few feet to the bus that would take us to a hotel. We would have just a few hours rest before setting off overland.

The road from the airport to town was lit by the amber lamps I'd seen from the plane. No other traffic. I smelled wood smoke but couldn't see much in the dark beyond the road. But Rabbi Zalman Schachter-Shalomi pointed to where a semicircle of white stones swelled out from the side of the road, like a breast. Our bus curved slowly around it. Inside the white half-circle was a broken corpse in a brown sari.

A fallen spark.

And not a kindred soul from all the multitudes to lift her up.

2

Flames

Delhi thrusts itself in your face, your hair, your nostrils and pores. Its smoke, sweat, noise, and flavors batter the senses. Hitting the streets before breakfast, I felt as wobbly as a bicycle rickshaw pulling a schoolbus. The streets and sidewalks have an intense scribbled-in quality, like the sets of *Blade Runner*—or a Bosch painting. No matter what level of detail you choose to notice, a square mile or a square foot, even outdoor space feels enclosed and saturated. A few feet of sidewalk house a dozen niches: a sleeping dog and a sleeping child; a shrine to Hanuman the monkey god popping out at your shins; a urinal; an orange salesman with his stack of green oranges; a beggar and British tourists and Delhi businessmen with briefcases. The more you look, the more you see, like those puzzle pictures in children's books where figures are hidden upside down in the bark of trees or inscribed in curling leaves.

After breakfast, I shared a cab with Reb Zalman and Blu Greenberg for a quickie tour of Delhi. Reb Zalman had been to India before; Blu was a gawker like me.

My first sight of Zalman Schachter had been in the JFK airport. Sitting on the floor, legs stretched out, he was scribbling in pencil on a small notebook. In preparation for the trip, Marc Lieberman had sent each of us *The Dhammapada*, a collection of classic Buddhist psalms. Reb Zalman was already at work translating them into Hebrew. I looked over Zalman's shoulder and read, "Animosity does not eradicate animosity. Only by loving-kindness is animosity dissolved."

This was a tenet Jews could really disagree on—and its wisdom was going to be tested even before we got to Dharamsala.

Near the Red Fort, a stately monument of Moghul rule, we saw a half dozen men lounging in a temporary shelter on what looked like a construction site. I took their picture. But Zalman mentioned a Talmudic caution. One must not call attention to the *mishkenot ohni*—dwellings of the poor—lest they be embarrassed. I *was* embarrassed. I didn't know those stacks of lumber and scraps of wood were dwellings. I thought they were the ruins of a lumberyard. These low fantastic camps, known as bustees, stretched for miles. Their residents were the lucky ones—they had shelter.

In the scatter of rubble, scat, and trash I deciphered the scene: with a coal brazier on the ground and a jar of white balls on a wooden table, the men sitting around were not simply idle. This was a restaurant. Those white balls, some kind of pastry. The man patting flour down on what I foolishly took to be a painted boulder was actually cooking on an earthenware stove. Cots were scattered here and there where men squatted, smoking. It was not just a restaurant, but an open-air hotel.

Ignorance swings the doors of perception back hard on their hinges. A flood of totally raw impressions overwhelms the nervous system. At first I made an effort to find names for all the new sights and scenes. But the first half hour of Delhi exhausted me. Soon all names escaped. I was reduced to an idiocy pure and delightful in its openness.

That is, until a leper thrust his stumps at my nose. I came back to my senses in a hurry. A few minutes later, outside a silk shop, a woman in rags pressed her infant hard against the window close to Blu. As Blu tore through her purse looking for rupees, I thought she might burst into tears.

Beggars waited at every corner, each demanding attention and care impossible to give in such quantity. You have few choices: harden your heart or look away. Or up, at the movie billboards. They represent the celestial realm, crowded, like the Hindu pantheon, with gods and goddesses. They also represent the political realm, for in recent years, movie stars are becoming successful politicians.

A mustached hero, two stories tall, brandishes a black bat—below him a policeman kicks a lesser deity. A villain thrusts an upright dagger into space. His costars glower and sneer, bathed in rose and chartreuse. A lovely starlet's head pokes above the trees, her ample bosom wrapped tight in a blue sari. She has the appropriate look: confused anguish. Between the billboard and the ground, a clothesline stretches, and a young boy pulls down a tangled dried sheet. The life of the bustees is all browns and whites, lived in dark shadows under the billboards' spectacular pastels. There's no separation between the two realms, one terribly constricted and impoverished, the other larger than life. In Delhi, even heaven crowds earth.

That fall of 1990, the tensions of such poverty, crowding, and squeezing were palpable. The billboard violence was baroque, but no more so than the violence on the street. Every boundary—ethnic, religious, caste—marked a dotted line for tearing. Sikhs murdered Hindus, Hindus murdered Muslims, states north and south were seceding. On the sidewalks of Delhi, upper caste students doused themselves with lighter fluid and set themselves afire, protesting the government's affirmative action plan. As our cab turned a corner I saw large yellow flames, with pointed red tips, burning hotly all over a billboard panel. Below in black: THIS SPACE RESERVED FOR INDIA'S MARTYRS.

The hard thing was knowing which martyrs.

Moshe Waldoks was also affected by the surroundings. "You come to India," he told me when I returned from our mini-tour, "you really feel how small we are. The Dalai Lama represents six million Tibetan Buddhists, but there are about three hundred million Buddhists in the world. We have only thirteen to fourteen million Jews. We're an infinitesimally small group."

Yet the relatively tiny Jewish world can look as divided as all of India. These days, Jews can get as fierce with each other as Sikhs with Hindus, at least rhetorically. The wars are mostly of words, but the passions are vigorous and often divide communities and families. There are Orthodox Jews who would never step into a Reform Jewish temple, and Reform rabbis who denounce the Orthodox as narrow-minded bigots. There are secular Jews who wish a plague on both houses. There has even been violence between competing factions of Hasidim in Brooklyn, groups in beards and black hats that most other Jews could hardly tell apart. A group of Orthodox Jews in Brooklyn calling themselves T.O.R.A.H. (Tough Orthodox Rabbis and Hasids) has painted a swastika on a Conservative synagogue! Very often in Jewish life today the sparks are not from uplifted souls, but from the clash of iron-clad identities.

The landscape of American Jewish life has changed considerably since my childhood, and the recent tensions between denominations seem much stronger. In the 1950s and 1960s, Reform Judaism loomed large, followed by Conservative Judaism. The Reconstructionists were hardly on the map. There was also Orthodox Judaism, but of a fairly lax kind, the residual Orthodoxy of Eastern European immigrants like my paternal grandfather.

Reform Judaism seemed the wave of the future. The denomination had secure roots in the successful and wealthy German Jewish immigration of the 1830s. Baltimore was one of its strongholds and impressive Reform synagogues dominated Park Heights Avenue in the 1950s, where the successful children of immigrants had moved uptown. Reform Judaism was sleek and streamlined, discarding needless rituals and emphasizing the great moral heritage of Judaism. Its sophisticated, intelligent rabbis addressed current social issues in their sermons, and its cantors used choirs and organ music to create a stately, dignified service that any Gentile would feel comfortable with. That was important, because Reform Judaism was a way for Jews to remain both Jewish and American. And since that is what most of the children of the Eastern European immigration wanted, Reform Judaism was where the action was in the 1950s and 1960s. Some of that generation preferred more traditional prayer, and they found a home in Conservative Judaism. But it seemed likely that as the immigrant generation died out their residual Orthodoxy would also fade.

That didn't happen. Increasingly since the 1970s, Orthodox Judaism has been resurgent, and Reform Judaism has been on the defensive. There are two significant movements in Orthodoxy that account for this: the Modern Orthodox and the ultra-Orthodox.

To the majority of Orthodox rabbis in Europe, America was a *trefe medinah*, an unkosher land, and those who emigrated there were basically the poorest Jews, and the least-educated about Jewish religion. Among them, however, came some with deeper religious commitments. On the one hand, they faced the difficult task of adjusting to life in America while holding on to basic Jewish observances, such as keeping kosher in the home, and remembering the Sabbath day of rest. On the other hand, they wanted their children to compete in American life. Modern Orthodoxy attempts to balance secular education with Orthodox practice. Its most important and characteristic institution is Yeshiva University and one of the movement's most important religious leaders has been the late Rabbi Joseph Soloveitchik, a deeply respected Talmudic scholar who also held a Ph.D. in philosophy from the University of Berlin.

Rabbi Soloveitchik was widely revered in the Orthodox world. His authority, however, was never fully recognized by another important group, the so-called ultra-Orthodox. (They would probably define themselves simply as Jews; other Jews, less observant than they, are considered *goyim*.) At their core, this group was the remnant of highly observant Jews who survived the Holocaust. The historian Arthur Hertzberg, who estimates that less than one hundred thousand of these Orthodox Jews came to America, characterizes them as "the first group of Jews in all of American history to come not primarily in search of bread but to find refuge for its version of Jewishness." In this sense, Hertzberg argues that they are the only Jewish immigrants comparable to the original Pilgrims in their commitment to purely religious values.

These later arrivals have transformed the Orthodox scene, and thereby the American Jewish map. Many of the leaders were the heads of distinguished European yeshivas who had always refused to come to America but had no choice after the Holocaust. Others belonged to Hasidic communities, the most well-known being the Lubavitcher Hasidim, led by Rabbi Menachem Mendel Schneersohn. Most of the ultra-Orthodox are extremely uncompromising in their Judaism and tend to isolate themselves socially from American secular influences, and also from most American Jews. Through the force of their commitment, they have exerted a strong rightward pull on Modern Orthodoxy, and on American Judaism in general.

As a result, in recent years Orthodox Jews in general have moved to an increasingly separatist position, avoiding dialogue with other Jews, for fear of legitimizing behavior they could not approve of. I'd had some interactions with both Modern Orthodox and ultra-Orthodox, in the United States and Israel, and had an uncomfortable sense of boundaries being raised higher and higher. I recall an evening in Jerusalem with a group of *baalei teshuvah*, Jews who had converted to Orthodoxy. To them it all boiled down to one proposition: either God had given Jews the Torah at Mt. Sinai or had not. And they asked me to choose. I felt like I was being grilled.

The emotional undertone of today's Orthodoxy, at least as I'd encountered it, seemed excessively self-righteous and self-isolating. It came down to little things, customs, such as the refusal of Orthodox men to shake a woman's hand. I knew there were reasons for it: if she were menstruating they could not touch her, nor could they ask her point blank. But it seemed to symbolize a self-enclosure, another barrier or boundary between men and women, and also between Jews and contemporary life.

I had imagined that someone obeying God's law would feel more joy. I didn't always feel that joy. There often seemed a neurotic quality to the obedience, a Judaism by the numbers that I couldn't relate to. Anyway, these were the prejudices I came to India with.

Because of the barriers between denominations, Moshe Waldoks told me, "the Jewish world has basically given up on interdenominational prayer. You go to any major Jewish conference, on Shabbat there will be four or five services. It's funny, but that's how 'pluralism' is understood in the American scene: everyone has the right to do their thing in separate rooms."

Waldoks has a black beard and a deep voice. He's stocky, as if he's so full of compressed energy that he's doubled up on himself. As the son of two Holocaust survivors, perhaps he has.

His parents met in a German Displaced Persons camp. His mother survived a labor camp. His father escaped the *Einsatzgruppen* because he'd been drafted by the Russian army. His father's family, and all the Jews of Lutzk, were annihilated. All that remains of their life together is a synagogue model in Tel Aviv's Diaspora Museum.

So Waldoks knows the stakes of Jewish survival. Educated in a Yiddish-speaking yeshiva, but holding a doctorate in Jewish history, he quit academia several years ago to freelance. He coedited *The Big Book of Jewish Humor* and is in demand as a Jewish lecturer, storyteller, and stand-up comedian. Part scholar, part rabbi, part comic, he can joke and pray at the same time.

More than anyone, Waldoks put the Jewish contingent together, and he was its social hub. He wanted above all, a *haimish* group—a warm group of Jewish homies. But as a bonus, he told me, the Dalai Lama would see "a quilt of the Jewish Diaspora, a microcosm of the wanderings of the Jewish people." He ticked the names off for me on his thick fingers, "Zalman Schachter born in Poland. Jonathan Omer-Man, an Englishman living in Los Angeles. Paul Mendes-Flohr, born in Detroit, an Israeli living in Jerusalem." Yitz and Blu and Rabbi Joy Levitt represented New York. Professor Nathan Katz, Florida.

To Waldoks, the polarization in contemporary Jewish life is the continual festering of a wound. "There isn't a serious Jew today, whatever denomination or affiliation, who is not still somehow traumatized that a third of our people were destroyed so viciously and in such a short period of time. It's like the amputee who still feels the phantom pain. The leg isn't there, but the pain is always there."

Waldoks characterized the basic split in Jewish life as between restorationists and secularists, those who want to re-create the past and those who want to abandon it. "It's ironic. You go to Israel and see the Orthodox right re-creating yeshivot based on the European model, with no attempt to redefine themselves in the new context of the Middle East. They say we have to be afraid of redefinition.

"And others say, 'Isn't the message of the Holocaust that we have to be totally liberal and work against any form of discrimination?' So Jews like that have been on the forefront of social action movements."

When Waldoks first met the Dalai Lama at the preliminary session in New Jersey, he felt challenged by him. "He got down to the brass tacks of what religious experience has to be. He asked us, 'Isn't the role of religion to create compassion in people?' And when religion stops creating compassion in people and unfortunately, we've seen religion as a source of divisiveness in the world, what's wrong?"

As to what might lie beyond the war of denominations, Waldoks said he personally feels most at home with the *chavurah* movement. A *chavurah* is a small group of like-minded *chevra*, or friends, who worship together, usually in private homes. The *chavurot* began establishing themselves in the late 1960s as a countercultural alternative to the established Jewish denominations, seeking a more intimate and fervent prayer experience, one that recognized the social changes going on around them. By stepping outside of the synagogue model, the *chavurot* were able to experiment with new forms of worship—and become seed centers for Jewish renewal.

Rabbi Zalman Schachter had been introducing me to Jewish renewal since we'd met. On the way to Frankfurt, we'd stopped off in London and shared Shabbat with a small *chavurah* there that had been inspired by his teaching. He was one of the founding members of the first and most widely imitated *chavurah* groups, *Chavurat Shalom*, which began in the Boston area. He told me he saw himself as "doing Jewish renewal, not Jewish restoration. We have to prepare for our next role in history, so I'm postdenominational. The issues over which the denominations quarrel and quibble are not as important as how we can meet the future unfolding and bring reality maps current to the situation."

Post-, pre-, un-, or multidenominational, our Jewish microcosm gravitated together that noon on the steps of the hotel in Delhi—having managed to pack in a few hours rest, a meal, sightseeing. The group certainly looked *haimish*. But then again, from what I knew of Jewish family life, "homelike" did not necessarily mean free of argument. A Jew who has another Jew to argue with can feel at home anywhere, even the Punjab. There would be plenty of time for discussion. Our three-hundred-mile trip north from Delhi would take two full days of driving. We grew closer during that trip, but the deeper divisions also came to light. We would be a Jewish microcosm for better or worse.

Initially, the group was united by the Dalai Lama's request. The delegates were eager to share whatever secrets of survival they understood—though in a very Jewish way, all did not agree on which secrets to bring, or if the secret was relevant, or even if there was a secret. As Rabbi Joy Levitt, a Reconstructionist, told me, "I don't know that we can tell the Dalai Lama, Eat chicken soup, send your kids to Hebrew school, and you'll be fine."

Dialogue presents special difficulties for the Orthodox. When Blu's father learned of the trip, for instance, he became so upset, that he made a special study of the Talmudic tractate, *Avodah Zara*. It has forbidding language about consorting with idol worshipers—including a requirement to kill them.

But over spicy yogurt in our Delhi hotel, Rabbi Jonathan Omer-Man, a gentle mystic, mused over a Buddhist text with a very different message. True dialogue, he declared, must change the speakers from you and me to we and us all.

Between true dialogue and *Avodah Zara,* there was obviously a huge gap, and a few hours later, our sense of where the group consensus lay would be tested directly.

Our Sikh drivers, led by the ever-helpful Tsangpo, lined up their white Hindustani Motors Ambassadors in the driveway of the Hans Plaza Hotel. Modeled on the British Morris sedan, their four-cylinder engines produced more noise than power. The tires were bald.

Since it's called the national road of India, Route One has a deceptive ring to an American's ear. I foolishly expected I–95, a nice interstate with a median strip.

But for much of the way through Haryana State, two lanes carried four lanes of traffic. The main road featured buses, cars, trucks, motorcycles, and moto-rickshaws. Large, slow trucks brought sand to construction sites. The sand was wrapped in burlap, in huge sloppy turbans that bulged into the oncoming lanes.

The shoulders offered no relief. They were crowded with their own parade: foot traffic, flocks of sheep and goats, huge lumbering ox carts with wooden wheels straight out of the Bhagavad Gita. At one point, we passed a quarter-mile-long Hindu Mardi Gras, with celebrants decked in red and gold robes, pulling a traditional temple cart. Inside was a man heavily made up around the eyes, who appeared to be in a light trance.

The direction of traffic was not uniformly observed. Travelers on the shoulders often meandered onto the main road.

Our drivers were extraordinarily adept, but as a matter of honor they occupied the passing lane for as long as possible, then swerved away from the centerline, avoiding the impending accident with a daredevil nonchalance. Brakes squealed, tires rattled, and horns blasted as our driver squeezed out the last bit of thrill before veering hard left.

It's customary for observant Jews to recite the *Shema* on their deathbed. In the first hour on the road dozens of *Shemas* escaped the lips of my fellow passengers. It was like the joke about the Israeli bus driver and the rabbi who arrived at heaven at the same time. A big fuss is made over the driver, while the rabbi is ignored. "What gives?" the rabbi asks. "I was a rabbi, he was just an Egged bus driver." And an angel answers him, "How many people did you get to say *Shema?*"

That's why some took comfort in the protective powers of the Torah, said to guard Jewish travelers, and which Paul Mendes-Flohr in turn guarded carefully on his lap. We Jews were bearing other gifts as well: prayer books and artwork for the Dalai Lama. We hauled candlesticks and matzahs, yarmulkes, tallises, and prayer books through the countryside. The drivers spent a good deal of time at every stop shifting our baggage around, balancing on the roof racks loads that threatened to topple. So the metaphor came up naturally: to Moshe Waldoks, who'd met with the Cardinal of Krakow, there was always baggage in dialogue with Christians, namely, the "overhanging history of anti-Semitism and supercessionist theory"—the belief that Christianity had superseded Judaism. "Yes, they're very kind to Jews now, but it's hard to forget the past."

In another conversation, in another car, Rabbi Joy Levitt, also active in interfaith dialogue, used the same metaphor, with a new twist. "We don't have any baggage with the Buddhists. We can meet them with open arms." But as she got to know her driver, Mr. Singh, a more basic problem came up. Sheer incomprehension. I can report the dialogue verbatim:

Mr. Singh: What do you do?

Joy Levitt: I am a rabbi.

Mr. Singh: What is it?

Joy: I am a priest. I am a teacher of religion. Do you know what religion is?

Mr. Singh: ?

Our Sikh driver had heard of Muslims and met some Christian tourists. To him, Jews were news.

That pricked my vanity. I didn't like to think that in vast areas of the planet, the story of my people is unknown.

But India's Route One was teaching me a whole new perspective on population politics. After all, Jews make up less than half of one percent of the world's population. There are as many Sikhs in the Punjab as Jews on the planet. In the span of a few hours, we had driven past, and through, an enormous exodus composed of individual human struggles: a huge ox cart with wooden wheels stuck in a rut, the driver tugging his ox alongside; thin women breaking up white stones into gravel, others carrying stones on their heads; a young girl in rags carrying her naked brother. Just outside my car window there was enough human tragedy, comedy, and heartbreaking struggle to fill a dozen Torah scrolls. At one point, near a bazaar crowded with shops and shoppers, I saw tens of thousands of people. Our driver lifted his hand and waved vaguely to a bus. Heads poked out of every window, and a score of passengers balanced on the roof. One of them waved back to our driver and smiled. They knew each other. On that road, in that multitude, this chance encounter between friends seemed a miracle.

I decided that the most important baggage Jews carry is an absolute conviction of our significance because we are Jews, because we have survived. On Route One, the whole grand story of Jewish survival, the tremendous importance I attach to my history, my Torah, shrank in perspective: to a single line, a single letter. I felt absurd: in the middle of India, did it really make any difference that we were Jews?

KARNAL, 5:30 P.M.

The drivers pulled one by one into a small restaurant in Karnal, not far from the plains of Kurukshetra, the great battlefield described in the Bhagavad Gita where a god taught the laws of karma to a noble prince. One car was missing.

We were being served our meals by the time Rabbi Zalman Schachter-Shalomi arrived, laughing and smiling. For travel he wore a dark blue beret, and with his white beard and glasses he bore a passing resemblance to Henri Matisse in his later years. Reb Zalman, the Matisse of religion, rearranged Jewish thought with decorative freedom. He carried what looked like a tallis and around his neck wore a new string of beads, like green grapes. At sixty-seven, he was our loosest, freest spirit—heir to the joy and zest of the legendary Hasidic masters. He was bursting to tell us about his adventure.

"The sky was getting bronze," he explained, "the sun was setting, and we were passing all these temples on the road. So I asked the driver if we could stop to say prayers. I could tell he wanted to take me to a Sikh temple, because he kept putting me off. 'Soon, soon, soon,' he said.

"So we stopped, went in, and took our shoes off. I stood near a pillar while they were chanting and davened *maariv*. At the same time, they were chanting and playing on their harmonium and doing their *maariv*."

"Do they have a regular evening service, too?" someone asked.

"That's basic. Dawn and dusk are basic times to pray, because then you have daytime and nighttime consciousness at the same time."

Reb Zalman turned to order some juice and Paul Mendes-Flohr told me, with uncharacteristic reverence for a self-professed secular Zionist, "They responded to Zalman's holy presence."

There'd been no big crowd, just six or seven people praying. "Coming in, first there was a little suspicion—who are those guys? what's going on? Then, a recognition that we were not there to make fun but to really somehow share and honor this place and that's great and we want to know these guys. When we finished the davening they were waiting to tell us, come follow us. The priest was in a beautiful white turban and white clothes. He had several of his people with him. We couldn't talk very much, a little English. He gave us a tape about meditation and some beautiful phosphorescent beads."

The guru tested Reb Zalman. "He said to me, 'You know God doesn't really need a temple or a Sikh priest, but nevertheless it's a good place to come together. What do you think about that?' I would give my response and each time he was happy he gave us another present.

"What we got to was, for 'us who know,' worship can happen any time, any place. But we also know that most people won't be able to take advantage of that. So as a concession to humanity, a temple is an important thing. We were professionals speaking one to another.

"We were eager to say something about being Jews, but it wasn't picked up. Our driver told him we were on the way to see the Dalai Lama. I could imagine some of the people being very curious. Could you imagine coming into a *shtiebl* in Brooklyn and someone saying, 'What are you doing here?' 'I'm on my way to the Dalai Lama.' 'Dalai Lama, what do you need a Dalai Lama for? Who's a Dalai Lama? Could you talk to this guy; after all, doesn't he wear little idols around him?' "

Reb Zalman's spontaneous davening in a Sikh temple had placed him squarely on the side of total immersion dialogue. Explaining to me later, he quoted from the Psalms, "I am a friend to all who respect you, O Lord." The Sikh guru and he are "in the same business, struggling to see holy values don't get lost. I see every other practitioner as organically doing in his bailiwick what I am doing in mine. When a non-Jewish person affirms me, I feel strengthened in my work. When I affirm a non-Jewish person, he or she feels strengthened in their work." Zalman also cited Isaiah's prophecy, "My house shall be called a house of prayer for all nations." Now that we are closer to having a temple in Jerusalem, Zalman thought, some day all people will be comfortable worshiping there as well.

I was electrified by his joyous crossing of boundaries, his davening chutzpah. It broke through my own neat categories. I associated Orthodox practice with insularity. Yet here was Zalman, making contact with another religion by davening *maariv*. I was conscious of the theatricality of the gesture, but that didn't diminish the effect. This was my fantasy of what Jewish renewal might look like.

I noticed that while others in the group seemed to share my excitement, Rabbi Greenberg, sitting at the end of the table, remained very quiet. Although he acknowledged Zalman with respect and courtesy, I could see flashes of the divisions in American Jewish life that Moshe Waldoks had been talking about. In recent years, under the influence of the ultra-Orthodox, even Modern Orthodox Jews have been pulled away from dialogue with other Jews, not to mention praying with Sikhs. As for Zalman, his extreme openness probably would have challenged many Reform rabbis, let alone Orthodox or Conservative.

On a more abstract level, I could also see this difference reflecting ancient competing impulses within Judaism: rabbinic and prophetic, legalistic and mystic, particularist and universalist. Clearly Zalman would continue to cross boundaries, and Yitz to defend them. I made a note to myself to keep on eye on Y and Z. Tension would run like a current between them until it sparked out into the open at the first session with the Dalai Lama.

With all present and accounted for, Marc Lieberman tried to open a discussion about plans for informal interaction with the Buddhists. But like a mischievous schoolboy, Reb Zalman unfolded the cloth he was carrying and wrapped it around his head. Then everybody had to take his snapshot—it was irresistible, the rabbi in a turban.

But Marc persisted, conscious that the Jewish group had to unify itself to be effective. He suggested that the visitors sponsor a public *Oneg Shabbat* in Dharamsala. "It would be nice to get the word out to other traveling Jews in the neighborhood. We can put some signs up in town."

That's when Reb Zalman got serious. "Do you think it would make sense to do that seder then?"

He proposed to give to the Buddhists the "shell" of a ceremony in which they could insert their own program, a seder built around the life of Buddha, four cups of wine, one for each stage of his enlightenment. Lieberman frowned. "The seder is going to be better if it's a bit more controlled." I made a note to ask him later what the problem was. If the Dalai Lama really wanted a secret of Jewish survival, the seder was a good one. It's the custom most widely celebrated by American Jews today.

Marc moved to a second proposal, "*shakharis* davening." Each morning, a different delegate would lead the prayers. That would be interesting—if Waldoks was right, this living quilt of the Diaspora might have a hard time praying together.

The discussion turned to inviting local Jews to join in. Marc Lieberman believed that a distant descendant of Henrietta Szold, the founder of Hadassah, was a Buddhist nun living in Dharamsala. Someone else added that there was an Israeli paratrooper who was a *bhikshu,* a monk. Moshe Waldoks was delighted. "Maybe we'll have a *minyan.*"

Finally Marc mentioned what he hoped would be an exciting interaction. Coincident with our visit, the Dalai Lama was hosting an international conference of Buddhist scholars, monks, and abbots from India and Nepal. The Jewish delegates would be welcome to observe the conference and some would be invited to address it.

It was getting dark. We left Haryana State at the crossroads town of Ambala and cut across a corner of the Punjab. At the border we stopped at a checkpoint manned by Indian soldiers.

Since January more than three thousand had died in battles between government forces and Sikh separatists. A week before, on the same road, a local Sikh surgeon watched his son gunned down by a drunken police officer.

At a second checkpoint just outside Chandigarh the soldiers took Mr. Singh into their hut. The guards said there was a ban on travel through the Punjab, and they wanted him to turn back to Delhi, six hours away. I told Singh to mention the Dalai Lama's name. The guards wavered and consulted among themselves. Finally, they waved us through.

"What did he tell you, Mr. Singh?"

"Some schoolchildren burned a school bus."

That sounded unlikely, but it was all we could get from him.

The roads into Chandigarh looked deserted, and the city had an eerie quality, as if dropped into India from another planet. The great architect Le Corbusier had built the place from scratch. This was brutalism at its most sterile. The poured concrete structures had weathered poorly—nothing Indian about them. Broad avenues swept into traffic circles, as in Washington, D.C., only here cattle roamed and the streets were smeared with dung.

The confrontation at the checkpoint had taken its toll on Mr. Singh. He got lost in the maze of streets radiating in spokes from identical traffic circles, but there was no one to stop for help.

Then we heard sirens. Police and soldiers ran around with automatic weapons. An upended car was burning hard. Singh threaded carefully around shards of glass while we contemplated the flames and what they might mean. Another problem in translation. I realized "schoolchildren" was a mistake. Mr. Singh had meant "students."

The students of Punjab were on strike and rioting. I remembered the poster I'd seen in Delhi with its stylized yellow flames, their red tips punishing the air.

THIS SPACE RESERVED FOR INDIA'S MARTYRS.

3

Roadblocks

The Hotel Sunbeam in Chandigarh was being remodeled. It seemed all of India was being remodeled, though at a maddeningly slow pace, chip by chip, stone by stone. The country was falling apart physically and politically at about the same rate it was being patched together, so the constant activity did not belie a feeling of stagnation. The Sunbeam, as a modernist building under the ambient influence of Le Corbusier, had started out ahead of the entropy game. But impermanence was catching up here, too. The second floor remained unfinished with untied wires and pipes poking out of the walls.

I milled around in the lobby with Mr. Singh and Shoshana Edelberg, a journalist covering the conference for National Public Radio. We heard loudspeakers from the roof of a low white municipal building across the street. Edelberg ran out with her microphone and I followed. A harsh official voice barked orders. I joined the hotel staff, a few bellboys and the desk clerk, a tall man in a buff turban. He explained we were under curfew. Four young men had been shot by the police not far from the checkpoint. In protest, students had burned buses and cars all over town. A few moments later the rest of our caravan arrived. At the checkpoint the guards had told Tsangpo it was against regulations for foreigners to travel through the Punjab. But he persuaded them to let our group spend the night at the hotel.

Nathan Katz, a professor of religious studies who'd been traveling in India since 1969, had never felt more concerned. With the Sikh-Hindu conflict, the affirmative action riots, and the Hindu-Muslim conflict brewing to the north of us, India was under triple siege.

But no one showed any fear. Most of the travelers were people of immense faith, even if of different kinds. As a Buddhist practitioner, Marc Lieberman was convinced no harm would befall us because of our good intention: we were on our way to see the Dalai Lama. The Greenbergs' concern was more for *halakhah*, the Jewish path, than the Indian road.

The Greenbergs were not the only Jewish delegates who kept kosher, but as Blu explained later, "That night in Chandigarh I began to feel the first bit of isolation as a strictly kosher Jew. Everyone else ate downstairs. We had to eat alone in our room. Everybody else was keeping kosher, but not strictly. Their definition would include vegetarian food cooked in pots used for other things. We couldn't eat from anything cooked in pots because something cooked in an unkosher pot absorbs the nature of the pot. So there was nothing we could have at the Hotel Sunbeam.

"I had brought food and a kettle. Vacuum-packed chicken from Kew Gardens Hills. When Marc Lieberman came to the door with a message, I felt ridiculous. My daughter had packed my food. There I was in Chandigarh with a huge bottle of Heinz ketchup."

Next morning at breakfast, Blu did slip down to sit while the rest of us ate in the dimness of pre-dawn. Tsangpo wanted to set off early before the police could stop us. Still, we paused after our meal to join hands and Reb Zalman led us in a *Hallel*, a prayer of thanksgiving ordinarily reserved for remembering miracles. Maybe getting past a checkpoint where others had been killed was miracle enough. We sang the Hebrew to the tune of "Michael Rowed the Boat Ashore." Tsangpo joined in, humming in a soft baritone and quickly learning the chorus of Hallelujah. Then we sat for a moment of silence.

We left Chandigarh without incident and followed the main route west through the native land of the Sikhs. At independence, this rich agricultural plain had been divided between Pakistan and India, as for centuries it had been divided between Muslim and Hindu. Five hundred years ago Guru Nanak, the founder of the Sikh religion, tried to heal this division, declaring, "God is neither Hindu nor Muslim." Apparently that had not settled the matter—the Punjab remains the scene of constant unrest, as we soon learned.

As our caravan pulled into the main square of Nangal, a town of ten thousand, a bus squarely blocked our path. A large crowd, mostly young people in their teens and twenties, milled about. More of Mr. Singh's "schoolchildren." There was a general sense of excitement in the air, like a cloud slowly condensing into storm. The protesters surrounded our caravan so that we could not move.

The sun was shining—a beautiful clear day. The town itself looked relatively prosperous with shops and restaurants lining the main square. We were more or less ignored, but I didn't think that would last for long.

Nathan Katz was told, "You'd better go back," and he heard "more than a little threat in their voices. I didn't feel they were likely to attack us, but I also felt we'd better get out of there. Tsangpo and Marc Lieberman had the brilliant idea to hire one of the leaders to get us to the back roads to Una. I felt skittish. I was spooked."

Marc Lieberman paid the student leader twenty bucks. "It was a win-win situation. He got his demonstration and the money, and we got out of town." The young man hopped into the lead car and took us out via the back roads of Nangal.

But we were now off the main route to Dharamsala. Soon the road petered out altogether where a bridge was under construction. We rattled across a gravelly creek bed and up the slope of the bank. On the other side two boys, no older than thirteen or fourteen, had set some boulders in the road. Marc Lieberman saw this as "a dharma situation: how do you deal with obstacles? Just go through." But his driver was too cautious and stopped. Money changed hands and they moved on. When our turn came, Mr. Singh was furious. He yelled at the boys in Punjabi, but they simply yelled back. I thought, Animosity does not eradicate animosity. Paul and I felt twenty rupees ($1.20) was a decent bribe to offer considering that political principles were involved. Another consideration was not receiving a rock through our windshield. The deal was struck, but Mr. Singh, anxious to maintain his dignity, insisted that the boys roll the boulders aside themselves. Then he floored the gas. The Ambassador shuddered and in a cloud of dust we left politics in the Punjab behind.

From now on we would be rising to higher things, as the landscape would teach us. We began a steep ascent through spectacular hill country. Paul had the good luck Torah in his lap. Equanimity, plus a bribe, had triumphed over animosity.

We approached the foothills of the Himalayas, the Indian state of Himachal Pradesh, a green land of orchards, goats, and sheep. On the winding switchbacks and narrow lanes, we soon learned new facets of Mr. Singh's driving talents as he made his way through a flock of sheep.

The road skimmed cliffs, spanned impressive gorges on very narrow bridges, then climbed rapidly the last few miles to the old capital, Kangra.

We stopped at a small shop for *chai*, the local tea mixed with milk, heavily sweetened and spiced with cloves. Across the way in an open-air schoolhouse, Tibetan children sat cross-legged on a porch learning their lessons. In the late afternoon chill the teacup warmed my fingers.

Kangra is no more than a block and a half of shops by the side of the steep grade to Dharamsala, but the town is the home of a civilization dating back to when Jews were slaves in Egypt.

We were anxious to arrive before nightfall. The road wound up and down another 23 kilometers before entering the narrow streets of Dharamsala. Our drivers had the same view of pedestrians as sheep: drive right toward them with no sign of giving way, honking the whole time. Even young children were practiced at leaping aside at a moment's notice, flattening themselves against buildings as we barreled past.

The town is laid out vertically, its streets no more than paved switchbacks. Lower Dharamsala is largely Indian with a bazaar, post office, and administrative buildings. Upper Dharamsala, which includes the Tibetan enclave known as McLeod Ganj, has a more impressive natural setting. Pine trees and cedars fill in the slopes, and the narrow road opens out onto magnificent views of the Kangra valley. To the east, a sheer wall of gray granite—the Dhaula Dhar range—towers with a supernatural presence.

At five thousand feet, the site appears refreshingly lofty, but for the Tibetans coming down from more than twice that height, life in India was actually a terrible descent into exile. Many suffered low altitude sickness. But back in 1959 the Dalai Lama's chief concern was the implication of his geographical isolation for the Tibetan cause. The difficulties of our trip underlined that point.

Compared to the glories of Lhasa—which once boasted some of the tallest buildings in the world—Dharamsala was a simple hill station, a vacation spot for British bureaucrats of the Raj. The Tibetan leader had moved from a great palace, the Potala, to a modest cottage.

But over the past thirty years the energetic and industrious Tibetans have built up their settlement in the neighborhood of McLeod Ganj, establishing shops and residences, as well as monasteries; an orphanage (the Tibetan Children's Village); a comprehensive library and archive of Tibetan culture; and Thekchen Choeling, or "Island of the Mahayana Teaching," an area that includes the main temple, the Dalai Lama's residence and compound, the Namgyal monastery, and the Institute of Buddhist Dialectics, a monks' debating school.

The Dalai Lama's large family has been helpful in these projects. His older sister, the late Tsering Dolma, first ran the nursery that became the Tibetan Children's Village, and she was succeeded by his younger sister, Jetsun Pema. His mother was established, until her death, at the Kashmir Cottage, where most of the Jewish delegates would stay and where we all met for meals, discussions, and prayers.

Kashmir Cottage, our new headquarters, was built of granite blocks, with several guest rooms that adjoin a porch with a magnificent view of the Kangra valley to the west. Set into the slope above us was the main house where the proprietors lived. The guest house was modestly furnished, but comfortable and homey. After the drivers pulled our packs and suitcases from the cars and we dusted them off, we were happy to sit for a while in the living room. I strolled around outside in the garden.

My exposure to India, though brief, had been staggering. I had traveled extensively in Mexico, Guatemala, and Honduras, so I knew what third world poverty looked like. But nothing could have prepared me for the total density of suffering. The immense need of the people, the vibrant anarchy of their lives, and the variety of costumes, physiognomy, and activity had left me drained. Certain images kept returning with an absolute force: the leper's finger stumps thrust into my face, the mother holding her infant up to our cab, and from our first hours, that corpse surrounded by a circle of white stones. My heart was torn and tender.

I believe in *tikkun olam*—that the world can be repaired. And that belief requires action: being a Jew means put up or shut up. In my own life that made sense. But in India, the idea that any individual could grasp, let alone modify, such a vast quantity of suffering felt absurd. The streets of Chandigarh smeared with dung, the tide of women and young girls carrying boulders on their heads toward a construction site, the multitude of beggars waiting to surround us at the airport at 4 A.M.—all accumulated into a sense of hopelessness.

If Jews are responsible for relieving the suffering of the world, knowing the size of the task is critical. I felt how much I ignore, how often I redefine the world as my world, and suffering as the suffering of the Jews.

I admit I was glad to leave the thick air of Route One for the thinner air of clarity and contemplation. At that golden hour I came upon Mr. Richard Gere, sitting on a lawn chair before a view of the Kangra valley, the setting sun illuminating everything below in a brilliant haze like a bowl filled with seething light.

I sat beside him and said hello. He nodded, natural, not unfriendly. Gazing with him into the valley, I could pick out the route we'd traveled through a thick choking cloud of wood ash, dung smoke, car exhaust, heat, and light—the great burning heart of the world. Sitting next to Richard Gere, I knew I was among the blessed. After I mentioned our problems with roadblocks and demonstrations, he remarked, speaking perhaps as a multimillionaire, "It's not a good idea to argue with poor people." Then he padded away, disappearing with a suddenness that made me doubt we had met.

The first order of business at Kashmir Cottage for Blu Greenberg was more practical: to investigate the kitchen facilities housed behind the cottage. Her commitment to *halakhah* gave her an enviable sense of purpose. Rinchen Khandro Choegyal, the proprietor, had carefully supervised the arrangements. Handsome and gracious, she was so warm and helpful when it came to solving problems—from making alternative travel arrangements to long-distance calls—that we all came to call her Rinchen-la. It was a small but delightful fruit of Tibetan Jewish dialogue to realize that both Yiddish and Tibetan share a linguistic quirk, the ending *L* plus a short vowel that makes a name more affectionate. Rinchen-la, bubbe-leh!

Like many of the Tibetans we would meet, Rinchen wears several hats. In addition to hosting the exile government's official visitors, she heads the Tibetan Women's Association, which fights the forced sterilization of Tibetan women, and raises funds for housing Tibetan nuns. Now, thanks to Blu, she could add to her resumé, *mashgiach*—kosher kitchen supervisor.

"I didn't have a problem," Blu told me, "because Rinchen kashered the entire kitchen. They poured boiling water on the floors. They bought altogether new pots and pans, all new utensils. Everything was totally new and their cooking surfaces they had totally kashered. They cleaned it out thoroughly and they *gli*'d it, raised it to its highest heat. We went over with them in advance what they should do and we saw what they had done. Rinchen supervised the whole thing. Somebody else might have looked at this and said it was ridiculous, but the Tibetans took it very seriously."

During the next few days, our meals were a blend of Western-style eggs, bread, coffee, and vegetarian versions of traditional Tibetan dishes. We were spared *tsampa*, a traditional ground barley staple but were treated to the great Tibetan delicacy, the *mo-mo*—a round, flat, fried pancake ordinarily stuffed with meat like a blintz, and a first cousin to kreplach in flavor. The vegetarian version we ate lost nothing in translation.

After supper on our first night, I walked around, happy to stretch my legs, wondering what other celebrated visitors I might stumble upon. In the dark around the cottage compound, by a rose bush, I nearly bumped into a familiar-looking man dressed all in black. I was speechless. The Dalai Lama in our garden!

"Excuse me," I said, and the Tibetan man smiled and extended his hand.

"Tenzin Choegyal," he said, "You can call me TC."

I introduced myself and we both laughed. TC understood what I'd been thinking, because the resemblance to his older brother is striking. Although TC was recognized in childhood as a *tulku*—a reincarnation of a previous lama—he had given up his monk's robes for the life of a householder and ran the guest house with Rinchen.

But now it was time for me and several of the delegates to be driven down to our lodgings. Since Richard Gere and another guest were staying already at the Kashmir Cottage, about half of our group was assigned to similar quarters about a quarter of a mile below.

After settling in, a few of us sat out on the veranda to talk. Marc Lieberman stopped by to check in on us, still mulling over the discussions he'd had en route. He feared that the Jews were so concerned with bringing their Torah to Dharamsala, that they would engage in a one-sided talkfest. There were some pretty good talkers in the group, so I could see the danger. Remembering his reaction to Zalman's proposal of a Buddhist seder, I asked him about his concern. He saw it as another example of what he feared, overreaching.

"Look," he elaborated, "the life of Gautama Buddha is totally irrelevant to the Tibetan Buddhists' Mahayana. To the Mahayanists he is one of zillions of Buddhas, and the life of the Buddha story isn't key. Second, the seder is a pedagogic technique that Zalman would like to insert into the householder life of the Tibetans. That's terrific, but we don't have the right audience. If he were to talk to a Tibetan PTA meeting it might work, but we're talking to celibate monks and nuns. They're not going to get together with the kiddies and make *tsampa* matzahs."

Rabbi Joy Levitt and I laughed at Marc's splenetic attack, but I also wondered why he was being so fierce with Zalman, while evidently very respectful of Yitz's more Orthodox position. I had assumed that as a Jewish Buddhist he would be more likely to embrace Zalman's universalist approach. This was a paradox I saw with other Jewish Buddhists. Maybe they wanted the Judaism they'd left behind to stay put.

Joy Levitt, while more open to Zalman's seder proposal, did wonder whether Tibetans felt their exodus was a memory worth preserving. "That's what Jews are about," she went on. "We're about remembering how shitty life was and how much better it could be. So do we want to say to them, you should sit down and tell the story of your trek over the Himalayas and do it with a *Haggadah* and have little games for the children?"

We laughed at that. But to be fair, Zalman was not proposing a parallel between the Jewish exodus and the Tibetan exile. Instead, his intention was to simply use the Passover seder format as a shell, in which to insert a message about the life of Buddha.

The point was, the Dalai Lama had asked Jews for help. So I asked Marc if the seder, with its emphasis on parents teaching their children, wasn't an important and enduring secret of Jewish survival.

Lieberman exploded. The tensions of shepherding us through India, and all the minor details he'd been saddled with over the past few days, like relaying phone messages and changing money, had evidently been taking their toll.

"We keep asking what they want to know. Why don't we ask what we want to know? That's why I'm here. I did not bring a Chautauqua Society to Dharamsala to lecture Buddhists or Jewish-born Buddhists about Judaism."

In his proposal, Marc had suggested topics for the Jewish participants. Rabbis Zalman Schachter and Jonathan Omer-Man would address kabbalah and Jewish meditation. Yitz Greenberg would cover the role of the Talmud in Jewish survival, Rabbi Levitt the synagogue, Dr. Blu Greenberg, the Jewish home, Professor Mendes-Flohr the role of secular Jews, and Dr. Moshe Waldoks the Jewish textual tradition. Professor Nathan Katz would cover possible points of contact between Judaism and Buddhism in the ancient world.

I thought the format itself practically dictated that Jews would teach and the Dalai Lama would listen, but Marc rejected that idea vehemently. "The topics were chosen because you could plug them in both ways. They are just as appropriate for Buddhists to talk to Jews about as for Jews to talk to Buddhists. How, for example, do the Buddhists really work? What's the reality of the Dalai Lama working with hot-headed Tibetans—keeping a lid on all the factions who urge violence and revolt against the Chinese? How do you work with that anger, that hatred of the oppressor?"

That interested Rabbi Levitt, who'd worked in support of the Israeli peace movement.

"Tell me about that," she said to Marc. "Who knows?"

"I think he will be able to show us."

But Joy was skeptical. She had been struck by the same phrase from *The Dhammapada* that I'd seen Zalman Schachter translating into Hebrew, "Animosity produces only animosity."

"My fundamental issue in reading Buddhist texts," she said, "is what it means to love your enemy. I have a suspicion that they have a much better take on those energies than we do. On the other hand, when I read this stuff about loving the Chinese, I want to know why. I don't get it at all. It seems unnatural."

Lieberman smiled. "It's totally unnatural. The whole Buddhist thing is unnatural. The natural way of *samsara* is the perpetuation of more and more suffering. Nothing could be more unnatural than cultivating the pure kind of mind where you get off the wheel."

"Yes, but I still don't understand that."

"I'm not trying to give you a flip answer. That question is a genuine meeting of Tibetan and Jewish experience, where their response is different from ours."

It had been a long day's journey, and it was getting cold sitting out on the porch. Tomorrow morning we would find new barriers on the Jewish side to overcome before such a genuine meeting could take place.

4

Heights

Refreshed after a good night's sleep and some vigorous morning prayers, the Jewish group sat around a long dining table at Kashmir Cottage for a hearty breakfast of eggs, milk, and cheese. Moshe Waldoks read to us from the Torah portion for the coming Sabbath, in which Abram journeys out from the land of Ur. He focused on *Bereshit* (Genesis) 14:18: "And Melchizedek, king of Salem brought forth bread and wine; and he was a priest of the most high God."

Then Moshe took us on a compact midrashic journey—through four thousand years of Jewish experience, from the terse biblical account to the rabbinic commentary to the Hasidic masters up to the present moment when, as we consumed bread and coffee, we thought about bread and wine.

To the rabbinic commentators, Salem is Jerusalem, and Melchizedek—as a priest of God most high—is intimating to Abram what his descendants will be doing there when they become priests of the Temple.

Then Moshe quoted a Hasidic take: "bread and wine" symbolize words of wisdom, and anyone who shares wisdom with another is as holy as the ancient priests.

That's how far we'd gotten when Zalman struck yet another blow for spontaneity with a zap of instant midrash. The story of Abram learning from Melchizedek, he proposed, is an image of the dialogue to come. Like Abram, we had journeyed far from home to learn wisdom from a great non-Jewish teacher.

I was impressed. Suddenly, the Dalai Lama was Melchizedek. This kind of vigorous interplay showed me how, in yet another sense, the Torah might bring this group together.

Then Zalman added another twist: just as Abram and Melchizedek had shared rituals, couldn't we share our seder with the Buddhists?

That was one twist too many for Rabbi Greenberg. He responded with an accumulating syntax of carefully qualified clauses—Talmudic inflections. He had "a theological reservation" about doing a Buddhist seder, "because it begins to raise questions of crossing the line, and also, maybe unintentionally, patronizing them."

Good-bye, Buddhist seder. The pattern would recur, the sides were shaping up. The traditionalists in the group, led by Rabbi Greenberg, spoke of preserving Jewish authenticity. But Reb Zalman believed that, in the Reconstructionist phrase, tradition should have a vote, not a veto.

The sides kept shifting partly because in moving into dialogue participants were loosening up. Joy Levitt felt unmoored—far from her husband, her two kids, and her Long Island shul. When our discussion that morning moved toward her expectations and apprehensions, she said they were the same. "I want to be completely open and that means I will be completely vulnerable. I want to be able go home changed. The more open you are about taking in new ideas, the more challenged you are about the ideas you already accept as true."

Jonathan Omer-Man quipped, "I've tried to purge myself of expectations, a process that was enhanced by the drive up here."

Blu Greenberg added, "Jonathan described himself as emptying out. It took so long that by the time we got here I thought we wouldn't have Jonathan."

A quiet, deeply reflective man, Omer-Man had spent eleven years in Jerusalem studying kabbalah and Jewish meditation. Very soft-spoken, he was often talked over in a conversation, especially in the boisterous exchanges this group engaged in. But he was referring to more than the volume of his voice when he spoke that morning.

"What normally happens to me in this kind of encounter is that through dialogue I learn to see myself through the prism of the other's experience, and I very much want that to happen. Paradoxically, I find it very hard to share my feelings with Jews. I have problems with the number of times I've been told by Jews what my experience is." His words would prove prophetic.

Michael Sautman, our Dharamsala connection, joined us. He was a somewhat mysterious figure. There was, for instance, the matter of what he did for a living, and for whom he worked. I knew for certain only that he was a trained private pilot, that he had done relief work with Tibetans in southern India, that he was the Dalai Lama's personal student. He mentioned that after the dialogue, he was starting up a cashmere factory in Mongolia.

Sautman was crisp, well organized, quick on the uptake, and very controlled. He was able to converse in Tibetan with Tsangpo or to bawl out our drivers in Punjabi if necessary. I sometimes wondered, in fact, how a practicing Buddhist could be so harsh with them. But he had reached very high levels of initiation in *tantrayana* and spent several hours a day practicing. He intimated to me that he was now able to visualize himself as a dragon-headed deity of some sort. His Jewish roots showed too: he'd worked very hard on this dialogue. His own dream was that the Dalai Lama would visit Israel.

More revealing perhaps about his own apprehensions and expectations, Michael Sautman had brought his parents to Dharamsala just for this occasion. It was their first visit. It seemed that Michael, like other JUBUs, was looking for a way to integrate his Jewish roots and Buddhist wings.

Sautman arrived with our schedule for the week. He was on his way to meet briefly with the Dalai Lama and wanted to hear what questions we might have him consider in advance. Like Lieberman, he was concerned that the Jews be open to learning from the Dalai Lama. "As far as learning what he's about," Sautman said, "it's a precious opportunity, in talking to a Buddhist master to gain some knowledge and wisdom."

But for now, much as Marc Lieberman feared, Moshe Waldoks and others seemed more interested in what the Dalai Lama would like to learn from the Jews.

Sautman sighed. "If you remember the first meeting in New Jersey, certainly there was an interest in Jewish mysticism. He is very interested in thought transformation—how one purifies afflictive emotions. In Buddhism it's done through *tantrayana*. He's also interested in issues of diaspora survival if there's some elaboration to be offered."

Then Sautman repeated his request. Zalman spoke first about how both groups were at a crucial place in history. "I would like to ask His Holiness, what is it he would like to teach to us for our own consideration and close cooperation with what's happening on the planet?"

"Give it to me in one sentence," Sautman said crisply.

Zalman didn't hesitate. "Give me dharma talk. Give me dharma talk addressed to Jews."

In the prewar Hasidic Polish community of his childhood, Zalman had been nurtured on Jewish mysticism. As a young man he'd been an important outreach person for the Lubavitcher Hasidim of Crown Heights. And later, earning an advanced degree in the psychology of religion, he taught at Temple University. Starting in the sixties, he'd become an increasingly charismatic figure in Jewish circles and was active at the inception of the *chavurah* movement, when young Jews from the counterculture began exploring their Jewish roots. He gathered many around him, organized as a religious fellowship based in Philadelphia known as P'nai Or, or "faces of light."

Since Zalman sees himself as "doing Jewish renewal, not Jewish restoration," he identified with the Dalai Lama as a colleague facing a similar challenge. The Buddhist leader had brought with him into exile a Noah's ark of practitioners. Just as Jews had their specialists—*mohels, mashgiachs, chazzans,* kosher butchers—so the Tibetans had brought with them oracular mediums, *thangka* painters, "inner heat" meditators. To have the "totality of our tradition accessible means to have people who live that tradition. It's not enough to have books; like in *Fahrenheit 451,* you need people who are living books. For every form of Tibetan practice he needs a living being that practices it." But now, like the Jews, the Tibetans faced the dilemma of restoration versus renewal, namely choosing "which tools to keep and preserve."

So Zalman had a second question to relay through Sautman.

"As the question of diaspora comes up for him, there is a sorting out of what is local and belongs to Tibet and what is global. I would like to know what he bases his discrimination on. This is our question in some ways too."

Sautman was getting more than he could hope to communicate to the Dalai Lama in a brief interview. He looked around the table—"If someone could write up these points . . . " Zalman's prolixity revived his concern about the dialogue, which was the same as Marc Lieberman's. He cautioned us that the Dalai Lama "always sees himself as the lowest person in the room. So it's important when you conclude your presentations to think of ways to bring His Holiness into the dialogue. I'm not saying he's shy. But you have to bring his participation in. It's very important."

Then Blu Greenberg raised a more basic matter of protocol: how to address the Dalai Lama. Michael Sautman suggested sticking to the conventional, "His Holiness." But to Orthodox ears that sounded problematic. Blu Greenberg commented later that although all human beings are holy in relation to God, because we are created in the image of God, "that's different from saying there's an entity of holiness that's independent of a monotheistic God." She saw a potential problem in "ascribing too much power, too much infallibility or eternality to a human being. There's holiness and there's finiteness of human beings."

"Maybe it was a fearful exercise," she admitted much later. Marc and Michael "were very generous-spirited through the whole thing, but in a way they took this as a bit of an insult. But I wanted to make sure, I wanted to satisfy myself about being halakhically correct."

This discussion was temporarily interrupted by the arrival of Karma Gelek, the Secretary of Cultural and Religious Affairs, who had taken charge of all the arrangements for our visit from the Dalai Lama's end.

We moved outside to meet with him, sitting on lawn chairs or along the garden wall. The late October sun was brilliant and warm, jungle crows made a racket in the trees, and dogs barked throughout the valley. Karma Gelek, who was very soft-spoken, could barely be heard, but his dry wit sometimes came through in the subtlest curl of his lip.

In greeting us formally, he expressed regret for our difficult journey. "Most of our foreign guests say that from Delhi to Dharamsala is much harder than from the United States to Delhi." His English was British, his manner very low affect and low-key. Perhaps partly because of the accent, I thought of him as Jonathan's spiritual cousin. Very quickly, the

Jewish delegates invited him into the rough and tumble of their discussion. (In talking about cultural cues in dialogue, Joy Levitt had joked earlier, "Jews have a signal when they want to speak—they interrupt.")

In answer to Blu's question, the monk explained that there were thirty different titles with which to address the Dalai Lama, but "if you could say His Holiness, that would be the usual way." He said this so matter-of-factly I couldn't gauge how strongly he felt about the issue. Soon he, Nathan Katz, and Michael Sautman began searching for more answers to this unique Tibetan Jewish crossword puzzle.

Kap gun was batted around, but turned out to mean "refuge" or "saving leader" or even "Savior," which rang funny in Jewish ears.

I was interested in how much the discussion with Karma Gelek had to do with translation. Robert Frost defined poetry as what gets lost in translation, but I'd go further: culture is what gets lost in translation.

It wasn't so much words as their historical resonances. How could Karma Gelek ever understand how Jews felt about "His Holiness," or the association Jews would make immediately with the pope and from there to the long history of persecution, proselytization, inquisition, and martyrdom? How to explain the peculiar tang of a title like *kap gun* once it got translated to "saving leader"? When Zalman heard it, he immediately asked, "Are there other forms, not weighted with salvation?" To a Jew living in a Christian world, this was a perfectly understandable reference, but in the ears of a Buddhist monk, Zalman's question must have sounded puzzling.

However, Karma Gelek did notice the various reactions and retreated on the "His Holiness" front, observing quietly, "If you would say *rinpoche*, nothing's wrong." (*Rinpoche*, which means precious one, is a general honorific for *tulkus*.)

But it was too late. Now Zalman Schachter was hot on the case, taking up Blu's cause as his own—driven too by his curiosity and loving to explain Jews, Judaism, and himself to Karma Gelek, "We would like to say a word in honor—it's not that we don't want to honor—it's like saying we understand, we honor you as a source of teaching and blessing for your adherents. Could we say, great teacher?"

By now, Karma Gelek had become totally flexible. "Yes, yes," he said, barely audibly.

But Lieberman and Sautman objected. "That's too low."

So Zalman raised the ante, "How about illustrious teacher?"

Unfortunately, "illustrious teacher" was not a traditional Tibetan phrase. "Jewel of wisdom" was offered by Michael Sautman, but finally Karma Gelek ended the discussion when he observed that all such names were very formal and that "His Holiness usually doesn't like formal things."

I took a walk with Yitz Greenberg after the meeting with Karma Gelek broke. We walked for a while in silence. Something about the whole focus on this tiny point bothered me. It reminded me very strongly of what I didn't much like about religious Judaism, an obsessive, niggling quality. Or as a young woman learning about Jewish culture had told me once, to her, Judaism is an old man saying no. With Jews so divided into factions, and some of the factions so self-preoccupied and self-obsessed with tiny points of practice and law, how could we reach out to other groups?

I knew that in some ways that same intensity about language was also what I relished and delighted in, in both Jewish religion and the Jewish mind. It had delighted me that morning with Moshe's and Zalman's midrash. But when the guidance system failed, Jewish verbal intensity seemed to nosedive, spiraling down into smaller and smaller circles.

I ventured to Yitz that maybe the discussion was really about how Jews could hold a dialogue with Buddhists while maintaining their authenticity. I thought this talk had to be about something more than an honorific.

He agreed, adding that, speaking for his group, "most Orthodox Jews feel religious dialogue is not possible. The number of Orthodox Jews involved in dialogue is not a *minyan*. But after twenty-five years—the more involved I am, the more comfortable I feel."

Yitz drew the line in quite another place, which explained why he'd been so quiet after Zalman davened in a Sikh temple. Dialogue was distinct from joint prayers or meditations. "Unlike Zalman, I see liturgy as an affirmation of being a member." He spoke of his teacher, Rabbi Joseph Soloveitchik, a distinguished professor at Yeshiva University and one of the foremost contemporary philosophers of *halakhah*.

"Rabbi Soloveitchik made the distinction: on social justice we have a universal language, but theology is a more intimate language. Liturgy conveys an affirmation that I'm in this system, so I would feel uncomfortable, for instance, in a Buddhist meditation." Or praying in a Sikh temple, no doubt.

On the other hand, there was no question in his mind that Judaism takes place in real history and that Jews had to learn from other cultures. "If you play in the minor leagues, you have minor league cultures. If you play in the major leagues, you have a major league culture." Rabbi Greenberg was particularly concerned that Orthodox Jewish culture had withdrawn into itself, shunning contact with the challenge of pluralism.

"The Orthodox Jewish community is third world in theology and philosophy. Having a political state of Israel now, I'm convinced the great religious challenge is going to be the pluralist issue. Each culture can no longer present itself as self-evident." Though he found this challenging, he also thought pluralism was positive. "First," he said, "because I think it is the will of God. The big question on the religious agenda is how are people rooted in their own religion able to respond to others. We must learn to affirm our truth while doing true justice to the other."

An open encounter with pluralism prevented any religious person from thinking he or she possessed exclusive claim to the truth. In dialogue, "you meet these people with tremendous force and openness, and they're not preselected, they're not prefiltered, or loaded in your favor."

I wondered if this was a risky game, particularly for people of faith. Pluralism can quickly lead to relativism and even nihilism. Because if there are so many different truths in the world, and each one is worthy of respect, why go through all the trouble of preserving any particular tradition. Why continue as Jews?

But for Rabbi Greenberg, "God's will is for us to learn how to affirm our full truth doing full justice to the other, not partial justice or twisted justice or a secondhand treatment."

With that challenge in the air, he left me to my walk. A Tibetan peasant woman, probably in her late sixties but with long black hair shining in braids, passed me on the gravel path. I smiled and said, "*Tashe delek*," joining my palms in the traditional greeting Michael Sautman had taught us that morning. She smiled and said, "*Tashe delek*," with a great deal of warmth, but didn't look directly at me, being a little shy.

When Karma Gelek had mentioned that this gesture of bringing the hands to the forehead was a sign of prostration, Blu had joked, "Let's not go into any meanings of it," to which Marc had added, kidding around, "The less we know, the better off we are. We didn't come all the way here to realize we can't say hello."

Yet the Tibetan woman and I had communicated, if only for a moment in passing. We didn't have the burden of representing any tradition or anyone but ourselves. *Tashe delek. Shalom aleikhem.* Peace.

Surprisingly, given their constant disagreements, it was Zalman Schachter who deepened my appreciation for Yitz and Blu Greenberg's need to preserve tradition even down to the finest points of speech and gesture. Perhaps as someone who himself has been mercilessly criticized in the mainstream Jewish world, Zalman well understood the kind of pressures the Greenbergs faced.

"How many people do you see," he asked me one night, "when you see Yitz and Blu? You see two people. Right? They are not two people. They are several thousand. That is the inner weight of who they are. So with such a constituency, how you act here becomes really important. He is bridging more tensions than any Jew I know at this point. Can you imagine how he gets scrutinized at every step? Because he certainly isn't Orthodox in terms of doctrine. So the orthopraxis of his life is very important: one step over the line and his credibility is lost."

The sympathy Zalman had for Yitz underlined the parallels in their lives. Rabbi Greenberg had received a secular education at Yeshiva University and been exposed to Rabbi Soloveitchik's brand of Modern Orthodoxy as well. His theology was one of the more original to come out of recent Orthodoxy, a reinterpretation of the covenant in response to the Holocaust and the establishment of Israel. To Rabbi Greenberg, both events meant that the human partner in the covenant had to take more responsibility for historic decisions. From this sense of human responsibility also came his opposition to separatism and his interest in dialogue, an interest that put him on the extreme edge of his group.

Zalman had gone over the edge. But he came out of Lubavitch Hasidism and spiritually I think he still belongs to it. Although ultra-Orthodox in practice, the Lubavitchers are rather unique, because they practice Jewish outreach, for mystical reasons. They basically view every Jew, regardless of denomination, as a potential Lubavitcher. By practicing *mitzvot,* one by one, the non-Lubavitchers could be brought along. Hence, young Lubavitcher Hasidim can be found in airports, or in the streets, in their vans known as "mitzvah mobiles," encouraging men to don tefillin and daven and encouraging women to light Shabbat candles. In deep Lubavitch thought, every Jew was redeemable, because every Jew had a *pintele yid,* a Jewish point in the soul. And I think some of their teachers really know how to touch that point.

I remember an encounter while in college with the singer Rabbi Shlomo Carlebach. He had come very late, and we'd been standing around waiting. But instead of beginning the concert, he came up to each of us individually and introduced himself, smiling and looking into our faces. It was a surprising gesture, a recognition that we weren't just a mass, that each of us was important. Yet the effect was to bring us all together with a certain warmth. Something Shlomo said—in the middle of a song yet—has always remained with me. I didn't even know precisely what it meant, but I've often thought about it. He said, "The whole world is waiting for Jews to be Jews."

Like Rabbi Carlebach, Zalman Schachter had begun as an outreach man for Lubavitch, shortly after World War II. He'd been a legendary recruiter for Chabad, helping to establish many centers and visiting college campuses, encouraging Jews to be more observant.

At the same time, like Rabbi Greenberg, Zalman had sought a secular education. The Lubavitcher Rebbe himself had studied engineering at the Sorbonne. Zalman received an M.A. in the psychology of religion from Boston University and a Doctor of Hebrew Letters from Hebrew Union College.

In the 1960s, Zalman separated from the Lubavitcher movement. His energy was probably just too much to stay confined within an ultra-Orthodox community such as the Lubavitchers, which is very intent on social conformity.

What he did retain was the ability to reach out to others, to Jews, but not just to Jews. And this he shared with Yitz Greenberg, who was himself on the edge of the Modern Orthodox movement and in danger of being pulled away.

So Zalman understood Yitz's situation very well. And from his explanation, I was gaining a tremendous admiration for Yitz's essential aloneness—what Blu, in a different context, called their "isolation."

For his willingness to dialogue, he risked condemnation, even expulsion, from the Orthodox community where his heart and family was. (Not long after our return Yitz faced a threat of *cherem*, or excommunication, from the Orthodox rabbinic association, the RCA, though fortunately it was forestalled.)

None of the other delegates faced such risks.

After lunch, Yitz and Blu would enter the Tsuglakhang, the Dalai Lama's main temple, a place most Orthodox Jews would view as a disgusting haven of idolatry. It was a place full of huge golden statues in glass cases before which Tibetans prostrated themselves. Could an Orthodox Jew justify being there?

The Greenbergs would make their own judgments, I was sure, with as much integrity and attention to detail as they had shown so far. The overriding issue for them was not the external appearances, but the Dalai Lama's own behavior. In his own setting, would he act like a god, or a man?

We arrived shortly after lunch at the opening ceremony of the All Himalayan Conference on the Five Traditional Buddhist Sciences. It was exciting that our visit coincided with this event, which drew on Buddhist monastics and teachers from all parts of Asia.

I had a hard time, actually, finding out, even from many Tibetans, what these five traditional "sciences" were. Evidently they were a decidedly medieval curriculum and included what we would call arts and crafts, such as making traditional Tibetan silk paintings of Buddhist religious figures, known as *thangkas*. Other sciences included astromedicine, or medical astrology, the science of healing related to the movements of the stars. All of these sciences—which we would probably call traditional learning—were ways to better understand and express Buddha's teachings, or the dharma.

The important thing was that we were finally entering fully into an entirely Buddhist world. After removing our shoes, we were ushered by some monks into the Tsuglakhang. From the outside I saw the clean lines of a Greek temple in its porches and pillars. But once inside, I felt the strange and colorful intensity of the surroundings. The walls were painted bright mustard, in glossy enamel. In a glass case behind the Dalai Lama's throne was the torso of a life-sized golden Buddha draped with a red robe and framed by jewel-encrusted gold and silver foil. If these jewels were real, and represented wisdom, then the Dalai Lama was very wise, for they were bigger than hen eggs. The throne was draped in golden orange silk brocade—the steps leading up to it framed with an inlay of golden lotus.

Our seating was less elaborate. In kind consideration of our Western spines, we were lined along the south wall on metal folding chairs. On the floor of the temple, about one hundred and fifty Asian scholars, monks, and abbots, mostly from the Himalayan regions of India, from Nepal, Bhutan, and from the exiled Tibetan community sat in neat rows cross-legged on woven mats. In the temple courtyard, a hundred more devotees, mostly young monks in maroon robes, listened in to the proceedings.

But ordinary Tibetan refugees, in simple wool *chubas*, also crowded in through the open windows just above our heads, simply to catch a glimpse of the Dalai Lama. You could tell by their faces he was indubitably, to them, His Holiness.

While we waited, a young woman and her mother, Tibetan peasant women, prostrated themselves before the throne, patting dust from the floor onto their foreheads. They bowed and prostrated before various images, which included Avalokiteshvara, a thousand-armed Buddha of compassion, Padmasambahva, who first brought Buddhism to Tibet, and Tsong Khapa, the Great Reformer of Tibetan Buddhism and founder of the *gelukpa* school, from which the institution of the Dalai Lama grew.

I looked down our row and saw Yitz Greenberg in his black knit skullcap. Blu sat beside him and I caught her watching the young woman and her mother intently. She told me later she felt "by the way they responded, they weren't in awe. This might be very offensive to someone else, but to me, their act was like kissing a mezuzah. It was like a formula. It wasn't that there was the essence of a god in those images, those things."

Marc Lieberman and Rabbi Jonathan Omer-Man both wore similar pillbox caps that could have been Guatemalan, Tibetan, or Indian. Next to me sat Rabbi Zalman Schachter-Shalomi, in a black *kappoteh* and a wonderful silver, tailored black *kippah,* and beside him, Richard Gere.

I'd seen Gere before lunch. He had added an ironic perspective on that morning's lengthy discussion when he referred casually to the Dalai Lama as "HH."

Then the Buddhist leader strode in, casting a special smile our way. Some monks bowed their heads, others remained seated upright. Blu Greenberg said this helped to convince her that not all his followers viewed him as a god. He sat in a lotus position on a red cushion in front of his throne.

Monks served us glasses of hot buttered tea and paper plates of sweet rice and raisins, traditional for the opening of Buddhist study—like the honey and apples given to me as a child at the Jewish New Year, a reminder that all learning should be sweet.

As we munched, the welcoming speeches began. Buddhists were not sparing of eloquence and the translation from Hindi to Tibetan added to the length. The Dalai Lama looked calm and benevolent, taking it all in, sometimes closing his eyes and swaying his body back and forth in a meditation posture Marc Lieberman described to me in a whisper as "a tree swaying in the wind." I wondered where his mind went, if and when it wandered. How boring to be a target of veneration, a vector of ceremony.

I was beginning to feel quite uncomfortable myself sitting through the barrage of incomprehensible language. I looked his way and our eyes met. Just a glance and a playful smile as if for a moment the whole scene, the afternoon's fading light, the hundred and fifty Asian scholars and monks, the speech, the plates of rice and raisins, the Buddha with a thousand arms had all come down lightly to rest and we were the only two in the room, sharing a private joke.

It was a simple human moment. He read my discomfort. Then, by a barely perceptible motion of his hand, he dispatched monks among us. They stooped in the aisle and translated the speeches in low whispers. That's where we first met Laktor, who would serve us as translator during our visit.

After a final formal greeting to the Dalai Lama, three Tibetan monks chanted with deep dignity. I closed my eyes and imagined ancient caverns, shadowed forests, yet within the notes was also a plaintive call, a longing for peace. Plangent chords filled the room—hell on the throat tendons. Occasionally one heard scattered coughs floating above like

ghost birds. They finished abruptly in a kind of "talking blues" effect—
the rapid recitation of a dedication prayer. The silence that followed
seemed purified.

The Dalai Lama spoke, his voice also deep. Laktor explained that he
was welcoming the Buddhist scholars from all over Asia who'd come in
spite of the civic unrest. Then in the stream of Tibetan I heard the word
"Jewish." I didn't have to wait for the translation. All eyes fell upon us.
I was fighting tears. For the first time in history, a group of religiously
minded Jews had come to the heart of the Buddhist world to teach and
to learn.

5

Blessings

Each morning before breakfast, the Jewish group assembled outside Kashmir Cottage for *shakharit davening*—morning prayers. The men strapped leather *tefillin* on the left arm and just above the third eye. In our brightly colored tallises and our headgear, which ranged from knit *kippahs* to sateen *yarmulkes* to Blu Greenberg's gray silk scarf to my own neo-Hasidic Indiana Jones fedora, we were quite a sight to the Tibetan kitchen workers, who always managed to break away for a glimpse. The davening was delightful: vigorous, lusty, witty and raucous, quiet and joyful.

This was all new to me. On any free association test, I'm sure after *prayer*, I would have checked *boring*. As a boy I'd served time in Orthodox shuls, where the Hebrew was babbled at supersonic rates, and I spent most of my time trying to figure out what page we were on or when it was okay to sit down. Of course, this was all my own ignorance. I'd been raised primarily as a liberal Reform Jew and had learned only a handful of prayers. My family belonged to a giant cruise ship of a synagogue, with comfortable wooden pews and lofty architecture. Huge concrete Jewish stars framed the windows and a lovely north light filtered through them down to the cool gray carpet. I used to watch the dust motes suspended in the air instead of following the prayers. The cantor and choir sang beautifully while the congregation sat in silence, like an audience at a concert. This is where Reform Judaism had gotten off the track in the fifties. It felt like our employees were praying for us.

My father's father, an immigrant from the Russian Pale, was, nominally at least, Orthodox. At family gatherings, he mocked our synagogue, which he called a church. But my father was the first in his family with a college degree, and the handsome and affluent Reform synagogue fit his sense of his place in the world. I'd been bar mitzvahed there, a terrifying and elaborate social event that most resembled marrying my mother in public—but one devoid of large religious significance. Our cantor worked hard with us, but the pressure on him was enormous: two bar mitzvahs a week. The extent of my Hebrew scholarship at that time was memorization of syllables whose exact meaning remained obscure.

In short, I'd grown up the typical liberal American Jew, loyal to his tribe and family, and very proud of the ethical heritage of the Jewish people. My Jewish identity was like a strongbox, very well protected, but what was inside it?

The interior meaning of being a Jew was indistinct, smuggled, inchoate—much like the Hebrew letters I could pronounce but not truly read.

The irony is, I had to travel halfway around the world to Dharamsala to discover the utility of Jewish prayer. Our davening brought us together and changed the environment around us, transforming Kashmir Cottage, a Buddhist guest house, into Beth Kangra, the open-air synagogue of the Himalayas.

Maybe Jews ought to pray outdoors more often. Our morning blessings echoed down and around the Kangra valley and were answered back by the call of barking dogs, the cackling of jungle crows, and the sweet chirping of sparrows in the cedars. Often eagles attended, floating overhead—soaring down from the great sparkling granite peaks of the Himalayas to the east as Moshe Waldoks chanted, "Hallelujah, Praise the Lord, praise the Lord from the heavens, praise him in the heights. . . . Mountains and all hills, fruitful trees and all cedars. Beasts and all cattle, crawling things and winged fowl. Kings of the earth and all governments, princes and all judges on earth. Young men and also maidens, old men together with youths. Let them praise the name of the Lord . . . " We became the prayer we recited.

Another great help to me was that Waldoks prayed with a running commentary, teaching and chanting in a baritone, sometimes bursting into aria for major prayers and other times transitioning with a peppery recitative, "We're moving now from verses of praise to *Shema* and its *brakhot* and some-would-say-*kaddish*-here-if-they-had-a-*minyan*-but-we-don't-have-a-*minyan*-so-we're-not-going-to-say-*kaddish*-here-but-I-wanted-to-bring-it-up-anyway-and-invite-everyone-who-is-along -to-come-along-because—" and then he chanted—"Blessed is the Lord, King of the universe, who forms light and creates darkness."

To Moshe Waldoks, who travels the country trying to enliven Jewish prayer, "The shul in Dharamsala was unique and shows how Jewishly sophisticated people could take advantage of being six thousand miles from Jewish politics and learn how to be human beings and Jews together." Each *shaliakh tzibbur*—prayer leader—brought a different style. Rabbi Joy Levitt favored us with quite beautiful singing whereas Jonathan Omer-Man, the mystic, conducted his service entirely in silence.

Zalman Schachter-Shalomi brought his unique combination of Hasidic energy and existential confrontation. The morning he led the davening, he came up to me during the last part of the *Shema*, touched me on the shoulder, looked straight into my eyes, and said, "Your God is a true God." I found that a powerful challenge.

I usually felt as I prayed in a group that I was assenting to ideas and images that were very foreign to me or that I didn't have time to check out. Zalman's gesture had cut through that in a very personal way. Something about his statement struck me in the heart as true, even with my intellect marshaling a thousand reasons why it couldn't be. My God is a true God? Which God was he talking about? Long white beard, old Daddy in the sky? Autocrat, general, father, king? Master of the Universe, doyen of regulations and punishments? These were the images that made me reject the very idea of God.

But in a funny mental jujitsu, the more I struggled with these images, the more what Zalman said came through. "Your God is a true God" meant to me that the images and the language weren't going to be supplied in advance. I would have to find them for myself out of my own experience, and in my own language

I wasn't the only one taken aback. Moshe Waldoks, an all-star veteran of Jewish prayer, was also moved by Zalman's direct challenge. He told me it was his peak moment Jewishly in Dharamsala.

"We always say it at the end of the *Shema,* but I understood it for the first time: that I ultimately will find the God that will work for me and it will be the true God. That was a tremendously potent moment. It gave me a lot of energy that I still carry with me. My eyes filled with tears. It was a loving act of support and affirmation that we live our lives and all we can do is help our people—all people—find what their God is and help them be true to it, live with a certain truth in their lives."

For Waldoks, that truth in his life was evident in the energy he brought to his prayers. But his chanted reference that Wednesday morning to not having a *minyan* touched on a sore point. Ten Jews, the required quorum, were present, but only if Jewish women counted. However, for Yitz Greenberg, the women did not count because the Talmud defines a *minyan* as ten Jewish males.

Moreover, he could not participate when Rabbi Levitt's turn came to lead the service.

I expected Rabbi Levitt to be upset. In fact, I expected her to come out fighting. After all, a prayer-illiterate like myself counted for the *minyan,* while she, who sang the prayers so lovingly, didn't. But she didn't see it as a civil rights issue. In fact, she asked not to be included in the rotation of prayer leaders, hoping to spare Yitz the embarrassment of being unable to join her. As she put it to me, "It's not a personal decision on his part, so there's no reason to blame him. He's following *halakhah* as he understands it, so I'm not personally offended."

The group rejected her request. Instead, on the morning she led the service, Rabbi Greenberg came a little late and stood a little apart.

It was an irony that for the Orthodox, interfaith work meant praying with Reform or Reconstructionist Jews. Another irony was that Yitz was the holdout at Beth Kangra, since no one in Orthodoxy had done more to promote Jewish unity than Yitz Greenberg's organization, the Jewish Center for Learning and Leadership. Its acronym, CLAL, recalled the ideal that all Jews belong to *clal yisrael,* the congregation of Israel. Yet *clal yisrael* often faded from sight, especially in recent years as a resurgent Orthodox movement challenged the legitimacy of more liberal Jews. There was no peace for a peacemaker among warring Jews. (Moshe Waldoks joked that a great benefit of the Dharamsala group was that "it gave Yitz a chance to be on the right for a change. He's constantly being battered by the right wing of his own group and seen as a traitor to his fundamentalist faith. Here was a chance for him to be the most conservative person vis-à-vis ritual and theology.")

That conservativism emerged again only hours before our first meeting with the Dalai Lama. Marc Lieberman, our reluctant leader, was anxious to tighten up the agenda, but that was not to be.

In the Talmudic tradition, young students often matched wits over theoretical fine points, arguments twisted like peppers, called *pilpul*. Example: If a child is born with two heads, which one wears the yarmulke? Long debate: some say the right head, some say the left. All quote Torah.

Now we were faced with a new age *pilpul*: what *brakha* do you make for a Dalai Lama?

True to form, Zalman had composed a brand new Hebrew prayer for the occasion, and Nathan Katz had prepared a Tibetan translation. But there were questions and objections. Rabbi Omer-Man wanted to know "the inner choreography" of the event, who we were saying the *brakha* to and what it meant. Rabbi Levitt thought the prayer too original, that it risked being "disembodied" from tradition. Blu Greenberg also disliked creating new *brakhot*, if traditional ones could be used. As the discussion dragged on, Marc Lieberman, obviously frustrated, broke in. "Folks, I think we're drifting into some real minutiae, and I'm not getting the big picture."

"This is not minutiae for us," Yitz told Marc firmly. "Deal with us two minutes. We're negotiating now with true respect for Buddhism that doesn't violate anyone's integrity."

Negotiating was an interesting word. I settled in for another long discussion. Zalman's prayer was attacked from right and left—perhaps logical, since he considered himself postdenominational. But Zalman, in turn, could quibble and quarrel with the best of them. Maybe this was the real secret of Jewish survival. We'd last forever because there wasn't time in the universe to finish our arguments. I felt like a kid in shul sitting on *shpilkes*. My deepest prayer was to go outside and play. The weather was perfect, and I wanted to hike the mountain paths winding up to Thekchen Choeling, the Temple mount of Tibetan Buddhism. It was a religious obligation to make solemn perambulations around the Dalai Lama's residence there, on a special path known as the *lingkhor*. From what I'd seen the day before, the paths would be full of Tibetan pilgrims, holy men, and beggars, whirling small Buddhist prayer wheels of wood and silver.

But my impatience partly abated as I came to understand the issues. It seems our encounter with the Dalai Lama presented a unique challenge in the long history of Jewish blessings. Their delightful variety covered almost every situation. There is a blessing on seeing a rainbow or an extraordinarily beautiful person. On seeing fruit trees in bloom or for an assembly of more than six hundred thousand Jews. There is a blessing on seeing the ocean and on seeing a mountain.

The Jewish tradition can stretch to accommodate new situations for blessing, but only by extension of old ones. There is probably no extant blessing for a computer chip, but there is a blessing for a pizza, fashioned from a blessing for bread.

In the case of the Dalai Lama, he could be blessed two ways, as a political or as a religious leader. There is a Jewish blessing upon seeing a Gentile king. There is another on seeing a Gentile sage or wise man. But instead of using one of them, Zalman proposed an entirely new *brakha*. He wanted to specially honor the Dalai Lama by blessing him as the equivalent of a *Jewish* sage.

The traditional prayer for a Jewish *chokham*, a wise Torah scholar, ends, "Who has apportioned of his wisdom to those who fear him." For the last part, Zalman substituted: "to those who honor his name." I did wonder how the Dalai Lama, who did not believe in a creator deity, nevertheless could be said to honor his name. But Zalman's point was that for the first time Jews would create a prayer to recognize the sacred in other religions.

He answered the objections about being too original by citing his source for the language, chanting the Hebrew from memory in an enchanting way. He claimed that the prophet Malachi had chartered a dialogue of spiritual equals when he wrote, "Then they that feared the

Lord/Spoke one with another;/And the Lord hearkened, and heard. /And a book of remembrance was written before Him./*For they that feared the Lord, and that thought upon his name.*" (Malachi 3:16)

Rabbi Greenberg delighted in the quotation. I could see that despite his differences with Zalman, he was closer to him in his thinking—at least about this issue—than I might have thought. Yitz felt the Dalai Lama, though his tradition has "direct cognitive dissonance with ours, is nevertheless thinking about God—*as we see it.*"

But Blu, who tended to work these things out through her gut feelings, still objected, and she eventually turned the tide. Now Joy Levitt declared that the situation was already radical, "so the liturgy doesn't have to be." Zalman was caught in a pincer movement—right and left, Orthodox and Reconstructionist.

So they came back to the traditional blessing of a Gentile sage. But Zalman objected that this blessing was a put-down, because it ended with the phrase *bsar vdam,* flesh and blood. The implication was that a Gentile, however wise, is only a creature of flesh and blood.

Yitz replied, "That he's human is not a put-down. First, because I don't believe he's a god. The fact that his own people do, I'm happy to dialogue with them, but I want to make clear where I stand on that." Yitz felt the Dalai Lama himself had removed such claims in his latest autobiography by describing himself as "a simple Buddhist monk."

In the end, Zalman agreed to recite the traditional prayer in Hebrew and his more innovative prayer in Tibetan. God presumably would handle the simultaneous translation with an appropriate sense of irony. The Tibetans would feel respected, the Jews uncompromised, and the dialogue could begin.

Unfortunately for Marc Lieberman's agenda, Yitz Greenberg's two minutes had stretched to a half hour and there was little time left for other discussion before lunch.

I understood Marc's frustrations. The Dalai Lama *pilpul* seemed a paradigm for the problems Judaism faces today. Yes, there are always dangers of becoming disconnected from the tradition. But there is an equally grave danger in ignoring contemporary realities.

For instance, the question of the *minyan*. Although I respected the difficulty of Rabbi Greenberg's position and admired the deftness of his maneuvers, I feel that to have to worry so late in the twentieth century about whether a woman's prayers count in the eyes of God is silly. Nor do I buy the explanation the Orthodox offer that somehow a woman praying with men is a distraction.

In fact, as the rabbis debated, I wondered if the Dalai Lama wasn't ahead of the game in facing up to contemporary realities. The previous afternoon, when he spoke at the All Himalayan Conference, the Buddhist leader had stressed that Buddhism had to find "a synthesis between modern science and traditional teachings."

His audience included rather conservative monks and abbots, who'd come to talk about traditional sciences. Yet he boldly counseled them to "find new ideas in Buddhism." Interestingly, the suggested method amounted to Buddhist midrash. Words "not fitting with reality if taken literally, should be interpreted."

The Tibetan people are in an entirely critical situation. The millions left behind to Chinese rule have lost their chief spiritual leader. Their monasteries and temples lie in heaps of rubble, their libraries and precious religious objects are destroyed. The Chinese are devastating a country that has been isolated geographically and politically and thereby, up until now, has preserved intact a tremendous treasure of ancient wisdom. Now that the great spiritual bank of Tibetan Buddhism has been broken open, its wealth threatens to be scattered and lost.

In this crisis, the burden of preservation falls heavily on the religious leadership in exile, and particularly to the Dalai Lama and his fellow monks and abbots living in Dharamsala.

One could imagine in this situation the Dalai Lama being a rather conservative restorationist, such as those ultra-Orthodox Jews Moshe Waldoks had referred to, who are busy reconstructing the *shtetl* in Israel and Brooklyn. Yet instead, he has become a Buddhist reformer. He has stated many times that if science can disprove a Buddhist doctrine—such as rebirth for instance—then the doctrine should be put aside. Modern science and Buddhism cannot contradict, because Buddhism is based on reality.

In some ways, the Dalai Lama enjoys a greater freedom to innovate than the rabbis. First, he is the undisputed leader of Tibetan Buddhism, a position no rabbi, not even the Chief Rabbi of Israel, could ever claim. There is no pope in Judaism. At a more subtle level, it appears that Jews and Buddhists have strikingly different attitudes toward language. In

Judaism there is a profound reverence for the written word—and a profound literalism. For instance, the Orthodox believe it is better to pray in Hebrew without understanding than to pray in one's own language. Even Zalman, at his most innovative, felt compelled to tie his prayer to a specific verse in Malachi. I thought again of the Frankfurt airport, how we'd been drawn to that Torah. I should think that anyone visiting a synagogue and seeing Jews revering and kissing their Torahs would think we worshiped our scrolls. Certainly my experience of Judaism was an experience with language—my quarrels, a quarrel with language.

Though we would learn that Tibetan Buddhists have a tremendous textual tradition of their own, the daring of Buddhist metaphysics is to defy all conventions, even the conventions of Buddhism. Words are labels, and even the Buddhist teaching, or dharma, has no ultimate reality. In fact, I have heard Buddhist scholars argue that a person who says, "I am a Buddhist," cannot be a Buddhist, because to be a Buddhist means to have no attachment to labels.

By contrast, the rabbis were very concerned with holding on to traditional language to preserve the continuity and authenticity of their Judaism. The words chosen for a prayer represented the consensus of *clal yisrael,* the unity of Israel. The discussion was not just a wrangling among denominations, or rabbinical showboating—though there were elements of that. Searching for the right words was a group attunement, a way to align all the energies of the Jews so they might face the Dalai Lama with a sense of unity. Now they could feel they were approaching the dialogue with integrity, working as Jews together.

6

Contact

As we entered the guard house, just within the Dalai Lama's compound, I remembered the Hasidic tale of a young man who journeyed many difficult miles to visit his rebbe. "Did you go to study Torah?" he was asked. "No, I went to see how the rebbe tied his shoes."

I was eager to see how the Dalai Lama tied his shoes. How he spoke, how he listened. I hoped to find in his gestures what it might mean to call a human being holy.

The Jewish group filled out forms, showed passports and visas, and registered with Indian military security, a reminder that the Dalai Lama was far from home, and not entirely safe.

We crossed a courtyard to the front porch of Bryn Cottage, bordered by roses and purple bougainvillea, and entered a small anteroom. Shoshana Edelberg, a professional journalist who was normally cool under pressure, nervously fiddled with her boom mike and cords. The rest of us were armed with cameras and cassette recorders.

The Samaya Foundation videotaped the sessions. To accommodate the fixed camera, the eight Jewish delegates sat in a horseshoe pattern around the Dalai Lama.

Michael Sautman led us in to the meeting room, which was more homey than royal. The participants sat in comfortable stuffed couches covered with blue cloth and the rest of us observers on folding chairs. Two stuffed armchairs were reserved for the Dalai Lama and whoever addressed him. Professor Nathan Katz would be up first, followed by Rabbis Schachter and Greenberg.

Behind the Dalai Lama's chair was a wooden shrine that looked like a fireplace mantel. On it rested twelve gold and silver bowls, brimming with water, as an offering, along with two vases of fresh roses and carnations. In a cabinet, behind a glass door, stood a golden icon of Avalokiteshvara. For the Tibetan faithful, the Dalai Lama himself is that Buddha of Compassion.

A curtain parted and he entered through a doorway beside the shrine. We rose to meet him, falling into a line that circled the perimeter of the horseshoe. Everyone grabbed the chance, video technicians, the reporters, Yitz and Blu's son, Moshe Greenberg, and Michael Sautman's parents.

Michael had instructed us meticulously on the protocol. Each of us approached the Dalai Lama—palms together in a sign of respect and a white silk scarf, a *katak,* draped over the wrists. The Dalai Lama took the scarf and draped it over our shoulders. Nathan Katz instructed us to remove the scarf quickly. To leave it on would be arrogant—to Tibetans the *katak* symbolized divinity.

"When you greet him," Michael Sautman had explained, "don't hurry. He'll want to make some contact with you. It's not just a ritual of handing him a scarf, it's a moment of human contact with him. He's just radiating then."

My turn came. The Dalai Lama smiled, radiant, yes, beaming so that I couldn't help but smile myself. Then he gave me a sharp penetrating glance. I turned my head away. I felt a little naked, in the soul.

Now a seasoned reporter would call this purely subjective, possibly nonsensical; a psychologist might say I was experiencing anxiety—and a cynic would laugh—and I had within me all those characters.

The Dalai Lama gathered his bright scarlet robe tightly around himself, joking to Professor Nathan Katz, seated next to him, that "it gives me some kind of warmth." Then he turned to the group at large and spoke in a deep voice.

"Welcome, our Jewish brothers and sisters. We are always very much eager to learn from your experience, and of course we are only happy to exchange our own experience with our Jewish brothers and sisters." He reached for some neatly folded yellow cloths on the armrest of his chair and wiped his nose. "Today I have a quite severe cold, so I hope you will not get it. I hope not to exchange this cold."

Michael Sautman asked Karma Gelek to introduce the three distinguished abbots of Tibetan monasteries, seated just behind Nathan Katz. Karma Gelek would translate for them.

The abbots were all men of the Dalai Lama's generation. Lati Rinpoche and Jiton Rinpoche were *tulkus,* recognized reincarnations of distinguished lamas. In Tibet they had headed important monasteries and schools.

Geshe Lobsang was the present abbot of the Sera Je monastery, in South India, now the biggest outside of Tibet. His title, *geshe,* means that he had studied advanced Buddhist teachings for decades—the monastic equivalent of a Ph.D. As he stood to be introduced, he bowed with deep humility.

These men at the Dalai Lama's back represented the anchor of his tradition, as surely as Rabbi Greenberg was bound to his Orthodox community back home.

Michael Sautman suggested we go around in a circle and briefly introduce ourselves and our affiliations. Then he called on Zalman Schachter to deliver the much-debated prayer. Reb Zalman wore his black rayon, full-length liturgical robe (in Yiddish, a *kappoteh*), and topped it off with a sable tail *streimel,* the fashion in hats favored by the Hasidim. Zalman was, strictly speaking, no longer a Hasid, and carefully referred to himself as "in the Hasidic tradition." But he wore the *streimel,* in part, he told me later, because Tibetan nobility wore similar fur hats. He believed the hats derived from a common source, the Mongols, passed on via the Cossacks and Tatars to the Polish and Lithuanian nobility and thence to the Jews.

"In our tradition," he told the Dalai Lama, " when we meet a wise sage and king, we have to recite a blessing to thank God for the privilege, and it goes like this," then chanted, "*Barukh ata adonai elohenu melekh haolam asher halak mikovodo umihokhmatov lebasar vdam.*" The melody was plaintive and my ears, schooled by that morning's debate, could pick up a hint of regret when he hit *lebasar vdam*, flesh and blood. He paused and the Jewish group added an amen.

While the Dalai Lama listened, he seemed to draw inward, and his face became impressively blank as if temporarily erased.

"And I will now try to say it in Tibetan." Zalman's tone was playful, a childlike delight, and the Dalai Lama responded with a big Santa Claus laugh. Zalman chanted his more innovative prayer in Tibetan, the Dalai Lama smiling to burst throughout; at the end he applauded and commented, "Oh, perfect." The room filled with laughter and applause and Blu Greenberg said with some pride, "No one else in the entire Jewish community could do that beside Reb Zalman." I thought, yes, very few had Zalman's breadth of knowledge, intellectual nimbleness, and sense of theater.

The Dalai Lama chuckled some more, then added, in low tones, almost a whisper, "Thank you." After so much debate the prayers had lasted less than a minute.

The Dalai Lama formally opened the dialogue. Perhaps Karma Gelek had made him aware of the controversy over "His Holiness," for he told the Jews that since this meeting came from "a genuine desire, a sincere motivation, an eagerness to learn from different traditions, there was no need for formality," which could be a barrier, "no need," he said, "for any hesitation. Whatever you feel you want to express here, please consider me as your own brother and I consider you as my own brothers and sisters. So, too, that way we can reach a deeper level." A palpable silence followed as we took that in and then, as if to make the point, he added, "That's all," and everyone roared.

The constant resort to humor was an unexpected meeting of the two cultures. Joking and kidding flowed from both sides. Laughter was never far from his heart. It just rocked out of him, rumbling along quite naturally, like cool water from a deep artesian well.

Nathan Katz, a bearded and rotund professor of Religious Studies from the University of South Florida, spoke first. He wished to demolish Rudyard Kipling's old saw that "East is East and West is West and never the twain shall meet." Instead, as a student of Hindu, Buddhist, and Jewish religion, Katz believed that Judaism and Buddhism had contact in the past. "The ancient Greeks," he declared, "knew about the Buddha. Ancient Israel also knew about India. The Buddha and our

King Solomon share legends. Words from Sanskrit and Tamil are found in our ancient holy book, the Bible. We construct memory in the present, and by constructing memory we create our identity. What we remember constructs who we are, and that's an insight of Buddhist philosophy also. What we forget also makes us who we are. Both of us, Jews and Tibetans, have forgotten we go back a long way together. It's only recently that we've forgotten."

Since we had all come thinking that this dialogue was unprecedented, Nathan was challenging some basic assumptions. In support of his argument, he reeled off intriguing evidence of contacts in the ancient world between Jews and Buddhists.

He noted that certain words in the Bible such as the Hebrew for ginger and ivory have Sanskrit roots. (Interestingly, so does *pilpul!*) He pointed to the trade between Israel and India in the time of King Solomon. He said that the tale of the judgment of Solomon also appears in the Jataka tales, stories of the Buddha's previous incarnations. He explained that the basic Buddhist concept of *shunyata*, or emptiness, which derives from Indian philosophy, was carried by a Jewish scholar into the Arabic world where it became the mathematical zero. The Arabic numerals were transmitted to the West by way of a Dominican monk. As Nathan suggested, the peregrination of zero from Hindu to Jew to Arab to Catholic monk represents a strong refutation of Kipling: "Jews were the first refugees to come to India [in the year 70 C.E.]. You are the most recent religious refugees to India. We both found havens in this tolerant land."

Given the burning cars and angry students we'd seen on the way up, I put a few mental quote marks around "tolerant land." But for all of its history, India has been highly tolerant of its Jews. Nathan had personal experience of this, for he had spent a Fulbright year in Cochin, researching a remarkable settlement of Jews on the south coast of India, who date back at least a thousand years. Moreover, as Katz explained, over the centuries there have been Jewish settlements in most of the regions surrounding Tibet, including China, Kashmir, India, and Mongolia. Hebrew manuscripts dating back to the eighth century have been discovered in Tibetan monasteries of Kucha in Mongolia. In the ninth century, a Muslim philosopher from Central Asia, al-Buruni, noted that the Jewish word for God cannot be pronounced and compared this to "the Hindu word *Om* and the Buddhist word *shunyata* because *shunyata* is beyond our language and the Hebrew God is beyond our language."

Still, Professor Katz had to admit that Tibetans and the Jewish people have no recorded history in common. As the Dalai Lama had noted in greeting the Jews the day before at the All Himalayan Conference, "There's no word in Gujarati for snow. No word in Tibetan for Jews." But Katz suggested that perhaps what had been lost was the memory of contact.

This seemed a highly speculative proposition for the moment, and I felt somewhat skeptical. In popular culture, imagination has sometimes run wild—there is a book floating around by a Russian author claiming proof that Jesus had spent his lost years in a Tibetan Buddhist monastery! It was only when I returned to Delhi and toured some of its shrines with Nathan Katz, that it would seem more plausible to me that Jews and Tibetan Buddhists might well have interacted, and even had a dialogue, four hundred years ago.

Throughout the presentation, the Dalai Lama fixed his attention on Nathan unwaveringly. I saw again how the master tied his shoes. It's not that he was always equally animated or fascinated by what he heard—but he always seemed completely there for the speaker, completely absorptive.

At the end of Nathan's talk, the Dalai Lama paused a few moments, digesting all he had heard, and then responded point by point.

This style of response derives partly from his monastic training. The *gelukpa* sect is very proud of its debating tradition. The Dalai Lama had made sure to house the monks' debating school, the Institute of Buddhist Dialectics, close to his home. Later that afternoon we would see the debating monks in action, which made a nice Tibetan bookend to the Jewish debating I'd observed all morning. In fact, as Professor Katz pointed out, the Tibetans and Jews are the sole religious traditions that incorporate formal debate as part of their religious training. As a very young man, the Dalai Lama had faced down the sages of Tibet in a day-long demonstration of his debating prowess. The requirement to absorb complex arguments and respond with appropriate quotations from Buddhist texts generously sharpened his powers of memory. Talmudic training has a similar effect, judging from the quotations that I'd heard flying around Kashmir Cottage.

But while Jews keep ties to the ancient world, it struck me in that room how much the Tibetans still belong to it altogether. Like the tallis, the Tibetan monk's robe is first cousin to the toga, and *gelukpa* pedagogy harkens back to the days of the first-century rabbinic sages. One morning in Dharamsala I was awakened near dawn by a woman's chanting. I listened for about a half an hour, impressed by the length of her prayers. But Nathan Katz explained she was actually chanting a Buddhist treatise on mindfulness, which she had mindfully engraved in her memory, page after page. I thought of the *tannaim,* who recited Mishnah in the early Talmudic academies before the oral law was written down. Again and again through contact with the Tibetans, I would feel in touch not with something exotic, but with an ancient memory in my own tradition suddenly springing to life.

The Dalai Lama's extraordinary ability to memorize and repeat every point he was told was also an act of respect. As was another gesture that I'd noticed with other Tibetans, which contrasted greatly with our conversational habits in Jewish culture: How kind it is, to take just a minute to reflect before responding to a question. It was a habit I vowed to cultivate.

After his talk, Nathan Katz pointed out that many Jews have studied Tibetan Buddhism. He asked the Tibetans to reciprocate and send some graduate students to his university to study Judaism. The Dalai Lama responded positively. As for the hypothesis of earlier contacts, the Tibetan leader admitted, with perhaps a hint of irony, "This is very, very new to me."

Although highly speculative, Nathan Katz's presentation had been animated and useful. By suggesting that history itself is always under construction, he made me more conscious of the history about to be constructed before our eyes when the more formal lecturing gave way to real give-and-take.

7

The Angel of Tibet and the Angel of the Jews

I don't know if anything could have prepared us for what happened in the next hour. The Dalai Lama threw a curve, and Zalman gracefully caught it. Together we entered unfamiliar realms, the four worlds of the kabbalah.

For months Zalman Schachter-Shalomi had prepared himself in his daily prayers and thoughts for this encounter, which he thought of crucial importance. "I was aware that inside of me there was a movement preparing for this event. All my reading, dreaming, talking with students and friends, praying and meditation, checking my chart for transits, reflecting on, discussing and packing the gifts, and sharing with other participants." This preparation was part of what Zalman called "getting there in *kavvanah* before actually arriving" in Dharamsala.

Kavvanah is an important element of Hasidic devotional practice. The term means "intention" and that is the sense of Zalman's statement. But the *kavvanot* are basically specific meditations or concentrations of thought designed to make prayer or a mitzvah more effective. For instance, one might visualize the unity of God through specific images before reciting the *Shema,* or simply take a moment to meditate in silence on the purpose of a given prayer before reciting it.

In a sense, Zalman's whole life could be seen as developing a *kavvanah* for his role in the dialogue, which was crucial. He would translate the esoteric language of Judaism into terms a Tibetan Buddhist could understand. This necessitated a rare combination of expertise. Zalman was not only thoroughly versed in the Jewish mystical tradition, but he had also studied Hindu and Buddhist thought.

He'd made specific connections with Tibetan Buddhism early on. When the Dalai Lama went into exile in 1959, Zalman fired off a telegram to David Ben-Gurion suggesting that Israel be offered as a place of refuge. (It wasn't.) Then in the early 1960s, he'd learned about Tibetan Buddhism through encounters with Geshe Wangyal, a Mongolian lama who taught at Columbia and founded a Buddhist monastery in Freehold, New Jersey.

As Blu Greenberg had noted, Reb Zalman is a unique figure—one of the most controversial rabbis on the American Jewish scene. He has been a guiding force in the whole countercultural Jewish movement since the late sixties. To his followers he has been both a canny and perceptive theoretician of Jewish renewal and a source of contact with the vast wealth of Jewish wisdom that might otherwise be inaccessible. To his detractors, he is flaky and irresponsible, condemned for his excesses, personal and doctrinal. I think that's a bad rap, but it's certainly true that Zalman crosses boundaries of all sorts. He has danced with Sufi masters and meditated with Buddhists and has been a general pioneer not only in interfaith dialogue, but in the kind of liturgy sharing that makes Yitz Greenberg uncomfortable. As early as 1973, Zalman had attempted to bring elements of *vipassana* meditation into a Yom Kippur service, as a way of enhancing prayer on that day of self-examination.

By this time, I'd seen enough of Reb Zalman in action to know that his talents and energies would be stifled in a role as socially constricted as congregational rabbi. When I met him, I finally understood the whole tradition of oral masters, who are best appreciated in person, and who inspire others through their incredible flow of ideas, images, and illuminating tales. Though he holds a degree in the psychology of religion, has taught at major universities, and published both popular and scholarly works, he is much more in the line of a classic teacher of wisdom or a holy man. He is charismatic and spontaneous, with a highly developed theatrical sense, and a touch of the clown. But he is far too open about his own spiritual struggles and failings to be a cult leader. This same openness has made him attractive to many otherwise disaffected Jews—by now a worldwide network of political activists, social workers, Buddhist meditators, writers, teachers, and rabbis who consider Zalman their rebbe.

In his home base of Philadelphia, he guides a Jewish renewal spiritual community, P'nai Or, or "Faces of Light." It is currently expanding into a network of Jewish renewal *chavurot* called ALEPH, Alliance for Jewish Renewal. Zalman has toured the world giving workshops, showing how the accumulated wisdom of kabbalah can be applied to today's life, trying to enrich and vivify Jewish practice, doing what he calls "R and D work in davennology," the study of Jewish prayer.

Today the Jewish mystical tradition is most actively transmitted within Hasidic groups like the Lubavitchers. Such ultra-Orthodox practitioners would probably feel prohibited from dialogue with Buddhists. So given the Dalai Lama's request to learn more about the Jewish esoteric, Zalman's unique role as an authentically trained disseminator of such teachings was crucial to our dialogue.

But Zalman's *kavvanah* arose also from a strong sense of identification with the plight of the Tibetans in exile. Because he carries a living memory of pre-Holocaust Hasidism, of a world and way of life consigned to ashes, he respected the Dalai Lama in a very intimate sense, as a colleague who bore on his shoulders a tremendous burden. Before his presentation, Zalman turned and looked into his eyes.

"I want to say that when a soul comes down to earth they show him first what he has to do here, that's our tradition. And I believe those who volunteer for difficult jobs deserve special consideration. When I think of the job you have to do, which is not only to guide your people through the crisis and, God willing, the restoration of your home, but also the risks you must take and the choices you must make of what is essential and what is to be left behind, I want you to know that I feel with you from heart to heart."

When Rabbi Schachter finished, the Dalai Lama grasped his hand between his two palms and thanked him softly.

I liked Zalman's personal gesture. It humanized the situation after so much grand talk—and worry—about formalities. And already he was showing us how the Dalai Lama could be seen as a kind of Hasidic master. Just as the Tibetans believed the Dalai Lama to be the fourteenth incarnation of his lineage, so the Hasidim also believe, in the words of Louis Jacobs, that "God sent down from heaven the lofty souls of the Baal Shem Tov and his disciples to illumine the darkness of exile" in the old Russian Pale.

Nathan Katz had stressed that we construct memory in the present to create our identity. If so, the mainstream American Jewish religious identity has become highly exoteric, with strong emphasis on ethnicity and the politics of Israel. In such a context, Rabbi Schachter explained, "our teachings have been kept secret even from Jews for a long time. So every day, when people get up and say their prayers, there is an exoteric order. But hidden inside the exoteric is the esoteric, the deep attunement, the deep way."

The deep way is the way of the kabbalah, "tradition" or "what is received." Kabbalah claims an ancient origin, has been passed from master to student mostly through an oral tradition, has drawn its inspiration from canonical texts, mainly Genesis, the Song of Songs, and Ezekiel, and has produced over the centuries a rich written literature, whose major works include the cryptic *Sefer Yetzirah* (*Book of Formation*), and the florid and lengthy *Zohar,* or *Book of Splendor.*

Hoping to show the Dalai Lama points of contact and similarity between kabbalah and Buddhist tantra, Rabbi Schachter framed his entire presentation in Tibetan Buddhist terms. "I have been told," he said, "that Tibetans want to know the view, the path, and the goal." As he spoke, he flipped the pages of a chart he'd prepared in magic marker on a poster-sized pad—the chart was full of annotations in Hebrew, English, and Tibetan—with smatterings of Sanskrit thrown in too. "And a friend did this here to say it in Tibetan "—the friend was Nathan Katz—"and I hope this is clear and transparent. I don't know what it means."

Everyone laughed and the Dalai Lama ribbed him, referring to the opening blessing, "You know Tibetan now, so you should get it right." It occurred to me that thanks to Nathan Katz, Hebrew and Tibetan had met for the first time as holy languages.

In Tibetan Buddhist teaching, the view is a fundamental orientation toward the nature, cause, and elimination of suffering. The path is a definite method of spiritual improvement through systematic meditations. The goal is to become a *bodhisattva*, a living buddha, whose great compassion will help all sentient beings eliminate their suffering.

Zalman wished to present the very different view, path, and goal of mystical Judaism. Where Buddhism begins with the nature of mind and its suffering, the kabbalistic view presents a cosmology. This map of the universe is based on a mystical interpretation of the primordial acts of creation in Genesis. When kabbalists read Genesis, they see not one, but four, worlds being created. The four supernal worlds correspond to the four letters of God's name—*yod, he, vov,* and *he.* The chart looked like this:

'	Yod	Fire	Spirit	Emanation	Intuition	Atziluth
ה	He	Air	Mind	Creation	Knowing	Beriah
ו	Vov	Water	Heart	Formation	Feeling	Yet zirah
ה	He	Earth	Body	Function	Doing	Assiyah

Zalman's interpretation of this cosmology had a decidedly psychological cast. "Each of the letters," he told the Dalai Lama, "represents a realm of the spirit or consciousness," namely the body, heart, mind, and spirit. "So the first part of prayer gets into the body and says to God, 'Thank you for the body,' and prepares the body. The second part of prayer takes you to the heart and it says, 'I want to attune myself to gratefulness to God,' to say, 'Oh, this is a good world, oh, this is wonderful, the sun is rising. I want to give thanks.' Up here in the realm of air you go to thinking, to wisdom, to trying to understand and to know. Then, going up to the highest place—the fire—there it isn't knowledge with the head, it is intuition."

The last word was unfamiliar and the Dalai Lama conferred with Karma Gelek in Tibetan. Zalman explained that intuition was "knowing by being rather than with your head."

"Knowing something automatically, spontaneously," the Dalai Lama suggested.

Zalman nodded. "And by identity." He pointed to the Dalai Lama. "I know you now as an other." He pointed to his palm. "You know yourself as a self. If I were to know you as you know yourself, that would be intuition."

Zalman's presentation correlated the four worlds with the elements: earth, water, air, and fire. When the Dalai Lama commented that in Buddhism there are also four elements, "and sometimes we add a fifth element, space," Zalman smiled like a teacher to an eager student, saying, "I'll come to that in a moment."

The four worlds cosmology comes straight out of the Lurianic kabbalah, as transmitted through the early Hasidic masters and finally formulated by the Chabad Hasidism of the late eighteenth-century rabbi Schneur Zalman, founder of the Lubavitch sect. Rabbi Schachter's update blended Lubavitch teachings with contemporary psychology, opening up to me the utility of an otherwise remote mystical doctrine.

Moreover, the complex road map Rabbi Schachter presented is not just for looking, but for traveling. It shows the destinations for which prayer is the vehicle. I had experienced some of this with Zalman first in London, and more in Dharamsala. Now I was hearing the theoretical underpinning for his davening practice. It certainly wasn't anything I'd ever been taught in Reform Jewish synagogue, where intense prayer would probably have been regarded as eccentric and embarrassing.

But in the Hasidic tradition, when one davens with true *kavvanah*, the four worlds of body, heart, mind, and spirit are called upon. Specific *kavvanot*, or meditations, are used to connect the words of a given prayer to the *sefirot*, thereby directing the prayer to the supernal realms. Through prayer, recited with inward intention, one rises from world to world to reach the goal of nearness to God.

There is an interesting connection to Buddhist thought when one reaches the level of nearness, or *atziluth*. But before Zalman could explain it to the Dalai Lama, the conversation took a detour. It happened this way. As Zalman gestured toward the second world on the chart, *yetzirah*, he mentioned casually that *devas* inhabit that realm, "according to our tradition."

The Dalai Lama interrupted. "What do you mean when you say *deva?*" In attempting to translate from Jewish to Buddhist, Zalman had used the Sanskrit term for a Buddhist deity. Though Buddhists do not believe in a single Creator Deity, they do speak of gods and goddesses. Some *devas* were depicted on the *thangkas* we had seen in Tsuglakhang as guardians of the dharma. Others are regarded as actual gods and demons belonging to the six orders of sentient beings. Still another interpretation is that *devas* are symbols or mental projections.

Zalman retranslated. By *devas,* he meant angels.

That touched off something magical in the Dalai Lama. For the next half hour the cosmic view was lost in a close-up of angels, angels, angels.

"When we speak of angels," Zalman explained, "we mean by that beings of such large consciousness"—he pointed to his forehead—"that if an angel's consciousness were to flow into my head right now, it would be too much for me." He raised his eyebrows, and his *streimel* started to slide off his head. It was right out of Charlie Chaplin. An expansive angel was flipping Zalman's lid.

The rabbi straightened his *streimel* and continued, "There are all kinds of angels. So that higher and higher for instance, we think each nation has an angel. Right now there's an angel of Tibet and an angel of Jews that are also talking on another level. So I believe if we do it right, the Angel of Jews will put words in my mouth and the Angel of Tibet will hear them in you—and vice versa. The dialogue is not only on this plane."

And with those words, it no longer was.

The Dalai Lama was full of questions. He leaned forward, and the robe he had earlier wrapped so tightly around himself slipped off his shoulder, revealing his bare forearm and shoulder.

"This angel . . . Do you regard just one angel or many angels?"

Zalman answered with great delight, "Oh, many, many, many. Realms of angels."

"When you say Angel of Tibet, Angel of Jews, there are many?"

"First, on the lower level, each family, each group, each city has angels, but on the highest level there is one who contains and represents the consciousness of the totality. If I were to speak in terms of mythic language, we act out what they are doing." As Zalman spoke the Dalai Lama responded, oh, oh, oh, to each point.

"So generally," the Dalai Lama asked, "do you consider angels as servants of God?"

"Yes, including the black one, including Satan. All are doing God's work. All is in oneness, nothing is outside of God."

"Between the angels there are positive and negative? Or generally positive?"

"It goes like this. Even the negative ones are positive. Their job is sometimes to create negative energy. For instance, as I look at *thangkas* and see wrathful deities, I have the sense that the wrathful deities are also in the service of the cosmos, except that their energies sometimes have to come with strengths and fire and severity. So that's how it's seen. There are angels for rewarding people and for imparting wisdom and angels also for punishing and for testing. This is in our tradition."

Zalman wanted to move on, but the Dalai Lama interrupted, "So even those angels, do you believe they have different colors?" (He'd picked up on Zalman's reference to Satan as the black one.) His voice rose with interest.

Reb Zalman answered warmly, "Oh, yes, yes. The description goes, there are fire angels, seraphim." He handed his charts to Nathan Katz and stood up to demonstrate. "Isaiah says there are angels with six wings." Zalman held out his arms, flapping his hands. "With two they cover their feet, with two they cover their faces, and with two they fly. And when the angels raise up their wings, they stand like a menorah." He lifted his arms into the air.

The Dalai Lama turned to his translator, Laktor. "Menorah?"

"Like a candleholder," the monk whispered back.

Rabbi Schachter added, "With six branches. So we say *kadosh, kadosh, kadosh*—holy, holy, holy is the Lord of Hosts." At each *kadosh*, Zalman moved his wings from thighs to face to flying position—and then finished the prayer, "the whole earth is full of his glory"—sweeping his right arm. He was an angel standing on high, viewing the whole earth spread below him.

The Dalai Lama was delighted. "Oh, beautiful," he said.

"The angels who praise God are called seraphim," Zalman continued. "Then there are angels that look like animals. One with a face like a lion. Another has a face of a bull. Another one has a face like an eagle and another has a face like the human being. These angels represent the signs of the Zodiac of the year. Each person has a nature. Sometimes a person has a bull nature, sometimes a person has a lion nature, or an eagle nature, and there's a person who is a human being. So all these natures are influenced by those angels." He pointed up to the heavens. "That's how we talk about it."

The Dalai Lama actually giggled.

"Right. And then below that, still more below, there are angels we call wheels. These angels have to do with shifting energy around. Sometimes we come into a room and the room feels flat, no energy. Sometimes a room is filled with energy. *Ophan*, one of those wheel angels is there and energizes the thing. But angels . . . " Zalman swept his hands in the air, as if dismissing the subject. But the Dalai Lama was undeterred.

"So these angels have some connection with the weather condition?"

"Yes, yes, yes."

"There was some small earthquake at seven this morning. So there was some angel?"

Zalman nodded. "That's right. They say not a blade of grass grows without an angel saying, 'Grow, grow, grow.' Angels are pushing fruit to ripen. So they speak of all kinds of beings, but when we use the word angel, that is only human speech because the number and variety of these beings is beyond being able to count. Okay. But I want to go away from the angels, I want to go higher." He made a sweeping away motion with his hands again, this time more forcefully, and then pointed upwards with his thumb as the Dalai Lama laughed.

"Oh," he said, looking slightly abashed.

"Okay?" Zalman asked.

But even then the Dalai Lama did not want to let the subject go. Instead, he steered the conversation toward a point of some subtlety. The Buddhist leader wanted to know if the action by these angels is ultimate. Do they have autonomy and authority or "did all their activities come through the creator's guidance?"

Reb Zalman answered, "If I would use an electrical image, I would say, the infinite needs transformers for lower levels." He built a transformer tower with his hands raised high and then represented the cascading down of energy with large spirals. "Ultimately there are no angels, ultimately there is God. But the garment God wears appears to us as an angel. So God has a little finger, and the little finger, as it were, has a glove, and the glove has another glove, and the outermost glove is what we would call an angel, or what we would call a wind or a force in the universe. But what moves them is always the power of the creator."

This discussion had taken some time, and Rabbi Schachter was anxious to get back to his charts. But just as Marc Lieberman had predicted, the real energy in the dialogue emerged in give-and-take with the Dalai Lama. The *ophanim*, the wheels, were moving around the room, exchanging energies all around.

I could see that the other Jewish delegates were getting a bit uncomfortable with that energy. Rabbis have egos too, and perhaps some were simply concerned that Zalman would use up most of the time that day. (As indeed he did.) But there was something else too. Although the group had already assumed Rabbi Schachter's material would be of interest, they could not have anticipated this absolute explosion of curiosity from the Dalai Lama. It hit with enormous force. Suddenly they confronted their own embarrassment about the subject, which was not just theirs personally, but endemic to contemporary Judaism itself.

Rabbi Greenberg, for instance, felt the need to add some spin control. "What you're hearing is the mystical tradition—actually there are two or three. Many in the more rational or more legal systems would not affirm all these beliefs." Then Rabbi Joy Levitt piped in, to general amusement, "And some of us are hearing them for the first time as well."

Even though her comic timing was impeccable, her remark defined in brief the whole mainstream Jewish attitude toward mysticism. Repression of angels had been going on for centuries, but somehow the Dalai Lama had cracked it open and released them.

Then Moshe Waldoks joined in. "There is no obligation to accept this, but if it helps you in reaching the higher levels, then you can accept it. Some people can reach higher levels maintaining a very rational position or ethical position without the use of angels. It's all an image, a colorful enjoyable image." He added, with unintended irony, "But some people get very frightened."

Yet the power of the angels could not be dismissed all that easily. Zalman's discourse partook of both belief and imagination. Though Moshe Waldoks was right to say that angels are an image, they are not *just* an image but how mystically minded Jews experience the living reality of God in everyday life. The question for the Hasidim is how to develop *kavvanah,* a strong spiritual intention, in order to lift everyday acts to higher realms. Visualizing a world in which every blade of grass growing has a cheering section of angels is a powerful help. At the rational level where contemporary Judaism tends to operate, it is important to discriminate. Logically, angels are either real or not real. But in the world of intuition, that logic no longer applies. Beautifully and profoundly, the image of two angels in dialogue captured the essence of the exchange between Rabbi Schachter and the Dalai Lama. Together they had raised the dialogue between Jews and Tibetans from the world of knowing to the world of intuition. And that was a very high place to be.

As Moshe Waldoks admitted later, the Jewish delegates had no reason to be embarrassed because the "esoteric is like gefilte fish to the Dalai Lama." It became obvious that the Buddhist leader had noticed the divisions in the Jewish group because a little later he joked about it. This, after a rather long consultation with the lamas behind him on a point of Buddhist doctrine. When he finished, he turned back to us and said, "I consult and they agreed. And they're the more Orthodox type." Over the ensuing laughter, I heard Yitz saying to Moshe Waldoks, "You see, it's the same world over. Covering your right flank."

Perhaps because of Yitz's spin control, the Dalai Lama looked for confirmation from Zalman. "What you are explaining about angels, do you find it mentioned in the Torah?"

"Yes," the rabbi affirmed. "In the five books of Moses it says when God closed off the Garden of Eden, he planted there an angel with a flaming sword. He sent angels to Avraham our grandfather, to announce the coming of a child. Our grandfather Jacob sent angels to his brother. The word angel also means messenger, so you can read it as messenger or as angel. If you have an inclination to mysticism, you say angel, and if you want to see everything as plain reality, then you say messenger."

But Zalman still had two more worlds to take the Dalai Lama through and not much time.

He had traveled from *assiyah* (doing) to *yetzirah* (feeling)—where the angels dwell. The realm above the angels is *beriah,* first creation. "If I were to borrow a word from your tradition I would say samsara is here." He explained that *beriah* is the beginning and source of the object world, the source of name and form and individuality, though it is "not yet object," but instead, "the divine mind conceiving of objects."

Above *beriah* is the realm of *atziluth*, emanation. *Atziluth* "is so infinite that it's both full and its empty. It's full of God and it's empty of everything, no object in it." This linking of God to a concept of emptiness was a crucial point of contact with Buddhism, as we would see.

Rabbi Schachter was giving the kabbalistic road map of God's creative processes. But because man was made in God's image, it is also a map of human creativity. The four worlds cosmology gave me a new vocabulary: one could speak of an intuition arising in the realm of emanation, becoming a thought in the realm of creation, being formed into a particular shape in the realm of formation, and eventuating in an action in the realm of function. There is a fifth level, as Zalman had hinted, above emanation—known to the Lurianic kabbalists as "Adam Kadmon"—but that was not discussed. Instead he turned from view to path.

Here Rabbi Schachter was going to address the second matter of interest to the Dalai Lama, what Michael Sautman at our breakfast meeting had called "thought transformation." This key element of Buddhist practice includes visualization, meditation, and as a preliminary to those practices, techniques of purgation such as prostrations. One Western Buddhist monk had told me about the one hundred thousand prostrations he was performing to purify himself to receive advanced teachings.

In Jewish terms, these activities correspond to prayer—in Hebrew, *tefillot*; in Yiddish, *davennen*. Not just prayer in synagogue, but the blessings or *brakhot* spoken throughout the day.

"Here is a very important part," Zalman explained. "Nothing we are to do should we do with instinct alone. Every instinct that we have can be gratified. But it always calls for stopping and becoming mindful. So we say a blessing before we eat. The blessing I said on greeting you is also part of this discipline."

With that, I understood better what Jonathan Omer-Man had meant by the inner choreography of that blessing. He was speaking of *kavanah*. Only with the proper intention would the blessing succeed in elevating our sense of the moment as we entered into dialogue.

"Here is where all the laws come in," Zalman continued, "to which all Jews are obligated. We speak of 613 of these laws."

"Six hundred and thirteen?" The Dalai Lama seemed impressed by the count.

"Six hundred and thirteen. So when a person in your tradition becomes a monk, he takes on 250. In the same way, when a boy becomes bar mitzvah, a girl becomes bat mitzvah—they take on the commandments. And from that time on there's an expectation of doing what leads to purification."

The next stage up the ladder from doing is formation or feeling. "Purification of the action isn't enough because what leads a person to do the wrong action is often the wrong attitude. So then on this level of formation or feeling comes the development of calm and of loving respect toward God and the universe—cleaning up the heart."

Borrowing a basic term from the Buddhist Eightfold Path, right aspiration, or right feeling, Zalman explained that "the laboratory for right feeling is prayer in the heart. Here is where we work, asking, Why did I do it? Before you go to sleep, you say, What was my day like? What did I do? Why did I do this? Once a week you do this deeper before the Shabbat. And once a year, at Rosh Hashana, you go though the year and you ask yourself, Why did I do what I did? and try to clean up all the karma, and this is where the discrimination of feeling comes in."

The Dalai Lama studied the chart intensely, looking it over like the detailed plans of a house. Zalman gave him time and for a moment the room fell quiet. Then he looked up and Zalman continued, "I can ask myself, Why do I hate that person? What's in my heart? Asking these questions, and working in the heart is what we do on this level of the path.

"But then we find out, that, why do I hate somebody? Because I have a wrong thought. If I would understand the context of that person's actions, I wouldn't hate him. So I have to now go to that realm of thought. And this is called *hitbonenut*, the contemplation of truth and also impermanence. This is where our traditions come very close. Our rabbis would be saying, 'Nothing of this world remains. Everything changes, everything falls apart.'"

"Yes."

"Yes. So at the level of thought when I understand this, why should I get so upset? The story about the wheel that turns—we use the same word, *galgal ha-hozer*. Today he is poor, tomorrow he is rich, it's all on the wheel"—Zalman's voice lilting, almost chanting—"it's all on the wheel. And the word that we use is *gilgul*, being on the wheel."

The Dalai Lama pronounced *gilgul* to himself a few times. It made an important contact between the two traditions—for Zalman was touching again on rebirth. He cited a bedtime prayer from the Art Scroll Siddur. "Before going to sleep: Master of the universe, I here forgive anyone who sinned against me, my body, my property, my honor, . . . whether he did it in this transmigration [*gilgul*] or another transmigration."

They would return to the subject, but the Dalai Lama had more questions about what he'd heard already. At the dialogue in New Jersey, the Buddhist leader had deferred any discussion about God or atheism, explaining that it was best to save such discussions over apparent disagreements until the two religions knew each other better. Now, evidently, that time had come. "Of course," he said, "you know Buddhism does not accept a creator. God as an almighty or as a creator, such we do not accept. But at the same time, if God means truth or ultimate reality, then there is a point of similarity to *shunyata*, or emptiness." *Shunyata* is also called by the Tibetans "dependent arising," the interrelatedness and interdependence of all things and beings. All phenomena that arise do so through previous conditions and relationships—nothing stands independently, permanently, or absolutely. All is interrelated. Such interrelatedness implies enormous individual freedom and responsibility. Perhaps that is why the discussion on angels had interested the Dalai Lama. It showed that in Jewish thought there is also a respect for different levels of creation, or "different levels of sentient beings." It corrected a simplistic notion—which seemed common among even Western Buddhists—of God as an autocrat, an all-powerful commandant.

Of course, many devout Jews do carry such an image of God. After all, in the prayer liturgy, God is described as a father, a king of kings, an almighty. But within the four worlds cosmology, the highest contemplations avoid such imagery. As Zalman had mentioned, the realm of nearness (*atziluth*) is both full of God and completely empty—because at that level there is no "thing" for God to be. The name the kabbalists used for God in *atziluth* is *ain sof*. This literally means no limit or infinite. Yet in some interpretations, *ain sof* is translated as *ayin*—nothing. For instance, the thirteenth-century kabbalist Joseph Gikatilla writes, "The depth of primordial being is called Boundless. It is also called *ayin* [nothing] because of its concealment from all creatures. If one asks, 'What is it?' the answer is, '*Ayin*,' that is, no one can understand anything about it." As the Dalai Lama had carefully phrased it, there is "a point of similarity" between the kabbalistic *ain sof* and the Buddhist *shunyata*. It would be exaggerating to say they are identical. The kabbalistic approach emphasizes that God is No Thing. But it still affirms an absolute existence—even if ineffable. In the Buddhist approach, all existence is empty because none of it has inherent reality, or absolute reality in itself.

Clearly though, by presenting the kabbalistic view, Zalman had changed the Dalai Lama's perceptions of monotheism. Now he saw that God is "the basis of all existence, not necessarily to create with a certain motivation or willingness."

"So personally," the Dalai Lama told Zalman, "when you explain it this way, it gives us a much wider perspective. When it becomes wider, or more sophisticated, then naturally there are more similarities."

I felt a tremendous excitement at this moment, a sense of a real meeting between the two religious traditions that Marc Lieberman must have had in mind for the dialogue all along. Zalman, who loves computer talk, would probably have called it a successful interface. The most obvious and fundamental difference between the two religions is zero and one, Buddhist nontheism and Jewish monotheism. But now that the angels were talking, *shunyata* had met *ain sof*. It was not necessary to equate the two concepts. But Rabbi Schachter and the Dalai Lama had narrowed the gap, and I felt the sparks leaping across the empty space.

The very word *God* had always been a stumbling block for me, but Zalman had made the concept much broader and more sophisticated, not only for the Dalai Lama, but also for me.

The Dalai Lama had mentioned creation and Zalman wanted to amplify. "I would like to suggest that the notion of a creator who comes from outside, who makes something happen, is not the way kabbalah spoke about it. Kabbalah speaks about emanation. It comes out of God.

There is nothing but God, so it all flows from God." He explained that there is a new feminine insight emerging that sees cosmology in female terms. Instead of seeing creation as "papa does and goes away, it is seen as more like mama, and child growing, and worlds begotten. Reality begotten—and arising out of. And so we speak of the womb of being, which could be seen as out of *shunyata*. Our theology is now very much in transformation because of the impact of feminist thought. People are saying the way you have expressed it up until now is how men think, do, and act."

This prompted a flurry of discussion about the role of women in Buddhism, a topic that would be covered more thoroughly at the second session. For now, the Buddhist leader wanted Zalman to complete his discussion of view, path, and goal.

So Rabbi Schachter explained that the goal of the Jewish mystic "at the highest level of all is not to come back in the world, but to achieve what is called the annihilation of the personal, to be totally drawn in to the being of God." This goal might be achieved over several lifetimes or reincarnations. So we were back to the wheel. And the Dalai Lama hadn't forgotten the angels. He wanted to know if angels could also experience rebirth, as *devas* do.

Reb Zalman answered, "Ravi Nachman of Bratzlav had a beautiful teaching. He said all of reality is like a spinning top. Sometimes that which is above becomes that which is below. That which was an angel becomes an animal, that which becomes a stone . . . "

The Dalai Lama interrupted with delight, "Oh. The same."

"When I first met with Geshe Wangyal in America," Zalman continued, "he asked me, is reincarnation only human or also in animals? I used to be a *shokhet*. It's one who kills the animals that are kosher. Before I would kill the animals I would send all the people out of the room. I would say to the animals, 'I don't mean to harm you, I mean to give you an opportunity to raise you up. When people eat you with mindfulness and they will open their hearts and their minds to God to pray, you will be able to experience human consciousness and move up on the level of incarnations.' That was part of the task."

The Dalai Lama did not linger over the image, but it made me smile—Zalman talking *gilgul* to poultry. I had to wonder how the chicken felt about the opportunity.

The Buddhist leader wanted to know how rebirth worked in Jewish doctrine. "What determines whether an angel in the next rebirth will be a bird or an animal? What is the main factor? Buddhists call it karma."

The term *karma* has entered popular American culture as a fuzzy synonym for fate. But serious Buddhists consider the theory of karma a science. Beginning with the simple idea of cause and effect; that is, every action produces a consequence, teachings about karma confirm that there is an ultimate overall economy of actions. In the long run, good actions will produce good consequences for those who do them, and likewise bad actions will produce bad consequences. Since this is not immediately obvious in the world we live in, karma in Buddhist thought presupposes rebirth. The long run includes life after life in various bodily frames, not only human, but also as animals, hell creatures, and *devas*. Rebirth is the Buddhist explanation of why bad things happen to good people. Our actions in one life plant seeds that may not flower or bear fruit until future lives.

For the Buddhist the goal of purification practices, such as prostrations and reciting of mantras, is to release one from the negative effects of previous actions, to purify bad karma. Unfinished karma provides energy for another birth, it keeps the wheel of rebirth spinning. The ultimate goal—known as nirvana—is getting off of the wheel. Now the Dalai Lama asked about the goal of the Jewish system.

"If an angel takes rebirth in animal form, is it due to the creator, or is it fate? How much is due to one's own behavior? How much is in God's hand?"

Rabbi Omer-Man spoke up. "Perhaps, I can give an image we use. Each soul has to create a garment. And each incarnation, each remanifestation, we make a little more or we undo a little more. Ultimately the goal is to complete the garment, which is a garment of light when it is finished. And some incarnations, we do more damage, we pull more threads out, in other incarnations we put more threads in. So how we are remanifest depends on what we have done in the past."

The Dalai Lama took this in and asked Jonathan, "The next reincarnation, what kind of reincarnation will take place, is that mainly due to the previous life's behavior?"

"Yes."

Now he appeared satisfied. This sounded very much like karma. The two mystical systems of rebirth appeared to have remarkable degrees of similarity.

Some monks came in with pots of tea, kneeling before us individually. I noticed we were being served by Karma Gelek and some of the other high officials, high lamas and sages, which was typical Tibetan Buddhist behavior—an effortless humility. For now, the dialogue at the mystical level was over. But it would be resumed in the next few days, and at the second session Jonathan Omer-Man would make an extraordinary presentation on Jewish meditation. A connection of surprising force had been made between the two traditions. I was now much more receptive to Nathan Katz's suggestion that they had somehow met before.

Yet Rabbi Schachter had gone very far in reaching out to Buddhism to make that connection. After all, mysticism is the front door of Tibetan Buddhism, but a very hidden back door of contemporary Judaism. I had no doubt that Zalman's presentation was well grounded in the Jewish mystical tradition. What I wondered, though, was how it connected to the Jewish present.

One part of me kept saying, Does he really believe all this stuff? Does a twentieth-century man with a computerized wristwatch believe in angels? Clearly not in the same way some of the Tibetan refugees in *chubas* believed in *devas*. I assumed their beliefs were premodern, Zalman's postmodern. The Tibetan agony is, in part, that of a medieval culture passing violently into the modern world. Jews have been wrestling with modernity ever since the Enlightenment, producing, among other things, the Haskalah movement, Zionism, and Reform Judaism. For most American Jews, very few of the old traditions have survived intact.

In its early triumphant phase, American Reform Judaism was particularly scathing, abolishing every thing from yarmulkes to bar mitzvahs. Even in these more observant days, if a Reform rabbi announced that he believed in angels, would the board renew his contract? To meet the Tibetans halfway, Zalman was doing a lot of translating, a lot of updating, a lot of psychologizing—he was pedaling pretty hard. But was the bike moving? Or was it all an exercise? There is a difference between understanding how a system works, or might have worked for certain

Jews in previous centuries—and the next step, which would be living that life today. Zalman had kept saying, "That's in our tradition." Yes, but where? And who has access to it now?

These are hard questions, not only for one who has stayed within Judaism, but maybe more for those who have left it. I was curious to hear from the JUBUs what they made of the angels.

For me, as for Rabbi Levitt, much of Zalman's presentation was news. But it was very good news. I decided to suspend disbelief and trust in the world of intuition what I could not yet confirm with my intellect. I stayed with my delight. After all, I had heard the Angel of the Jews speaking to the Angel of Tibet.

8

Always Remind

Rabbi Irving Greenberg's presentation would take us away from the supernal realms of *ain sof* to a much more familiar deity, a God who acts in Jewish history.

Less theatrical than Zalman, Rabbi Greenberg brought just as much passion to his presentation. Teaching Jewish history to the Tibetans, he believed, was a religious obligation, one that could be found in the Torah passage of the week, *Lekh Lekha* (Gen. 12:1–17:27). (It was getting to be a very rich and useful *parasha*.) Because when making a covenant with Abraham, God promises that the Jews will be a blessing to other nations.

So Rabbi Greenberg spoke with great warmth to the Tibetan leader: "All of us came here with a sense of wanting to learn from you, but also with a feeling of love. The love is identification, for we have suffered some of the tragedies you have suffered, and we would like to help in some way. So we asked what learning might be helpful."

Yitz was keenly aware that the Tibetans faced a crisis that could mean their end as a people as well as the end of their religion. Jews have faced similar crises, not only during the time of the Holocaust but also two thousand years earlier.

Actually, we Jews have a rich menu of crises to choose from. The expulsion from Spain in 1492, the Inquisition, and the Crusades were all terrible disasters. And the Babylonian captivity provides fascinating parallels to Tibetan history. But all of us were thinking most about the Holocaust. Seeing photographs of the Chinese destruction of Tibetan Buddhist monasteries, temples, and libraries, I recalled the systematic Nazi destruction of synagogues. When I read about celibate Tibetan nuns and monks being humiliated and tortured, I remember the SS forcing rabbis to spit on the Torah before shooting them. And the death of more than a million Tibetans as a result of the occupation brought up the inevitable charge of genocide. As Rabbi Lawrence Kushner had told the Dalai Lama when they met in New Jersey, "The Chinese came to your people as the Germans came to mine."

The parallels are not exact—how could they be? The Holocaust took place quickly, and extermination was the conscious goal of the Nazis. The Chinese are not seeking a "final solution," though by favoring Han, or ethnic Chinese, over Tibetans, a strong element of chauvinism is playing itself out. Their principal aim is to dominate and exploit the Tibetan territory, to make Tibet part of China by eliminating any vestiges of Tibetan resistance. But the result of their suppressing Tibetan nationality, culture, and language through decades of brutally repressive rule may well be a genocide played out in slow motion.

One-third of the Jewish people were murdered while the world stood by. Much the same is happening right now to the Tibetans, and not a single nation is protesting with any force. Though many Jews wish to reserve the Holocaust as a unique historical event and object to its use as an analogy for other people's suffering, that doesn't trouble me so much. My problem is, the analogy offers the Tibetans too little in the way of hope.

Perhaps Yitz might have chosen to discuss the Babylonian captivity instead. At about the time of the Buddha, in 586 B.C.E., the Babylonian king Nebuchadnezzar had sacked Jerusalem, destroyed the Temple, and led fifteen thousand Jews into captivity in Babylon. The intellectual leadership of priests and scribes left the country while the poor Jews remained on the land. This resembles in some ways the Tibetan case. In exile, the educated Jews carefully compiled their sacred writings—as the Tibetans are doing today at the Library of Tibetan Works and

Archives in Dharamsala. Jews kept their religious teachings alive and, within a generation (by 516 B.C.E.), were able to return to the land and, ultimately, rebuild Jerusalem and its Temple. Upon their return, they reformed their religion and democratized it further, much as the Dalai Lama is attempting to adapt his religion to contemporary circumstances.

Obviously the Babylonian story offers much more hope. But I knew why Yitz chose instead to make a parallel with events surrounding the Roman destruction. The Tibetans might well be facing a long exile. And not far from his mind also was the Holocaust and the theological questions it raises.

I would put these questions simply. How can Jews affirm faith in God and his covenant with the chosen people after Auschwitz? The question is settled for most secular and liberal Jews—they can't. Obviously such a position is unacceptable to an Orthodox Jew. While some simply drew inward and clung to a reactionary faith, Rabbi Greenberg had seen that new answers were demanded.

Perhaps it is true, as Jewish sociologist Arnold Eisen has noted, "that not much creative work has been forthcoming over the last two decades" in Jewish theology. In part, as Eisen explains, Jewish theology demands a unique combination of skills: someone deeply committed to Judaism but with a secular education. Among the most important postwar thinkers have been Rabbi Abraham Heschel and Rabbi Joseph Soloveitchik, Rabbi Greenberg's mentor. Heschel, for Hasidim, and Soloveitchik, for Talmudic Judaism, each represent in their thinking an encounter between Jewish tradition and modern philosophical thought.

In contemporary Orthodox Jewish theology, Rabbi Greenberg's own substantial contribution has been the concept of the "voluntary covenant." According to Eisen, "The word 'voluntary' is crucial to Greenberg. It emphasizes that the initiative—now, more than ever—is on the human side rather than on God's. It suggests that we will be faithful, we will uphold the covenant, even if God in the Holocaust did not."

Therefore, Rabbi Greenberg told the Dalai Lama that the covenant is "the most seminal idea" in Judaism. The covenant that began with Abraham has not been abrogated—even at Auschwitz. Instead, he affirmed to the Buddhist leader his own faith: "The creator God seeds the universe with life. Humanity can become a partner with the divine in making the world better or perfect."

What has changed is the human role in the partnership. And that happened, not in recent times, but "about nineteen hundred years ago, halfway in the history of the religion. The Jewish people in Judea were conquered by the Romans and their Temple destroyed by the Roman empire. It was devastating." Rabbi Greenberg explained that Jews could no longer make pilgrimages to Jerusalem, offer sacrifices, or receive divine messages through the priestly oracle. They were cut off from direct access to God.

"Then within a century or two the people lost the land altogether. So it was a major crisis. We lost many great teachers and important religious figures."

In the first century, many interpreted the Roman destruction as abandonment by God, the end of the covenant. "And since the whole Jewish idea of covenant is that the world can be made better, this would be such a victory for evil that many Jews simply gave up. They assimilated and joined the very dynamic culture around them, Hellenism. Another large group, the Zealots, put all of their energy to recapturing and rebuilding the Temple. They reconquered Jerusalem for two years, but then they were crushed again." The final revolt against the Romans ended in the mass suicide of the Zealots at Masada in 73 C.E.

The Romans not only destroyed Jerusalem, they renamed the capital and drove her people into exile. More than one million Jews died at that time, and Jews did not regain sovereignty in the land until 1948. But Judaism did not die. The religion was saved by the first-century sages, known today as the rabbis, the teachers.

Yitz explained, "There was one great rabbi of the time, Rabbi Yochanan ben Zakkai. The Talmud says, when the Romans had Jerusalem surrounded and were about to destroy it, he was able to break through to the Roman emperor and was given one wish. He said, 'Give me Yavneh and its scholars. I want to set up an academy there.'" There he told his students they would outlast the exile by teaching, interpreting, and preserving the tradition.

"Yochanan ben Zakkai basically said, 'If we don't have our Temple, but we have our learning, our texts—our Bible with us, we have the power by learning to create the equivalent of the Temple. It's a portable homeland.'

"It's not enough to preserve. His power was to say that as partners in the covenant, fallible humans have the authority to add new insights, so that their activity was the equivalent of a renewal of the convenant. Their courage to renew preserved the past."

After Jerusalem was laid waste, the rabbis found a home in Yavneh, a tiny town near Ashdod. There, in a vineyard, their leader, Rabbi Yochanan ben Zakkai, declared the academy of rabbis successors to the Sanhedrin.

As Yitz told the story of the first-century sages, I felt the power of our being there, as Jews. Dharamsala, as much as one can argue by analogy, is surely the Tibetan Yavneh. In this small Indian town, with no more than five thousand souls, lies the main hope for the survival of Tibetan Buddhism. And I could see—with a little squinting—the Dalai Lama and his leading abbots and monks as the Buddhist equivalent of Yochanan ben Zakkai and his sages.

The Dalai Lama interrupted Yitz's history lesson to ask the inevitable question about the covenant, "The concept of the chosen people, is it right there from the beginning, or later developed?"

Rabbi Greenberg answered that it was relatively early—and begins with the first Jew, Abraham. "Chosenness means a unique relationship of love. But God can choose others as well and give a unique calling to each group. Each has to understand its own destiny and can see its own tragedy not simply as a setback but as an opportunity."

"Certainly," Yitz added, "I never thought I would learn from a Buddhist monk until you came to the world. In the same way, the Jewish people in their tragedy had an opportunity to be a model of how one persists, how one takes suffering and ennobles it. In essence, this was the challenge they faced in the first century."

Yitz returned to his topic. He said the strength of the first-century rabbis came from their basic analysis. They did not choose to believe that God had abandoned them, and they insisted that the Torah was still fully binding and valid. They interpreted God's nonintervention with the Roman destruction as a sign that, henceforth in history, the human partner in covenant must take more responsibility for the outcome. In the past God might have parted seas, rained down manna, performed signs and wonders to save the Jewish people. But God was no longer going to step in and do the miracles for his human partners.

Listening to Yitz, I had to reflect that the first-century rabbinic remaking of Judaism was an extraordinary feat. For six hundred years, after the return from Babylonian captivity, the Temple in Jerusalem, the site of pilgrimage and sacrifices, had served as the mainstay of religious life. Then, in one blow, Temple, Jerusalem, and priests were gone. Along with them went all the magic and grandeur of ritual—the incense and sacrifices, the awe of the High Priest entering in the Holy of Holies. In their place, the rabbis evolved the text of laws and the stories and debates known eventually as the Talmud.

The memory of the Temple was never lost—but it was turned into literature. More than two-thirds of the Talmud is devoted to descriptions of Temple rituals and implements. In that sense the Talmud is much more an imaginative literary text than a collection of laws. The rabbis declared that reading about the Temple laws was now the equivalent of Temple service. And this sort of sleight of hand, though brilliant, is a step back from the immediacy of ritual, what we'd seen, for instance, the day before in the Dalai Lama's temple, with its rich incense, colorful banners, and deep throat chanting.

More—the magical side of religion, especially the yearning for a messiah—was subdued, if not basically suppressed, by the rabbinic sages. And this became a dominant cautionary note in rabbinic thought for centuries to come, extended not just to messianism but to mysticism in general. It is still dominant in Judaism today, in all of its branches. Reason became the keynote of Jewish religion, and though some of the rabbinic sages were themselves mystical practitioners, the Talmud certainly expresses strong cautions against too much interest in mystical topics.

Rabbi Yochanan ben Zakkai had had good reason for such caution. He had seen that excessive messianic faith had led the Zealots to challenge Rome, only to bring destruction on all of Israel. He is quoted in the Talmud as saying, "If you are holding a sapling in your hand, and someone tells you the Messiah has come, plant the sapling first, then go look for the Messiah." Maybe I'd been in Dharamsala too long, but I could almost hear Rabbi Greenberg saying much the same to Rabbi Schachter.

Yitz had another point that he wanted the Tibetans to consider: democracy. The rabbis succeeded because they had democratized religious education. "If God is not going to speak in visible ways, if we don't have the Temple that's so awesome to the average person—then we have to educate every single Jew."

This was another interesting proposition to thrust into the Tibetan exile context, especially as the Dalai Lama and his high lamas were more Sadducee than Pharisee, more aristocratic high priest than democratic rabbi.

Like the Tibetan *gelukpa* monks, the first-century rabbis became an elite religious group and held themselves to a higher discipline than ordinary Jews. I suppose they were a little like Yitz and Blu, keeping strictly kosher while others kept plain kosher. But at the same time, "they taught everyone to study and brought everything they knew to the people."

Without mentioning it too pointedly, Yitz brought up another difference between rabbis and monks. "The rabbis are not celibate, so that in their answers and teaching, they would speak with the credibility of sharing the problems of everyday people."

What the rabbis did in teaching the people—they often traveled from town to town—was to utterly transform and reinterpret every feature of the old Temple cult.

He told the Dalai Lama, "Each of the holy days was reinterpreted to bring in a stronger historical element, and additional holy days were added to remember the tragedy. On Tisha b'Av, they would retell, relive, and reenact the actual destruction. Why? So that no Jew anywhere would ever forget the destruction or accept the world as it is. Such holidays reminded the Jews, 'We are in *galut* [diaspora], we are in exile, we are not in our homeland.'"

In the New Jersey session, the Dalai Lama had already expressed admiration for Jewish home ritual. Now Yitz explained in detail how keeping kosher or making blessings over bread and wine became the equivalent of the original Temple rites. He offered them now as potential models to share.

For instance, he said, the weekday blessings after the meal include the psalm "By the waters of Babylon we wept." "Six days a week, before you thank God, you first cry, 'I am not home here, this is not my land, I'm in exile.' But on Shabbat, on the seventh day, the perfect day, we use a different psalm, a psalm of Israel. 'When we were in Zion, we were like dreamers and God restored us.' With that psalm, I'm back in Israel. . . . "

The Dalai Lama interrupted, "So it's a visualization."

The Tibetan Buddhists, in their meditations, practice prodigious feats of visualization, such as have not been seen in the West since the time of the great memory theaters of ancient Roman rhetoric. They regularly envision colorful arrays of deities and bodhisattvas, with their precise clothing, jewelry, and gestures.

Obviously the traditional Jewish mental technology was different, but Yitz agreed with the Dalai Lama's characterization. "For twenty-four hours they made believe they were living in Israel—visualization—which was so real that it kept alive that land."

But this went beyond prayers to customs. "Every Jew is to be reminded of the exile in the sacred round, during the holidays, and daily life. At the end of every wedding, we break a glass. Why? To remind people they cannot be completely happy. We are still in exile, we have not yet been restored. When you build a new home, you leave one little place unfinished. Why? As beautiful as the home is, I am not at home."

The Dalai Lama listened with great attentiveness, nodding thoughtfully, and then responding, softly, almost to himself, "Yes. Always remind." Remind the people that they are in exile and they must return.

But then Rabbi Greenberg took this thread further, by explaining that these practices were not only devices for memory. In time, especially in mystical thinking, Jewish exile took on a deeply spiritual meaning: the world is broken. God is in exile.

That last phrase puzzled the Dalai Lama, who asked for an explanation.

First, Rabbi Greenberg made a comparison to the bodhisattva who cannot accept a personal nirvana while others are suffering. Likewise, God cannot be happy or satisfied but is also in exile. Then he turned to Zalman's turf, the tradition of the Lurianic kabbalah, for Isaac Luria and the sages of Safed had reexperienced the bitterness of exile after the

Spanish expulsion in 1492. In response, Luria had developed a new teaching in which exile is a central metaphor. Luria stressed that Jews lived in a broken world.

Earlier, during his presentation, Zalman Schachter had outlined the Lurianic kabbalah. "Rabbi Yitzhak Luria, great kabbalist of the 1500s, taught that in the first part of creation God made light and made vessels for the light. The vessels were too fragile, they broke, and from the broken vessels of the supernal lights, the material world was created. So when I sit in this chair with mindfulness, the spark of God that's in it gets raised. It all begins with a cosmic catastrophe, because bringing energy from the infinite to the finite is very hard. Even God had to try a few times in creation, and the first few times it didn't quite work the way in which it needed to be, according to the Lurianic tradition. And it says God creates worlds and destroys them. So depending where the spark was in the great scheme of things, it falls down and then has to go up and be raised. It's the purpose of human beings to come and find the sparks here and raise them up."

Now Yitz added his explanation, "In trying to create a world, the infinite cannot fit into the finite; the vessels break, and therefore there is something wrong with the world. It's the equivalent, if you will, of Buddha's discovery that the world of appearances is all wrong, out of sorts, not functioning properly." Yitz was referring to Buddha's first noble truth, that the nature of existence is *dukkha*—unsatisfactory.

"In somewhat the same way," he went on, "the divine fullness of being cannot be as long as the world is disturbed. Or one can have a historical version: the world as God intends it to be is not here yet."

The Dalai Lama was visibly moved by Rabbi Greenberg's presentation, especially the emphasis on customs and prayers. He told Yitz, "The points you have mentioned really strike at the heart of how to sustain one's culture and tradition. This is what I call the Jewish secret—to keep your tradition. In every important aspect of human life, there is something there to remind, We have to return, we have to return, we have to return, to take responsibility."

The Dalai Lama had grasped an essential Jewish secret of survival—memory. In the Dalai Lama's words, "Always remind." The Torah is full of exhortations to remember—to remember the Sabbath and keep it holy, to speak of the law constantly and teach it diligently to your children. The sacralization of memory has been an essential feature of Judaism throughout its history. We can see it today as Jews work hard to keep the memory of our Holocaust victims sacred.

The Buddhist leader had now gained a more specific understanding of how Jews transformed the painful memory of exile into a source of strength and hope. For almost two thousand years, Jewish rituals and prayers constantly reinforced the same message—we have to return to our homeland. This tenacity had its reward, and this was the Tibetans' favorite part of the Jewish story—the happy ending. Soon after Israel's success in the Six Day War, Jamyang Norbu, then president of the Tibetan Youth Congress, published a history of Israel, meant to inspire the Tibetans by example. The Jews had recaptured their homeland, why not the Tibetans? And Nathan Katz recalls in 1973 seeing a banner in Dharamsala that read "Next year in Lhasa"—a clear reference to the perennial call at the end of the Passover seder.

The glow from the Six Day War has long since faded, and these days many young militant Tibetans find more immediate analogies to their situation in the struggle of the Palestinians, which shows how fickle and complex the uses of history are. But the Dalai Lama made it clear: he still found the example of Israel inspiring.

But can the Dalai Lama and the conservative lamas and abbots behind him transform their religion as Yochanan ben Zakkai had transformed his? Yitz focused on several possible problems. He seemed to be suggesting that the monastic isolation from ordinary life could be a problem in the new situation of exile.

"Judaism," he declared, "takes this-worldly activity much more seriously than Buddhism historically has. But I hear in your teachings already the recognition that it will never be the same. One of the new elements is this affirmation that the liberation of the Tibetan people—the improvement of the human condition, improved ecology—is a valid religious activity. This is in essence what the rabbis said. We are affirming life, we are called to take this responsibility, and we are going to correct this imbalance, we are going to get back to Israel. The genius was, you don't surrender to force. So if you prepare properly, whether it takes nine years or nineteen hundred years, you'll make it."

The Dalai Lama pronounced the presentation excellent and practical. And I wondered at that moment if Zalman's Buddhist seder hadn't been dropped prematurely. But the Tibetan leader's curiosity did not end there. He wanted a little give-and-take.

"So according to new circumstances," the Dalai Lama said, "a certain new idea developed. How was it developed?"

I could see that as the central figure in the Tibetan drama for the past thirty years, he was thinking about the rabbis from his own position, wrestling with the questions of leadership Yitz had raised. How, he asked the rabbi, could profound changes be made in a religion, except through a single leader? How had the rabbis succeeded in democratizing religion?

Each of the various Tibetan Buddhist sects could trace their lineages back through a hierarchy of elite masters. In the thirteenth century, the Sakya Pandit, leader of the *sakya* sect, became the religious tutor of the Mongol emperors, the descendants of Kublai Khan. In exchange, the Sakya Pandit was given political rule over Tibet, while acknowledging China's authority. A century later, with the decline of the Mongols, Tibet regained full independence. But the same pattern was reestablished in the seventeenth century, this time by the *gelukpa* sect, and its leader, the Dalai Lama.

In this way, the XIV Dalai Lama combined spiritual and temporal roles as the head of a religious hierarchy. Yitz Greenberg saw some advantages to this, since the person most exposed to the new realities also had the most authority. But at the same time, he was also challenging the Tibetan leadership. He told the Dalai Lama that Yochanan ben Zakkai had saved Judaism not because he was its most profound sage, but because he had worked democratically, transferring the burden of religious practice from a hereditary Jewish priesthood, the Levites, to every Jewish household. "His secret was to get the average Jew involved."

In turn the Dalai Lama showed that he could challenge as well as be challenged. He asked a question, which if properly considered, really cut to the heart of the contradictions in American Jewish life. "So after Israel was established, did some of these traditions change—or not yet?" He wanted to know if contemporary Diaspora Judaism continued to emphasize exile in its prayers and practices now that the problem of exile has presumably been solved, now that there is a state of Israel to return to.

He smiled mischievously. The Dalai Lama's sect is artful in dialectics and he had touched a Diaspora nerve, though in such a gentle way that

Yitz was delighted by the question and the rest of the group broke into laughter. I'd often thought that "Next Year in Jerusalem" had utterly changed its meaning now that Jerusalem is only an El Al ticket away.

"I think we are going to vote for you for Chief Rabbi of Israel after you finish here," Yitz said with delight. "I mean it." Rabbi Greenberg admitted that today's Diaspora Jews are living through a theological crisis as profound in its own way as the original exile and dispersion two thousand years ago. Because the entire structure of remembrance built up by the rabbis is obviously undermined if exile is no longer enforced by outward necessity.

He explained that the Orthodox Jewish community is deeply divided over how to interpret the Jewish state. Many traditionalists resist the recognition that "Israel is a transformational point that asks Jews to take more responsibility for their fate today." Rabbi Greenberg and others see that "as two thousand years ago, we are again being forced to face a major moment, where religion is called upon to its limits, where a people stretches its mind to preserve its past and its future."

For every Jew in the Diaspora, observant or not, the fact of Israel raises gritty, personal questions. Most of us in that room had at one time or another seriously flirted with aliyah. But relatively few American Jews are willing to give up their material comforts for a life of struggle in the promised land. One exception was the next presenter, Paul Mendes-Flohr.

He'd made aliyah as a young man, on the idealistic principle that this was the most authentic path for a Jew in the twentieth century. His idealism also showed in his politics: he is a peace activist and had organized an interfaith dialogue group, Rainbow.

As Professor of Modern Jewish Thought at Hebrew University, and a prolific scholar, Paul specialized in the work of Martin Buber. The author of I and Thou had emphasized dialogue in his work, and I sometimes felt Buber's spirit was hovering over our dialogue. There's also some evidence that Buber flirted with Buddhism in his youth. I first read him as a teenager, mainly his Tales of the Hasidim, and I also felt some affinity with his religious position. Buber had rejected halakhah as the basis for a Jewish spiritual life. As a result he'd won little favor with Orthodox Jews. But with his strong and early commitment both to

Israel and to peace with Israel's Arabs, he would be a model for Paul. As a secular Zionist, Paul made a point of telling the Dalai Lama that he did not wear a yarmulke. Later, when the Dalai Lama sneezed, he said, "Although I'm a secular Jew, I'll say, God bless you."

As an Israeli, Paul had a very different answer to the Dalai Lama's artful question about continuing the memory of exile. Unlike Rabbi Greenberg, he did not interpret the return of Jews from exile as a problem in theology. It meant, instead, the reentry of Jews into the political world, "a source of joy and of pain. The joy is the ingathering of our peoples from the four corners of the earth, of seeing our children dance and sing in Hebrew. The pain: our return has been accompanied by a tragic conflict with another people."

He pictured for the Dalai Lama what it would be like when his own people returned, if they had to face conflict with the Chinese now living in Tibet. "We have a similar problem with the Palestinian Arabs."

The Dalai Lama asked him about violence. "The use of force, from the spiritual viewpoint, what would you say?"

"A necessary evil. We're not proud of it, we're not happy about it." The Dalai Lama reflected. "This is reality, because of your own survival."

I felt that subject would need a lot more ventilation but Yitz Greenberg, an ardent defender of Israel, steered the conversation around to a different point.

"I was thinking about how the resistance in Tibet began with some of the Khampas fighting." The Khampas are fiercely independent tribesmen in eastern Tibet who began an active guerrilla attack on the Chinese in 1956. They are the Tibetan Maccabees.

"I'm not asking you to betray your tradition of nonviolence," Yitz said, "but in a way the reassertion of Tibetan dignity and the right to have Tibet began when certain Tibetans saw the oppression as so overwhelming that they had no choice but to fight. I know it's a conflict but . . ."

The Dalai Lama took it from there. "Yes, from the Buddhist viewpoint, theoretically speaking, violence is considered just a method, so the method is not very important. What is important is motivation. The goal.

"Violence is like a very strong pill or drug. For a certain illness it's very useful, but there are a lot of side effects. So then the worst thing, at the moment when you are about to decide, is that it's very difficult to know what the result will be. Only when things happen, then afterward, time goes, then you see whether war or violence really produces satisfactory results. Like the Second World War or the Korean War, I think there were some positive results. But the Vietnam War, now the Gulf War, nobody knows what the result will be. So therefore always it's better to avoid, this I feel."

As I interpreted it, the Dalai Lama was not saying that violence is justified. Justice and justification are very much Jewish and thereby Western concepts, foreign to the Buddhist worldview. Violence is a tool, a drug, only permitted if the perpetrator could know that there would be satisfactory results. The catch is, who would be in a position to know in advance the outcome of a violent act? Really, only an omniscient Buddha.

Paul Mendes-Flohr would state at the end of the trip that what really moved him in his encounter with the Tibetans was living in a community that so absolutely abhorred anger. He had worked for peace for years at the political level, and he was painfully conscious of the effect of constant war and conflict on the Israeli psyche. He particularly grieved over its effects on Israel's children. So he was speaking from the heart when he asked the Dalai Lama for advice about "learning how to deal with our conflicts in a more imaginative and nonviolent way." Unfortunately the dialogue had run an hour overtime already. There was a long pause. "It's almost five now," the Dalai Lama noted and called an end to the session.

Michael Sautman thanked the Dalai Lama for his presence, adding softly in Tibetan, *tujaychay*—thank you.

We were all thankful—touched, moved, stimulated. As we filed out through the anteroom, I introduced myself to Alex Berzin, who'd sat in to help with translation. A Jewish man in his forties, he'd been living in Dharamsala off and on since 1968. The Dalai Lama called him "my rabbi" and with his glasses and short curly hair, Alex definitely looked the part. That day, it was hard to tell whether he was prouder of being a Jew or a Buddhist.

He was impressed by the preparation of the Jewish group and the creative ideas they offered. Evidently other dialogues had been more off the cuff. He thought "His Holiness showed a great deal of interest. It was very lively."

Alex spoke very formally and languidly for an urbanized Jew. It did cross my mind that maybe he'd spent too much time on the meditation cushion. I asked him what the purpose of dialogue would be from his point of view. He thought it might help "His Holiness to explain about Buddhism back to the Jews in a much more knowledgeable way."

Was he talking about proselytization?

Alex denied that vigorously, and I could see why we were making each other uncomfortable. He was using "His Holiness" in every other sentence and that was giving me the creeps. I knew too that he'd gone around the world teaching Buddhism. So he probably heard in my questions about proselytization a note of reproach. At that point, I had a certain prejudice that maybe Jews who went over the deep end into Buddhism would lose their individuality and become like zombies. But I'd get to know him better later, along with an interesting group of Dharamsala JUBUs.

In the meantime, I turned to Michael Sautman. He thought, if anything, the dialogue might help the Dalai Lama explain Jews to other Buddhists. "Everything is utilized by a master like that to bring others to enlightenment."

I asked Reb Zalman why he thought the discussion had lingered so much on angels.

"In all likelihood that is the material that needs the most confirmation. To hear that, especially about reincarnation to animals, nobody else believes that like the Tibetans do. To find that Jews do too, that was a delight."

Yitz Greenberg told me he remained impressed by the Dalai Lama's extraordinary humanness and total unself-consciousness. "It's very hard not to take oneself very seriously when you're surrounded by people who think you are probably God."

I was also trying to sort out the power I had felt emanating from the Dalai Lama. The whole debate about "His Holiness" had now shifted in my mind. I was thinking about the Tibetan honorific for the Dalai

Lama, *kundam*, his presence. That is what Michael Sautman had thanked him for, and it made a lot of sense. There was a power to his presence that went beyond his sharp intellect, his fine sense of humor, and his capacity to digest a great deal of material.

In the course of three and a half hours the Dalai Lama was introduced to topics as challenging and various as kabbalistic angelology, contemporary politics in Israel, the response of the rabbinic tradition to the destruction of Jerusalem, and evidence of early historical encounters between Judaism and Buddhism. Yet he followed them all. His normal attention was extraordinary, but it was clear when a subject wholly absorbed him. He would lean forward in his chair and seemed to magnetically draw from the speaker what he needed for his nourishment. Zalman Schachter told me, "There were times I was close to tears just from the intensity of his listening."

Also astounding was his modesty. Several times, he prefaced an allusion to Buddhism with "our weak point is." He certainly didn't attempt to promote the superiority of his religion or viewpoint.

The specific questions he asked about Judaism were truly outstanding. "How did the rabbis develop new ideas?" or "After Israel is established, do you still follow the same traditions?" These are not obvious questions to jump in with from another culture. It was uncanny how much he was able to think like a Jew. He seemed to operate very easily in the realm of intuition, what Zalman had called thinking through identification.

Perhaps the direction of his questions also revealed his own preoccupations with how to reform a religion while in exile. About 115,000 of his people are now living in a new situation, some in Dharamsala, more in the rest of India and in Nepal, others scattered in Europe and North America. They are the first generation of a Tibetan diaspora, and Yitz Greenberg had noted that they face two crises at once—the crisis of exile and dispersion and the problems of modernity.

Young Tibetans growing up in India or in Europe are not always interested in cultivating Buddhist practice. In that sense the Dalai Lama and the rabbis share a problem: how to keep religion relevant in a highly materialistic and secular culture; how to renew without losing continuity.

That was also the question Yochanan ben Zakkai faced, and Rabbi Greenberg had made me appreciate the relevance of first-century Jewish history, especially hearing this remarkable story told in the presence of the Dalai Lama and his monks. For those moments, Dharamsala was Yavneh, and I was powerfully moved that Jewish history could be so relevant to another people. All the suffering, the martyrdom that had always been so bitter and difficult for me to accept, now appeared a lesson hard earned, and a precious knowledge, even a Jewish secret of survival. That was very exciting.

I recognized that Rabbi Greenberg's lifelong dedication to dialogue, within the Jewish world and with other religious leaders, is a key to renewing Jewish life, and keeping Jewish history alive. His belief that our history is meant to be—must be—a blessing for others is inspiring, unlocking old resentments and releasing the stored energy of our Jewish past.

The history Yitz told the Dalai Lama was, inevitably, simplified. The rabbinic party had its origin in the Babylonian captivity, when Jews learned to live without a Temple. And so Jews had the fortune—or misfortune—to rehearse exile and develop its theology for more than six hundred years before the second, and longer lasting, exile began. Yochanan ben Zakkai did not appear out of nowhere.

What is true enough is that the Talmudic project as a whole represents a radical change in Judaism. As much as Yitz, as an Orthodox thinker, might want to emphasize Jewish continuity, I saw in his parable of Yavneh an important lesson in Jewish discontinuity—and Jewish renewal. I noted Yitz's words to the Dalai Lama, that to preserve tradition, the rabbinic sages had to find the "courage to renew." This linked Y to Z, Yitz to Zalman, tradition to renewal, in my mental alphabet.

It is an Orthodox article of faith that the essence of the Talmud was given to Moses at Mt. Sinai as an oral teaching—and then passed down to the time of the rabbinic sages by word of mouth. This belief I cannot share with Yitz. I view it instead as myth, affirming a necessary sense of continuity in a religion that has changed completely between Sinai and Yavneh.

At a crucial juncture, with survival at stake, Judaism made a quantum jump across a historical discontinuity, and thereby released an enormous sustaining energy that has outlasted two millennia of exile.

Now, post-Holocaust and with a state of Israel, Jews in the Diaspora are looking at a huge gap between the claims of their tradition and their lived experience. How to leap across it? How to renew Judaism again as in days of old?

Overall, I felt satisfied at the end of that first magical encounter that both Rabbis Schachter and Greenberg carried part of the answer. Neither had all of it. The angels Zalman had unleashed in that room had impressed me with their beauty. I knew they had wings—now I wanted to know if they had legs. I felt the mystical tradition was a vital component of a renewed Judaism. But I had doubts about the groundwork. Was it possible that Jews today could ever revive a state of mind where the Hasidic tradition was truly usable, truly available?

I didn't know yet. But something vital in those few hours made me rethink my received ideas about Judaism. I had to give great credit to the two rabbis, who had come so well prepared to teach. Their *kavvanah* was obviously powerful. But I also gave credit to His Holiness. Both Zalman and Yitz, each in his own way, had sought to bring a blessing to the Dalai Lama. But in asking so sincerely for the secret of Jewish survival, he had also given a blessing to us.

9

Debating Monks and Angels

Rabbi Greenberg and I walked out into the broad flagstone courtyard of the Thekchen Choeling, or the "Island of the Mahayana Teaching." The entire area served as the center of religious life in Dharamsala. The Tibetan refugee faithful gravitated here, solemnly perambulating its outer precincts in a repetition of an old rite once performed around the Dalai Lama's palace in Lhasa.

But we were in Yavneh now and behind us stood the Dalai Lama's modest cottage. About twenty yards ahead was the Tsuglakhang, the three-story main temple where we had first seen him at the All Himalayan Conference.

Yitz Greenberg hoped his message had been useful. "We Jews lived through certain experiences in the first century which the Tibetans are now beginning to live through. Maybe they can learn from our experience then, maybe they can adapt it."

I wondered if he shared my sense that the dialogue could benefit Jews today, particularly since both groups are now facing the problem of squaring ancient wisdom with contemporary life. He did.

"All religions," he said, "not just Judaism, are now being placed in a new situation. At first I thought the culture was forcing us. But I've come to believe this pluralism is God's will. Can you learn to propagate your religion without using stereotypes and negative images of the other? If we can't, all religions will go down the tubes—and good riddance—because we're a source of hatred and demolition of other people."

One thing Yitz had done was demolish my own prejudices about Orthodoxy, at least his brand of it. His Judaism was not an old man saying no, but rather an extremely intelligent and very real engagement with contemporary life.

Other, more fundamentalist Jews, as well as Christians and Muslims, resist pluralism as yet another seduction of contemporary life to be shunned. They view themselves as pious keepers of the faith in a world of sinful secularists.

By contrast, Rabbi Greenberg was finding true piety in dialogue. He told me that afternoon at Thekchen Choeling, "Dialogue is an opportunity to learn the uniqueness and power of the other and then see if I can now reframe my own religion to respect that power, to stop using negative reasons why I'm Jewish. It leaves me no choice but to be a Jew for positive reasons." Pluralism challenges Jews to discard old stereotypes about themselves and about others.

My own barriers against Gentiles had been based more on ethnic pride than religion. Actually, ethnic pride was a large component of my religion, a heritage passed down to me by my father. He grew up in an entirely Jewish neighborhood—the same one depicted in Barry Levinson's film *Avalon*. It was the era of restrictive clubs and beaches, and he remembers a sign in the Baltimore suburb of Catonsville: No Jews or Dogs Allowed. My aunt told me she never even met a Gentile until she was a grown woman.

Along with this isolation came a Jewish counterculture. Since Jews were a minority, anti-Gentile attitudes seemed like fair revenge. A lot of it came out in humor. I remember my father's joke, "Why did God create Gentiles?" Answer: somebody has to buy retail. Or my grandfather, who used to comment in Yiddish whenever anyone made a bad business decision—"*goyishe kopf*"—Gentile head. There was a similar contempt for the dominant religion of the other, Christianity, a mockery of the "dumb goyim" for believing anything so absurd as that a Jewish guy could be God. I remember once in Jerusalem, a concentration camp survivor told me, "They took this nice rabbi—and made him fly!"

I grew up in the fifties in a suburban neighborhood so Jewish, the public school closed down on Simchat Torah for lack of attendance. So I picked up my share of stereotypes, too. Jews were smart. Gentiles were dumb. Jews were good in business. Gentiles weren't. Jews had a great sense of humor. Gentiles couldn't tell a joke. At the same time, my life offered me constant opportunities to assimilate and exposed me to wider realms than the self-imposed ghetto. In high school and college, I met all sorts of smart, savvy Gentiles who could tell great jokes—and plenty of dumb Jews who couldn't make a dollar. That didn't matter. The stereotypes remained part of my identity—part of who I was.

As an American Jew, I was the un-Cola: not Christian. And that carried with it all sorts of received ideas and stereotypes.

In a sense, Christian anti-Semitism makes it easy for Jews to get away with these sorts of attitudes. But what I had just witnessed persuaded me to take a second look. I could even understand why Yitz believed that pluralism is God's will. His experience was that dialogue with other religions could be deeply clarifying of his own.

He told me, "Jews have been the victims so much we forget that we have a lot of negative images of others. Rav Kook, the great chief rabbi of Israel, said that every hateful or negative image of other traditions that's in our own should now be seen as a mountain we have to climb over as we try to reach God."

We were looking at a mountain as he spoke. The gray granite of the Dhaula Dhar peak sparkled in the rosy light of the setting sun. Within Jewish teaching itself there are certain negative images of other religions. Some of the rabbis speak as though Gentiles are not fully human or do not have souls as Jews have. By contrast, others insist that the righteous of all nations will have a share in the world to come—the Talmud is full of competing voices.

And so was I. I visualized the obstacles in my own thinking, whole Himalayas of aggression and defensiveness that formed a rock rib of my Jewish identity. I had to wonder if the strongest elements weren't the negative ones.

By forging a reactive identity, I had failed to see that there might be something more to Judaism than simply an opportunity to be sarcastic, precious as that was.

Because in denying spiritual power to other religions, particularly Christianity, but also Buddhism, Hinduism, and Islam, my own Judaism—as a religion—had also become a very dry and unexamined affair. (As an identity, it was quite juicy.)

The image of a mountain blocking a view was really hitting me and not just because the Dhaula Dhar range was so gorgeous in the setting sun. Zalman's teaching about four worlds and angels was all new to me—and not just me. That glimpse of angels made me realize that I had missed tremendous areas of a living spiritual depth in Judaism. Why had I missed them?

Part of it was that I identified spirituality itself with Gentiles. Perverse but true. If they had faith, they gave faith a bad name. In my stereotyping, I included the idea that Gentiles were credulous and superstitious, that the whole realm of being holy and godly was something for Catholics in their confessionals and for the evangelicals I called Holy Rollers. I grew up near a convent and remember being both frightened and somewhat in awe of the nuns there. I knew they had given themselves to God—I never thought that way about my rabbi.

After all, as a child I didn't know many spiritually minded Jews. I knew rabbis, of course, but they were affable, or highly intellectual. None of them struck me as full of religious enthusiasm. That would have been embarrassing. Religious enthusiasm I consigned to the distant Jewish past, the shmaltzy world of *Fiddler on the Roof.*

So I understood Rav Kook very well—the contemptuous attitudes I had toward Gentile spirituality had blocked me from ever looking for spirituality in Judaism. They were the mountains I had to climb over to reach God.

Yet I don't think a dialogue with Christians could have led me to this place. I had too many resistances there—I was too aware of how many times in the past Christians had killed Jews in the name of their savior. The beauty of dialogue with Buddhists, as several of us had noted, was they had no baggage with Jews. Tolerance is a very strong Buddhist tradition.

In ancient times, strangers meeting along the Chinese Tibetan border would greet each other, "Sir, to which sublime tradition do you belong?" That was the spirit in which the Dalai Lama approached Jews. And that was the key to the success of the dialogue so far. He had asked us for our "secret." It was good that he asked, but that he thought that we had such a secret was sweetest of all. He had reflected Jews back to themselves with an uncommon generosity of spirit, with no hostility, grievance, anger, certainly no contention. In that reflection, Judaism was revealed more fully and beautifully.

Yitz Greenberg found that a great bonus of every dialogue he had ever been in over the past twenty years was seeing a new constellation of yourself and your fellow Jews. Part of that new constellation for me was Yitz Greenberg's emphasis on the power of interfaith dialogue. And another new star was the Jewish esoteric that Zalman Schachter had introduced.

I thanked Yitz for his comments and, as we parted, saw Zalman, who characteristically had gotten out ahead of the rest of us. A crowd of monks on the temple porch caught the last sunlight on their broad faces and maroon robes, while below them this tall rabbi with a white beard in a fur *streimel* and a white turtleneck, half beatnik and half Hasid, was raising his arms. It looked like a serious discussion, and I saw Marc Lieberman listening in. But I just had time to take a photo of Zalman and the monks before the whole tantric debate school poured out of the temple. The Jewish visitors took seats to the back while the monks assembled to demonstrate the ancient art of Buddhist dialectics.

They faced each other in long rows on the porch, chanting. The deep sound ringing in the courtyard cleared the air of any lingering fatigue from the hours we'd spent indoors. The debate master, a senior monk, posed a question to two young contenders. The first made his case, rattling off an argument in great bursts of syllables. As punctuation, he wound up his right arm like a baseball pitcher and slapped his palm down hard on his extended left hand, smiling in triumph. (Symbolically he was raising up wisdom with the right hand, crushing wrong views with the left.) Then the young monks urged him on with a cheer, one long Wooooooo, peaking in pitch like a passing train and sharply punctured by three shouts and claps of the hand.

It was very animated and medieval, metaphysics as football. The debaters pushed and shoved or grabbed each other's robes to take the floor. One monk pulled his *mala* beads slowly back over his forearm, stretching his bow and releasing an arrow of argument. Then several monks jumped into the fray, all gesturing and arguing heatedly at once, lifting their arms into the air and pointing in ten directions. I had no idea how the judges could sort this out.

Zalman Schachter grabbed Moshe Waldoks's sleeve. "Give me the two reasons why you have to kosher meat with salt!" he cried. "Tell me the two authorities and what do they say!" Then he slapped his hands and these two ex-yeshiva *bucher*s broke into laughter.

Karma Gelek offered us a more solemn play-by-play. The monks were debating a commentary on a Buddhist root text, the *Pramanavar-tikkam* (Valid cognition commentary), written by the Mahayanist, Dharmakirti. "At the moment, their topic is how to establish through logical reasoning, the cause of the future life." Their rough verbal jousting over sublime metaphysics showed both sides of the Tibetan character, fierce nomads subdued by a gentle religion. According to their myth, the first Tibetan was the son of a bodhisattva and a monkey demoness.

A few minutes later I found myself riding back with two more firm believers in a future life. Though happy the first dialogue session had gone so well, Michael Sautman had picked up an implicit challenge from Zalman: Why be a Hindu? Why be a Buddhist? We have everything we need in Judaism.

Marc Lieberman responded with a joke. "Since Zalman includes in Judaism all the religions on the face of the earth he's right." Their discussion took off from there as our car twisted down switchbacks from McLeod Ganj to the lower part of town.

Sautman: I don't know anything about kabbalah or Jewish mysticism.

Lieberman: Well, I certainly can't compete with him on the level of his rabbinic knowledge, he's a scholar and I'm not.

Sautman: That's right.

Lieberman: But I can tell you also that he's eclectic and imaginative and doesn't draw distinctions between his own experiences, be they induced by trance, meditation, inspiration . . .

Sautman: Oh, I see (chuckling) . . .

Lieberman: . . . or whatever, and the traditions of the past. I think he feels it's one continuum of experience and that any symbols or signs or traditions that can help express that experience go along with his energy, which is that of constant creation. He's like a Hindu god.

Sautman: But if in fact there was a lost tradition of Jewish mysticism, meditation, reincarnation, it's great that Zalman is here to re-create that.

Lieberman: No one else has the courage to talk about it other than to quote it as a scholar, and he's quoting it to you as someone who actually believes that this stuff could be real.

According to Lieberman, when Zalman spoke to the debating monks, one said, "How do you believe in reincarnation?" He said, "Well, I know it's there." The monk just smiled at him without missing a beat. "That's not a logical answer, why do you believe in it?"

He thought this illustrated the weakness of Rabbi Schachter's approach. "Zalman says: 'The truth is, I may not believe it tomorrow. Every day I believe something different.'" To Marc, that really summed up a lot.

The JUBUs' critique of Zalman hit home. Because, in the days ahead as I talked to Jewish Buddhists, I came to realize that the key problem for them with the Jewish esoteric was its inaccessibility. In effect, Marc and Michael were saying that Judaism may have this great stuff in its attic. But Buddhism has it here and now.

For all the talk among the Jewish delegates about authenticity, and being representative of Jews back home—the JUBUs were sensing a major gap between theory and practice. Certainly this was true of Zalman's presentation. As he himself had made clear, very few Jews know much about the deep way, the hidden way, of kabbalah.

But the same critique could apply as well to Yitz's more traditional teaching. The fact is, the vast majority of American Jews do not celebrate Shabbat the way Yitz had depicted so beautifully. Nor has the survival of Jews in America, by and large, rested on their always remembering the Promised Land. Throughout our history, most American Jews have dumped both Shabbat and *kashrut* as fast as you can say assimilate.

What gave Rabbi Greenberg's presentation a firm footing was that he spoke with great integrity of the Judaism that he lived and that represented a solid community of Jews back home.

Zalman's case was different. I felt he was representing a Judaism that once was, and that yet might be. For that reason, I didn't care that he interpreted the tradition as flowing into his own experience, his imagination, his dreams, his everyday life. He was agenting for change, for Jewish renewal. To me, renewal seemed exactly what was called for today in all traditions. What good was the rich storehouse of the esoteric in Judaism if it was only available in freeze-dried scholarly packages?

As Yitz Greenberg knew well, true dialogue goes both ways. If the Jews had come as missionaries of the secret of survival, that mission was now being transformed. The Dalai Lama's presence—his "holiness"—was a living affirmation of the power of Buddhist teachings. That was unsettling because up until that point, despite a certain lip service to the concept of dialogue, the Jews had largely conceived of themselves as bringing their Torah to Dharamsala.

But Zalman Schachter was not surprised at what was unfolding. He told me that evening over dinner, "I didn't come just to sell, but also to buy."

10

Shabbat Shalom and Tashe Delek

Friday morning after prayers, Yitz and Blu Greenberg, Paul Mendes-Flohr, Joy Levitt, Marc Lieberman, and Moshe Waldoks returned to Tsuglakhang, the main temple in Thekchen Choeling, for the All Himalayan Conference on the "five traditional sciences."

This would be another historic first: a formal address by Jews to a group of Buddhist religious leaders from all parts of Asia. But as we were settling into our seats, a debate broke out over our presence. Some monks argued that Buddhists should not associate with alien *sanghas,* to avoid contact with negative people and negative thoughts. Ironically, the negative person who was the subject of the discussion was that champion of dialogue, Rabbi Greenberg, who was scheduled to address the group.

We were seeing firsthand that the Dalai Lama's brilliant tolerance was not practiced universally in his community. In fact, it has been said that were he not the Dalai Lama, he would be considered a heretic. Faced with the immense task of preserving Tibetan religion in exile, some monastics have become ultraconservative restorationists. They seek to preserve tradition by rebuilding Tibet in India. They are the counterparts of ultra-Orthodox Jews such as those settled in enclaves like Mea Shearim in Jerusalem. Moving to a modern—and hot—Mediterranean country, they nevertheless replicate an eighteenth-century Jewish ghetto, down to black clothing and fur hats!

The restorationist impulse is strong among a people facing the shock of losing their home, whether they are Jews after the Holocaust or Tibetans fleeing the Chinese invasion. More than two hundred monasteries have been reestablished since 1959, many taking the names of old destroyed monasteries in Tibet. According to what the chair of the conference, Tashi Paljor, had told us at the opening session on Wednesday, "keeping the dharma tradition alive is their most important task."

But in contradistinction, the Dalai Lama at the same session had stressed that preservation meant more than buildings. It meant a cultivation of inner resources. "When you have faith you should have understanding, otherwise you have blind faith. So a beautiful monastery is not enough. Understanding is important, understanding the essence of Buddhist thought, and keeping it alive in inner thought."

For this reason, the Buddhist leader liked to enrich himself with different kinds of learnings and thus invited scholars and lamas to teach him different traditions. That is why he had invited the Jews to Dharamsala. He emphasized that "this is a personal practice." But clearly he valued it because to the Dalai Lama, "religious life should be a mixture of faith and analysis." Tradition cannot be conserved with a closed mind. Now, as the monks argued, I looked at Rabbi Greenberg and wondered what would happen if a Buddhist monk came to address a yeshiva. Fortunately, a young Nepalese monk brought the debate to an end. He said it isn't what you are but how you act that makes you negative or positive.

Rabbi Greenberg is tall and thin. He has a haunted look—and striking blue eyes. For a movie, I would have cast him as Søren Kierkegaard, not a New York rabbi. He towered over the Buddhists who sat at his feet on mats. His task was not easy, explaining Judaism in fifteen minutes. Like Zalman, he spoke in terms of view, path, and goal, but he presented a more mainstream approach, quoting the Talmud, that "the world stands on three foundations—Torah, prayer, and deeds of loving-kindness." The Jewish path is study, prayer, and good deeds; the goal, to serve God.

Once again, he briefly related the history of the Jews, the parallels to Tibetan exile. Geshe Lobsang, the stocky abbot of Sera Je monastery, whom I'd seen bowing with such deep humility the day before, responded graciously now. He thanked the Jews for giving the Tibetans an example to follow. "Your speech reminds us of our responsibility and encourages us in our future action. We use different terminologies. When it comes to practices, we are doing exactly the same thing."

One highlight was that Paul Mendes-Flohr also gave a brief address, the first ever to such a group from an Israeli. This was a good contact in India, a country with one of the world's largest Muslim populations. Paul spoke on behalf of Israel and for freedom for Tibet.

Meanwhile, Nathan Katz and Zalman Schachter were playing hooky in McLeod Ganj, shmoozing with George Chernoff, a Chicago native and Buddhist monk studying in Dharamsala. George asked Zalman what a kabbalist does for a living. Zalman replied, "The same thing everyone else does, only with extra windows opened." When George asked what that meant, Zalman put one hand on each side of his head and said, "Windows here—open to other realities."

Zalman also shared with George and Nathan what he called "an interactive meditation practice" being developed by kabbalists. One suspected, knowing Zalman, that the kabbalist was himself and the development was taking place on the spot in the streets of McLeod Ganj. Zalman would start a sentence with "In the world to come . . ." and the others had to complete the thought. Reb Zalman explained that "This is a kind of meditation to make you into *Hashem*'s messengers." (*Hashem,* or "the name," is an Orthodox way of referring to God.)

Later that afternoon, the angels-in-training and the other delegates caught up with one another at a meeting with senior Tibetan abbots and *geshe*s.

In a dimly lit study in the Tibetan library, we sat around a long wooden table. The Jewish delegates had lots of questions, but the abbots seemed very reserved. They deferred to their oldest colleague, who carefully traced his lineage, in mind-numbing detail. In a somewhat stuffy room, the pace of the past few days caught up with more than a few of the Jewish delegates. It was hard, frankly, to keep eyes open.

The discussion picked up when we got into methods of training young *tulkus,* those recognized at an early age to be the reincarnation of a highly realized master. Of the more than four thousand *tulku*s in preinvasion Tibet, only a few hundred escaped. When such a child is recognized—most all *tulku*s are male—he is taken into a monastery and trained to assume his position.

The Dalai Lama himself was the greatest advertisement for the *tulku* idea, for in the current situation one could hardly imagine a better Dalai Lama.

But the system must have its flaws, for when Marc Lieberman asked, "What happens when a *tulku* turns out to be a dud?" even the most ceremonious of the abbots laughed.

He and I took a pre-Shabbat stroll back to Kashmir Cottage, passing through the back streets of town. The Tibetan refugees live under difficult conditions, whole families crammed into a single room. We came upon an Indian traveling musician, sitting on a dirty poured concrete porch, his crutch propped against the step. Two puppets danced on a small crate while he played the mandolin. The Tibetan children, all three and four years old, were gorgeous. They squatted, giggling, but hid their smiles behind folded hands, shy beauties.

I was thinking of my own kids when I saw Blu Greenberg at Kashmir Cottage setting candlesticks on the Shabbat table. It felt as if we Jews had come together, like a family, that we were inviting guests home for Friday night. When the senior lamas and abbots arrived, joined by a few Western Buddhists, Moshe Waldoks began the davening. Jews usually pray facing east toward Jerusalem, but we faced the setting sun. Two abbots were having an animated discussion with Laktor. They thought they had learned the true secret of Judaism—we were sun worshipers.

The davening was getting intense and Zalman exclaimed, "I feel the saints of both of our lineages are dancing around us." When that was translated, the abbots laughed out loud. Zalman added, "Most of the time we speak of God as more male than female. But in Shabbas the divine presence comes like a queen, so we sing and dance to greet her." Then we sang "Lekha Dodi," to welcome the Shabbat bride. We sang it with the words, and then in Hasidic scat: Yi di di di di . . . The monks, by the terms of their vows, do not sing or dance except to their own liturgy but allowed themselves to clap their hands to the tune. Zalman explained that "we call an additional soul into ourselves when we chant."

Moshe Waldoks chanted the *barkhu*, the traditional call to prayer. He explained that in ancient Jerusalem, the priests would stand on the parapets of the Temple and call the *barkhu* down to the crowd gathered below, to proclaim the evening sacrifice. "Blessed are you, God the most blessed." The people would answer back, "Blessed is the Lord for ever and ever." Moshe added, "But the replacement of sacrifice by prayer has been for many Jews considered an improvement." Karma Gelek translated and the monks laughed.

As darkness fell, Moshe read the prayers by flashlight. In the chilly mountain air, some of us retrieved blankets from the cottage and wrapped them over the bare arms of the elderly lamas. They were fascinated as Moshe, our prayer leader, threw his *tallis* over his head during the silent meditation, rocking gently side to side.

As the service concluded, we greeted the Tibetans one by one with "Shabbat shalom." Very quickly they learned to reply back with the same words. Then, spontaneously, they recited their own dedication prayer, The Word of Truth, "composed," Laktor told us, "by His Holiness the Dalai Lama for regaining Tibetan freedom." Zalman Schachter stood with his palms pressed together Tibetan style, a broad smile on his face.

He was noticing that just as the Jewish group had their interpersonal dances so did the Tibetans. "You could almost get the sense of one person saying, 'I told you so,' and the other one saying, 'No, it doesn't count.' They also have some arguments about, Is there truth in other ways?"

We walked up to the porch for the candle lighting, lamas and Jews alternating, Jewish Buddhists and Buddhist Jews, making a circle around the table. Blu Greenberg, in her gray scarf, recited the blessing over the Shabbas candles and Moshe chanted kiddush over a cup of grape juice. Buddhist monks don't drink alcohol. When we recited *shehekheyanu*, Moshe explained it "was a special prayer because this is the first time we've ever celebrated Shabbat like this in Dharamsala." The monks raised their cups and added another word to their quickly growing Hebrew vocabulary, "*l'chaim*."

Instead of challah, Blu Greenberg used matzahs. The bread of affliction expressed solidarity with the Tibetans in their exile—and was the closest we would get to a Buddhist seder.

We scattered through Kashmir Cottage to eat. It was a wonderful opportunity to meet more informally with these men who collectively represented the exiled wisdom of Tibet.

I found myself sharing bread and wine—a meal—but also wisdom, with Geshe Sonam Rinchen and his student Ruth Sonam, a longtime translator at the Library of Tibetan Works and Archives.

Geshe Sonam was in his early sixties, tall and rather handsome. When he leaned toward Ruth there seemed to be a special communication between them, and as Ruth translated, they even looked a little like father and daughter.

I asked Geshe Sonam a question that had already come up several times in the Jewish group. Is it possible to practice Buddhism and Judaism together?

He thought so. He found many things that "would harmonize very well. For example, the practice of generosity and ethical discipline." There were differences in philosophical view, "but when it comes to practice, there's so much common ground." He thought though that in some cases "we use similar terminology, like love and compassion, but we mean something different. When we understand the deeper meaning clearly, then we will find much common ground."

I turned to specifics. What was the Buddhist explanation of the Holocaust?

He answered, that "from the point of view of the Buddhists, the Holocaust itself is a result of past karma. Those people were not necessarily Jews in their past lives when they created the actions that they reaped in that form. But when your karma ripens there is nothing that can protect you."

A young Israeli visitor joined in and asked if the *geshe* viewed the Holocaust as a national karma, like the exile from Tibet.

"This is a common karma. If you purify actions before their ripening, before their fruition occurs, then one doesn't have to experience the results. On the other hand, once the results have ripened to manifest, then it's too late, there's nothing that can extenuate, you have to experience them, that's the only way to get rid of that negative momentum."

I was taken aback by the *geshe*'s explanation of the Holocaust, because it sounded like blaming the victim. The issue would come up again in my conversations with Jewish Buddhists. It bundled several points of contrast between the two religions. How does one respond to evil? What is essential for survival of a people? What is the meaning of terrible group suffering?

Exile was another karma both peoples shared. So I was touched when I overheard Zalman's midrash on the week's Torah portion.

"Now the Lord said unto Abram, *Lekh Lekha*—remove yourself out of your country, your birthplace, and your father's house to the land which I will guide you." After Zalman read, Ruth Sonam translated for the Tibetans.

"So the commentators asked a question. The order doesn't seem to be right: country, birthplace, father's house. The order should be go out from your father's house, from your birthplace, and then go out from your country.

"So you have the question. So when we study this, we go, Woo." He clapped his hand like the debating monks, which the *geshe*s enjoyed very much.

"I give you now the short answer, coming from one of the teachers of our tradition. The word 'from your country' also means from your earth-bondedness, from your involvement in the earth. So the first thing we have to clean up is that which we got from our regular earth life, that is the body.

"And since people are made because the father and mother beget them, in the act of begetting they bring something into life, and that is the second stage of purification they have to deal with. So that is how they interpret birthplace.

"The father also means desire. So the house of your father can mean, the source of your desire. So it says, after you've cleaned up your earthness, and your birthness, you can go to clean up the source of your desire. Then you come to the golden land, the promised land which God shows you."

It was great to hear Zalman teaching this particular midrash to these Tibetan holy men. The idea of cleaning up the source of your desire sounded like the Buddha's second noble truth, that the cause of suffering is desire. At the opening of the All Himalayan Conference, the Dalai Lama suggested finding new ideas in Buddhism, by interpreting "words not fitting with reality." Zalman was demonstrating the Jewish method. Through the midrash, Abram's leaving his homeland became a paradigm for every spiritual journey. This was a deep thing he and the Tibetans had in common, this *Lekh Lekha*, this "going forth." Their task was the same: to transform exile from a physical to a spiritual journey.

Perhaps, as the Dalai Lama had suggested to Nathan Katz, "some such exchanges between Buddhists and Jews had taken place" in the ancient world. Now they were taking place before my eyes.

And there were remarkable similarities in the theology of exile. Nathan Katz told me once about a time he was staying in the Drepung monastery in southern India. "It's out of the way and they don't have so many foreigners as in Dharamsala. A monk said to me spontaneously—he didn't know I was Jewish—'We have the same idea as the Jews had. They had all this exile, but they know God was leading them into exile, and we know that because of this exile the whole world is learning dharma from us. If it weren't for what the Chinese did to us, we wouldn't be spreading dharma, which is more important than our suffering.'"

The geshes and Zalman got down to a serious exchange over techniques of meditation and visualization. Rabbi Schachter was interested in the phenomenology of the experience. He asked them, "What happens in vipassana [insight meditation]? Should you let the mind go along with the dream that it gets into or should you let go of the idea?" They told him, "The answer is, in vipassana, gently bring the mind back to the subject, which is the mindless space. . . . "

Vipassana is a term that belongs, strictly speaking, to Theravadan Buddhism, which is the older form of Buddhism practiced principally today in Sri Lanka, Thailand, and Burma. Vipassana is an advanced form of meditation that involves becoming aware of the processes of the mind through careful observation. It is also known as insight meditation.

Later Zalman told me, "We got into a discussion of sitting, and watching the breath, and seeing the bodhisattva looking at you, and I raised the question, does the bodhisattva come off the yantra [the image], does he really breathe and look at you, do you make that kind of a mind form, or is he more like an icon? And he said, no he's living, breathing, he's really there."

So Zalman shared with them a visualization practice from the Hasidic tradition, as taught by Rabbi Elimelech of Lizensk.

He explained that you visualize "a great and awesome fire burning in front of you," and you, for the sake of sanctifying the name of God, "overcome your lower nature and throw yourself into the fire as a martyr."

As a young man Zalman had been trained in this visualization to the point that "there's this person staring at you, looking at you, scrutinizing your behavior and each time shouting out at you. You hear the voice. They're building in the voice of the rebbe. . . . "

The *geshe*s described their own training, the rote learning, the twenty years of sutra reading, the one hundred thousand prostrations, as Zalman put it, "all kinds of austerities people have to do to get into it." For instance, the young monks at the Institute of Dialectics spend five to ten hours a day for twenty years memorizing, studying, and debating basic Buddhist texts.

Zalman told them in response, "First of all, I'm the last of the Mohicans from our end. I still have some memories from before the Holocaust of what spirituality was about and you guys are the last from yours. And you're looking ahead, you're getting old, so the urgency to hand over what you have received, without change, to make sure it is authentically absorbed, I can understand in full.

"But the other side is it still takes too long. Because our technology outstrips our spiritual and moral development, we need to hurry it up. We can't take twenty years to do the sutras. We have to break it out for people." So Zalman, with characteristic chutzpah, suggested that his fellow teachers do some research and development by exploring the relationship of their practices to contemporary thought, especially to transpersonal psychology and planetary consciousness.

At that point, Zalman's translator told him, "We don't need this stuff. Buddhist practice doesn't have to be psychological or ecological." But Zalman, who'd taught psychology of religion at Temple University, disagreed. The role of the contemporary teacher was to help students find their way to the riches of tradition.

He told the *geshe*s a story about how he once took a group of people to the Lubavitcher rebbe. One of them asked the rebbe, "What are you good for?" And he said, "I'm not talking about myself, I'm talking about what my master was for me. He was for me the geologist of the soul. There are great treasures in the soul: there's faith, there's love, there's awe, there's wisdom, all these treasures you can dig—but if you don't know where to dig, you dig up mud—Freud—or you dig up sto Adler. But if you want to get to the gold, which is the awe before and the silver, which is the love, and the diamonds, which are the then you have to find the geologist of the soul who tells you where to dig." The rebbe added, "But the digging you have to do yourself."

When Zalman told them this story, they were full of stories, too: how to deal with students, the role of the teachers, their methods of training.

At one point Zalman explained to the *geshes* an important teaching of the founder of Hasidism, the eighteenth-century rabbi Israel ben Eliezer, known universally as the Baal Shem Tov, or "Master of the Good Name." It is the doctrine of "strange thoughts."

"The Baal Shem Tov says when you are praying and you have a thought of a beautiful woman, lust, such a thought comes to you begging to be raised. You raise it by saying, 'Oh, where does the beauty, where does the charm, where does the attraction come from?'—it comes from the source of beauty. He would say, Don't get scared, don't push it away, such symmetry, such beauty—what was it in this ideal that drew you on? Where did it come from?—it didn't make itself. It's so sublime, so beautiful, that's why it draws you, so take it back to its divine root."

I wondered what celibate monks made of this teaching on "strange thoughts." According to Zalman, they loved it. "It was such a gratifying thing. Then I started pushing again on the research and development. There are ways to hurry ahead. . . . " By such prodding, Zalman felt he was "agenting for the next level of the dialogue" when *geshes* and rabbis would meet to exchange techniques of meditation and training.

What was delightful was that such conversations were taking place all over Kashmir Cottage, living room, dining room, porch. When we reassembled for after meal prayers, we had traveled light-years from the formal interaction of that afternoon. We had blown on the spark lit when the Dalai Lama called a Shabbat psalm a visualization. Now Rabbi Joy Levitt led us in the very psalm Yitz had cited. "When God returned us to Zion from exile, we thought we were dreaming. . . . "

She expressed the hope that the Tibetans too would "return . . . again to freedom." The lamas responded, putting their palms together and chanting a low-throated dedication that the good energy of the evening would go out to the aid of all suffering sentient beings.

As the two groups parted in the dark, the Jews formed a receiving line and the Tibetans wished each of their Jewish friends "*Shabbat Shalom*." The Jews responded in Tibetan, "*Tashe delek*." Sabbath peace.

Peace to you. The Angel of Tibet and the Angel of the Jews were surely listening in just then.

Rabbi Greenberg had explained to the Dalai Lama the power of Shabbat in theory. But I was deeply moved to see how powerful the Shabbat could be in practice. Clearly the *geshes* were also impressed, as were some of our Jewish-Buddhist visitors. Among them was Ruth Sonam, Geshe Sonam's translator and student, who it turned out had grown up Jewish in Ireland. I also met the Venerable Thubten Chodron, who had made the amazing journey in her life from American Jewish housewife to Tibetan Buddhist nun.

On their way home, Chodron and Ruth talked about the Shabbat. They'd noticed that the *geshes* were sitting stone-faced while the rabbis were dancing and singing. That shared joy was very attractive, Chodron told me later. "It seems to create a stronger sense of community than if you're meditating."

I asked her what the *geshes* thought of the davening.

Chodron laughed. "They were probably wondering how you can maintain control of your mind while you are singing and dancing."

The Jewish Sabbath is above all a family affair, and as it turned out, we had gathered to us an extraordinary group of Jewish Buddhists living in Dharamsala. The next day would take on all the joy and some of the pain of a family reunion.

11

Jewish Buddhists, Buddhist Jews

A stroll through the Tibetan market at McLeod Ganj on Friday morning had already convinced me that a good number of Jews were seeking spiritual wisdom in Dharamsala. On a narrow street crowded with shops, the Tibetan merchants sold mass-produced *thangka*s, for two or three hundred rupees (about twenty dollars), and other rarities such as a yak horn snuff box (good for a perfume bottle, though you can also buy the snuff). The street ran uphill to a view of the Dhaula Dhar range, where it looked as if you could step off the edge of McLeod Ganj into a vast mystical depth. Since the sixties Dharamsala has been a way station for spiritual travelers, including Thomas Merton, Gary Snyder, and Allen Ginsberg. Now a new generation, the long-haired and the monastically shorn, mingled freely with Hindu beggars by the steps of the Lhasa Guest House.

Marc Lieberman bought some very handsome *mala* beads, dark circles of wood strung on a leather thong, with inlays of Himalayan coral, silver, and gold. The beads were the size of a man's knuckle, heavier than the ones around the Dalai Lama's wrist—108 per string, used for counting mantras. During breaks in the dialogue Michael Sautman had been clicking away on his. Hundreds of thousands of repetitions were required at certain stages of the practice.

I bought some beads of my own from a wrinkled Tibetan woman who sat in front of a card table. Marc said they were very old. "What kind of wood is this anyway?" I asked him. "Mahogany?"

That's when I learned those dark little wheels had been bored out of a human skull—intended to make you reflect on impermanence. It sure worked for me. I gave them a sniff and they smelled slightly salty, a faint perfume of their previous owner.

The Tibetans made quite a trade in human bones: in various shops I saw trumpets made from a human femur, with skeleton intaglio. In old Tibet a dead body would be carried up into high places for a sky burial—to feed the vultures. Ground burial was impractical in frozen soil, but the custom also reflected a Buddhist view of the body—as an impermanent frame that the mind stream entered and left, one with no personal value. Buddhist texts argue, I am not my body, nor does the body belong to me.

I was tempted by the novelty of a ceremonial skull bowl, imagining it brimming with Cheerios. But I settled for an embroidered hat with fur ear flaps, and a pair of brass *ting sha* bells joined with a leather thong. They made a sharp soul-awakening sound that gradually diminished into silence, along with the noise of the mind.

I overheard some voices speaking Hebrew, then saw Moshe Waldoks in front of a T-shirt shop in an animated conversation with three Israelis in khaki shorts. Moshe was buying Tibetan yarmulkes for himself and his kids: beautiful pillbox caps with fancy, thickly threaded embroidery and bits of blue glass glued in. They were very princely. He introduced us and told the Israelis about our meeting with the Dalai Lama, but they'd already heard about it from the buzz in the streets. Moshe told them that all of Yiddishe Dharamsala was invited to the Saturday morning service, and they promised to come. According to what Thubten Chodron told me later, there'd been a flood of Israelis in Dharamsala in the past few years.

Still, when I hiked the quarter mile up from my quarters to Kashmir Cottage Saturday morning, I was surprised by the size and variety of the crowd we'd gathered. More than a *minyan*.

Traditionally, the Torah portion for the coming week is divided into sections, intended for daily meditation. It had made a running commentary on our week—or was our week just the latest midrash on the story? Melchizedek and the Dalai Lama, *shalom* and *tashe delek*. Having opened myself to the beauty of the Buddhist spiritual tradition, I was reawakening to my own as well.

Rabbi Schachter and Rabbi Greenberg officiated at Congregation Beth Kangra in delightful sunshine. Our old traveling companion, the Sephardi Torah, stood upright in its case, once more showing its power to bring Jewish sparks together. Rabbi Greenberg announced the portion we'd been mulling over all week, *Lekh Lekha*. The Hebrew means: Take yourself out. Go travel. Seek foreign lands. So Reb Zalman announced an aliyah for "those, like Abram, who travel, those who seek truth in other places." Most of our guests identified with that one and crowded around the Torah, including an academic couple from Massachusetts traveling through India with their kids, some backpacking spiritual seekers from Los Angeles, a young Israeli doctor, and four Jewish Buddhist nuns in maroon robes and close-cropped hair. From Hadassah to Dharamsala in three generations! I was only disappointed that Max Redlich, the former Israeli paratrooper I'd heard about, bailed out at the last minute. He sent word that he was working hard on building a *stupa*, a Buddhist reliquary. But Ruth Sonam came, and Alex Berzin, and Thubten Chodron. So did George Chernoff, the monk from Chicago, looking for more lessons on how to become one of *Hashem*'s messengers.

With the mass aliyah of Jews and JUBUs assembled, Yitz and Zalman chanted the Torah. They spot translated the Hebrew into English. At the same time, they maintained the Hebrew cantillation. It was a gracious and nimble performance that showed a remarkable command of the text. I realized that whatever their differences in outlook, they shared a deep reverence for the Torah.

Sitting around on lawn chairs, and in the cool grass, we later discussed a passage from the Torah portion. One nun asked if Abram's wars against the kings of Sodom could be interpreted as spiritual struggles against delusion.

But to Rabbi Greenberg at least, the wars were real. They illustrated an actual struggle to establish religion against violent opposition. They were like the wars Israel has to fight today. For Yitz, "Humans live in history. We have to make choices, sometimes painful choices."

A Western Buddhist challenged him. "What are we faced with in our present culture? Many of us see that Buddhism provides the balance we need in this world today."

Yitz Greenberg admitted being impressed by the Buddhist commitment to nonviolence. But he felt pacifism was only possible in the context of a balance of terror between larger nations. Neither Buddhists or Jews could afford to be pacifists if their survival was at stake. For instance, on analogy to Israel's battles, Yitz very much supported the Tibetans fighting for their freedom and was skeptical of their winning in any other way. Likewise, to Dr. Isaac Bentwich, the young Israeli I'd met the night before, spiritual growth was always colored by historical circumstances. He compared the Dalai Lama to Abram, and the kings of Sodom to the rulers of China.

The discussants tried to resolve the conflict between survival and spiritual values. Could Buddhists fight to preserve a tradition of nonviolence? Many Buddhists thought not. Chodron put it this way, "If you get angry and you start acting unethically to protect a doctrine that preaches patience and ethics, then are you protecting the doctrine or by your own behavior are you destroying it? If all the Buddhists start becoming terrorists, then what's the use of preserving Buddhism? The preservation of Buddhism is preserving your own internal heart. If Tibetans became terrorists they might win back Tibet, but Buddhism would be destroyed by that attitude."

We moved on. The Jewish Buddhists had some of the same questions I had. They wanted to know if Judaism was flexible enough to adapt to our times. Could it respond to feminism, the ecological crisis, and the need for individual spiritual growth? Zalman Schachter, in the Hasidic style, offered a story as an answer. "A man opens a bank account in Switzerland. He's dying and he believes in reincarnation. Thirty years from now, he tells the bank officials, someone will come with a syllable. I want you to give him control of the account.

"Thirty years later a man comes and asks to withdraw all the money. When they question his judgment, saying that, after all, the original depositor told them to hold on to it, he says, 'I gave you the order last time around, but now I want to do what I want to do.'

"We're invested in a tradition so we have a continuity. The best people to invest in tradition are conservative. But the best people to spend it are those willing to take a risk.

"Our treasures—what a fantastic bank account we have grown. The past and the tradition have a vote but can't have a veto, because we are in unprecedented conditions. Now there's an understanding emerging that we are an organic part of all species, that religions are the organs of humanity."

The Jewish delegates and Jewish Buddhists replayed an old family quarrel. Jewish Buddhists felt that the bank account of Judaism had been empty for them when they came to make a withdrawal, whereas they had found real spiritual wealth in Buddhism.

I knew the immediate defensive reaction to that, it was the mountain or barrier I had put up in my own thinking: the Jewish community tends to dismiss such people as flakes or apostates. I had come to Dharamsala with a few of these attitudes myself.

But in the Shabbat sun, those mountains were melting. I'd been deeply impressed with the Dalai Lama and the other Buddhist masters, and having felt firsthand the attraction of another religion, I could no longer be judgmental about Jewish Buddhists. I'd been moved when the Dalai Lama addressed our group as his Jewish brothers and sisters. Well, the JUBUs were certainly my brothers and sisters! So I was eager to talk to them, to learn in depth about their Jewish backgrounds, how they came to Buddhism, how they feel about Judaism.

Extremely open about their lives and beliefs, what they had to say that morning seemed revealing not just about them, but about the problems of gaining access to Jewish spirituality—and the need for a new way of teaching it, for a Jewish renewal.

I approached a tall woman in her late thirties, in a maroon robe and with shorn hair. She'd seemed to enjoy the service and had participated in the discussion afterwards. I wanted to hear more from a Buddhist nun with a Brooklyn accent.

She told me her name was Thubten Pemo; her family name was Landsman and she "grew up in Brooklyn in a middle class Jewish neighborhood." We sat in the shade and I scribbled her answers in a notebook.

Her grandmother was the chief Jewish influence in her life. "I remember she was always praying. She'd get up before sunrise, pray all day and at night. She was extremely strict and she followed her rabbis. She kept kosher, and on Saturdays she wouldn't turn on a light bulb." As for synagogue, "I used to enjoy it. I'd go and feel happy that everyone was praying."

Yet her formal Jewish education was a disappointment—though she did learn to read, write, and speak Hebrew at age eight or nine—because she was the only girl in the class. Eventually she gave up Hebrew school.

Even as a young girl, Pemo had been deeply concerned with spiritual issues. "I used to lie in my bed and think about my life. I would make up rules of morality: I'm not going to kill. I'm not going to steal. I'd make up all these rules. I didn't want to have any children. I thought that marriage was suffering. I decided, I'm not going to get married, that means I'm going to be a nun. Then I'd have to be a Christian nun, but I didn't know anything about Christianity. I had a very strong wish to have wisdom."

Later, at Brooklyn College, she had some contact with Hillel. But in 1967 her mother died suddenly. "One day she had a heart attack and she was gone. Then I had to support myself. I switched to night school. I had a full-time job. That went on for years. My aunts and uncles couldn't take care of my grandmother and they put her in an Orthodox old-age home in Brooklyn."

She dropped out of school and in 1970 decided to quit her job and travel for six months. "I went with some girlfriends. We flew to Japan for the World's Fair and started traveling west." However, soon she found herself alone in India. She was twenty-seven. "I got on a third-class train to Nepal. I thought I'd go for two weeks and look at a snowy mountain. I went to a Tibetan lama for a teaching. I didn't know what Buddhism was.

"Lama Yeshe sat and spoke for two hours in horrendous English. But Lama was radiating love at everybody. I thought, this is the nicest man I've ever met in my life and I'd like to be like him. That was twenty years ago. His point was: the ego was a demon and had to be destroyed. I thought, gee, they'd never taught me that in my psych class.

"I ended up staying for two years in the East. I went back to New York to earn money. I'd heard there would be a Kalachakra initiation." (This is a special teaching about the cycles of time.)

"I wrote Lama Yeshe, 'Should I come?'" The answer was yes. And then, after a one-month meditation course, this Jewish woman from Brooklyn shaved her head, took vows of celibacy, and became a Buddhist nun. Now she was Thubten Pemo, and she had vowed to cut herself off from worldly things. She went to Brooklyn to dispose of her furniture, jewelry, and personal items, still hoping her relatives would understand. But her aunts and uncles refused to see her. And her final encounter with her grandmother took on a poignant and comical aspect. "I visited my grandmother in an old-age home. She didn't notice I was wearing my robes.

"'When are you going to tell me the good news?' she said, meaning, When are you going to get married? There was no way to tell her I was a Buddhist nun. She was just happy to see me."

I was impressed by Pemo's intense preoccupation with religiosity at a very early age, her search for some way of living a spiritual life, a search unfulfilled for her in Judaism as she knew it. Growing up in the Eisenhower years, she knew no women rabbis or cantors. She had no access to a spiritual life outside the traditional roles of wife and mother. When I asked her about her knowledge of the Jewish mystical tradition, she said she might have been interested but it was never taught to her.

But Pemo's new path had not been easy either. Though I'd heard questions about the Jewish response to feminism, from Pemo's account I gathered there were also problems for women in the Tibetan Buddhist monastic world. Tibetan and other Asian cultures give women a very low social status, and this is reflected in the treatment of an *ani* or female monastic. In any case, all Western Buddhists had to be self-supporting. For Pemo that meant years of hardship.

Sometimes she had to return to secular life. "I worked in New York and saved money to last for twelve years. It lasted six. From 1979 to 1989 I had nothing. Sometimes I had no money for food. In Switzerland the monks wouldn't give us nuns anything. I went to the cook for the food he was throwing in the garbage. I lived on the carrot ends for a month."

She had medical problems as well. "You get hepatitis. Diarrhea. Tapeworms." Yet she didn't want to give up her nun's vows. She was afraid that living with laypeople, she would "get sucked into attachment."

"I found I had to rely on faith. Certain deities we pray to in the Buddhist tradition can help us. One is Tara, the female Buddha. You pray to Tara to get you safely on a plane. When I have no money for Buddhist practice, I pray to Tara."

Despite all her difficulties, Thubten Pemo remains convinced she has found answers to life in Buddhism. "Most religions teach morality. A lot of religions say to love others. The special thing in Buddhism is, we are given the methods of development. We aren't just saying to have compassion for others, but how to train your mind for compassion."

I thanked Pemo and took her photograph. Cutting her Jewish roots had caused her enormous pain from her family. Although I could understand their reactions, this total rejection seemed cruel and unnecessary. I was also impressed with how she had stuck to her convictions. And that she had a gentle sense of humor.

I'd met Thubten Chodron at the Shabbat the night before. Born Cherry Green in 1950 in a Los Angeles suburb, she received a B.A. from UCLA in 1971. In 1975 she attended a meditation course. Lama Yeshe had struck again, and Chodron decided not long after to put on the robes.

There's something definitely vibrant about Chodron's demeanor. She seemed assured, happy with her choice, radiant. "I felt very comfortable," she told me Friday night, "making the switch from Judaism to Buddhism. I thought I was finding answers to my questions and also techniques that helped me get along better with people and a direction to help make my life meaningful.

"From my parents' point of view, they didn't understand very well. I was married, I was beginning my career. 'She's going to have a career, she married a nice Jewish boy, she's going to have children.' Then all of a sudden their daughter left her husband, shaved her head, went to India, and became a Buddhist nun. It's completely out of their American Jewish suburban experience."

Both Chodron and Pemo have found work as teachers of meditation. Chodron has written several books on Buddhist practice and regularly gives lectures and classes in the United States. (Among her recent books are *Open Heart, Clear Mind* and *Taming the Monkey Mind.*)

Now I saw her seated on the garden wall, having an animated discussion with Rabbi Joy Levitt. Chodron told Joy that she had been really apprehensive before coming to the Friday night service, worried about how the rabbis would feel about her. But she felt relieved now.

Chodron and Joy started comparing notes—how each had found her way onto a spiritual path. It was fascinating, because the rabbi and the *ani* were about the same age and had similar backgrounds.

"I asked to go to Sunday School as a teenager," Chodron said. "I was really searching for something. Sunday School turned me away from Judaism. What I learned there I couldn't accept. I wasn't able to understand it in a way that brought meaning into my life.

"I went into a period of agnosticism and atheism. In college, I joined Hillel for social reasons. Later, I saw a poster for a meditation course. What they were talking about started to provide answers to questions I'd been asking a long time: Why am I alive? What's the purpose of life? What does it really mean to love people?"

Rabbi Levitt listened intently and then answered, "Astonishingly, I had an identical experience of asking questions as a teenager. But I got the answers. It's dependent on personality, community, and place, what answers are out there."

In Joy's case, "My anger was transformed. My purpose in life was to end suffering in the world. The quality came from my people. I was part of a people who had suffered and said I am responsible for you because you are in my community. That leap of action required further leaps of action—beyond the community."

Rabbi Levitt learned that as a Jew, "you are part of a people who have experienced pain and salvation, rejection and acceptance. You have a choice to accept the experience. . . . Our choice as a generation was either to opt out of society or be totally cynical. But I found a third alternative in the Jewish community, some texts, and teachers."

Chodron also felt that her feeling of responsibility for others came from her Jewish upbringing.

"But," she complained, "there was so much emphasis on Jewish suffering. First our group, then others. The Jews are living well in America. What about the suffering of the blacks, the Mexican Americans? I wanted to reach past Jewish suffering."

Joy replied, "The point of understanding Jewish suffering was only that it gave you insight into the suffering of others."

"But," Chodron said, "I fit in. I didn't feel that same defensiveness in American life as my father did, experiencing anti-Semitism."

Then Chodron smiled and just looked Joy over. The rabbi had led the singing of prayers that Shabbat morning, and she was still wearing a petite, blue knit *kippah* pinned to her hair. Finally Chodron said, "It's so incredible for me to see female rabbis. Hurray for you. It must be difficult."

I thought of the difficulties Joy had faced in Dharamsala leading prayers. She admitted to Chodron that "our religion is still patriarchal." But she found some real advantages in that.

She explained, "I go to Orthodox services on Saturday to daven. I love *not* having to sit next to men. I find it much easier. There's no sexual overtones. I find it a relief I won't be called to do anything. I'll be fundamentally unequal, but I won't be pestered. I want to choose the environment in which I pray."

As for the questions about the meaning of life that so haunted Chodron, Joy said, "Jews are supposed to live as though each day were their last." She paused, smiled, and said, "I'm depressed a lot." We all laughed, but she added quite seriously, "As a child I felt very much— and still do now—that death is an end."

Later I asked Joy to elaborate. She told me, "My sense of where Chodron and I divided probably has to do more with our psyches and upbringing. She found it impossible to accept the fact that when you die you're dead, that's it. And I never had that question. I don't know why I didn't have that question and she did. And she found that question resolved in Buddhism, which is when you're dead, you're not dead."

The sun was getting quite warm, and I decided to go into the living room of the cottage, where I found Alex Berzin chatting with Ruth Sonam, the translator for Geshe Sonam I'd met the night before. It tickled me, in a way, that the Jewish folks all knew each other and seemed to have formed a society within a society. It was a silly game of Jewish geography, but there were times I felt, the Jews are doing very well here in Dharamsala.

Certainly Alex and Ruth were. Both are very conscious of their Jewish background and identity. Alex quite explicitly thinks of himself as a Jew, though he has been a practicing Buddhist for many years. Berzin grew up in Paterson, New Jersey, attended an Orthodox Hebrew school, and was a bar mitzvah. However, this scholarly man, who has something of the demeanor of a metropolitan rabbi, told me he was taught Judaism "without any intellectual stimulation." Though he went on to be a professional translator and knows Tibetan, Chinese, and Sanskrit, he never mastered Hebrew because "they never explained the grammar."

"I attended graduate school at Harvard. I was always interested in how Buddhism came into China from India. What was the translation process? To really understand it, I had to study the Indian side as well. I studied Sanskrit, then Tibetan. I've studied translation and transmission, the bridging of cultures back and forth."

But when Berzin came to Dharamsala on a Fulbright in 1969, this interest changed its character. "I came in contact with a living, accessible tradition. It wasn't a matter of academic detective work to decode the ancient texts, but of people who have a full oral tradition going back unbroken."

Berzin returned to Harvard to complete his Ph.D., but he changed from an academic studying the transmission of Buddhism to something of a transmitter himself. He serves at times as the Dalai Lama's interpreter and edits and translates Tibetan Buddhist texts for the Library of Tibetan Works and Archives. "Because of the love of clarity and scholarship, one feels at home in this tradition. This has allowed Jewish people to make a contribution here."

Ruth Sonam, an Irish Jew born to German parents fleeing Hitler, has also devoted most of her time in Dharamsala to translation work. Ruth feels that Jews bring something special to the task of explaining Buddhism to the West. "We bridge," Ruth Sonam said.

She added that given her parents' background as refugees from Hitler's Germany, "the concept that there is suffering was most alive to me and opened me up to the Buddhist concepts."

Alex said, "The Jewishness of my background adds something to my Buddhism, a life-affirming, creative approach. This is one of the main contributions we have given to Buddhism, being more creative with it to help make it more accessible to Western people, and more affirming, more secular." Alex has made two world tours, teaching Buddhism in more than twenty-six countries.

As a translator, Alex took as his particular task the job of finding exact English equivalents to Buddhist concepts. The first people to translate ideas from Sanskrit were Christian missionaries, who used terms like sin, salvation, and suffering to translate the Buddhist concepts of *klesha, nirvana,* and *dukkha.* In part Alex has devoted himself to de-Christianizing Buddhist English, which somehow seems apt for a Jewish Buddhist.

Despite their serious commitment to Buddhism, both Ruth Sonam and Alex Berzin were moved by the Jewish visit to Dharamsala. Following the Shabbat service, Ruth mused, "Maybe I could have been a Talmudic scholar if things had been different." Alex said, "After the audience with His Holiness the only way I could explain it to my friends was that it made me so proud to be Jewish, to see Jewish customs presented in such an intelligent and open way."

Meeting Alex at Shabbat, my view of him changed. He seemed more comfortable and relaxed, more flexible than I'd thought after our first encounter. Although I didn't understand how a Jew could also be, in effect, a Buddhist missionary, I could see that he really felt he was both Jewish and Buddhist, however contradictory that might seem.

I was curious to learn more about Israelis in Dharamsala. Recently India had issued the first visas to Israel and several of the Jewish Buddhists had commented on the influx. Pemo told me of a meditation course she taught in Nepal. "We had several Israelis, including one who is becoming a rabbi. A great person, strict, he wouldn't come to the teachings on Saturdays. He'd pray in his tallis. When I gave the lecture on Emptiness, he interrupted, calling out that I was wrong."

She spoke to Max Redlich, who'd fought in the Six Day War. "He'd leapt from a plane into a ditch and they shot off his boots. In Australia he became a millionaire butcher, exporting meat to Canada." He met Lama Yeshe there, and now, as a Buddhist monk, "he's purifying his killing karma."

She asked Max "to speak to the Israeli in Hebrew. Afterwards, the boy apologized to me for being rude. He was quite interested in meditating, still wearing the yarmulke. One day he fainted. He'd had an experience of emptiness—the one he was fighting against—and passed out. At Bodh Gaya, he took refuge in the Buddha. But he saw no contradiction with being a Jew."

Not every Buddhist practitioner in Dharamsala had left Judaism behind. Friday night I'd met Isaac Bentwich, a twenty-nine-year-old Israeli and a recent graduate from the medical school at the University of Beersheva. He insisted that studying and practicing Buddhism "does not diminish my Jewishness. I'm much more Jewish than I was before."

Bentwich was spending several months in Dharamsala, learning about *tantrayana*, the advanced visualization practice of Tibetan Buddhism. Yet for him, "Judaism is an extremely profound heritage, philosophy, religion, way of living, way of looking at the world. It's an extremely spiritual path not inferior to any other."

Instead he finds that studying Buddhist practices helped him "to understand better hidden and dormant parts of my religion. For example, the philosophy of Maimonides is extremely similar to Buddhist philosophy."

Both Maimonides, a twelfth-century philosopher, and Buddhists advocate the virtues of following a middle path, balancing between extremes of behavior. In the *Mishneh Torah*, Maimonides also advocates certain practices for curing the ills of arrogance or anger. "If one is irascible, he is directed so to govern himself that even if he is assaulted or reviled, he will not feel affronted. If one is arrogant, he should accustom himself to endure much contumely, sit below everyone, and wear old and ragged garments that bring the wearer into contempt, and so forth, till arrogance is eradicated from his heart and he has regained the middle path, which is the right way."

But Bentwich, descended from a distinguished Israeli educator and knowledgeable about Jewish wisdom, was an exception. The Jewish Buddhists felt they had chosen a more complete and richer path in Buddhism. To Pemo, "Buddhism includes all living beings. Any person can come to my teacher. He has compassion for all of them. In Judaism, I'll help you because you are the same as me. As long as we have a discriminating mind, we are going to harm each other."

Alex Berzin, who is something of a historian of Jewish Dharamsala, felt that a remarkably large number of Jews had been prominently involved. For instance, he mentioned that the first foreigner ever to receive the title of *geshe* is a Swiss Jew named George Dreyfus.

Later that evening over dinner, I asked Joy Levitt how she viewed the loss to Judaism of such sensitive, intelligent, and spiritually motivated people. She said, "I don't feel they represent a symbol of some kind of Jewish failure. Their impulse has more to do with the nature of those individuals and their souls in a free and open society. There is enough richness and spirituality in Judaism to go around tenfold. Although we can always teach it better, for some people it will simply not resonate.

"The Jewish problem is not that a few people find Buddhism attractive. The Jewish problem is that most people don't find anything attractive. I don't know why we pick on the people who are spiritually alive and blame them for not helping us. Alex Berzin, from the standpoint of the world, seems to me a fulfilled person. Is he a loss to the Jewish community? Sure. But when you put the Jewish commitment in the context of the repair of the world, *tikkun olam,* he's participating and lots of other people aren't."

Joy's was a familiar complaint. There is a very strong streak, especially among more liberal and secular Jews, against anything that smacks of excessive concern for God or piety, against any overt religious display. When asked their religion in a recent survey, one out of five Jews answered "none." It must be terribly frustrating for rabbis to encounter such Jews and have them complain about too much Hebrew, too much praying, too much Jewishness in the synagogue. And she was being quite generous to say that an Alex Berzin, because of his spiritual commitment, was at least participating in *tikkun olam.*

Still, after the Shabbat was over, others in the Jewish delegation reported greater ambivalence and even anguish about the JUBUs. After eleven years of studying and writing about mysticism in Jerusalem, Rabbi Omer-Man had been invited in 1981 by the Los Angeles Hillel council to set up an outreach program for religiously alienated Jews, especially those involved with alternative religions, such as Buddhism and Hinduism. He worked for a number of years on a one-on-one basis. In fact, while Zalman debated with the monks, Jonathan had struck up a conversation with some Jewish kids from Los Angeles. When they heard that Jonathan would soon be opening a school of Jewish meditation, they immediately signed up to study with him. Jonathan found that episode more than ironic.

As for Professor Katz, his Shabbat encounters with the Western Buddhists he called dharma people had been very unsettling. Before the trip began, he had told me, "I came to Judaism through Buddhism." He explained that in the seventies he had studied Buddhism with Chogyam Trungpa at the Naropa Institute and had taken bodhisattva vows, as well as receiving a number of tantric initiations.

Yet in the end, Trungpa had encouraged Nathan to explore Judaism more deeply. Following his teacher's advice, he had eventually made his way back to Jewish life and for many years now has been a very committed Conservative Jew in his own personal practice.

So it was with some anxiety that Nathan Katz had encountered the Western dharma people, many of whom, such as Alex Berzin, he'd known for years. He thought Alex was doing marvelously well. Perhaps he saw in him the path his life had almost taken. Nathan had also been tested by the ubiquitous Chodron in an intense dialogue that afternoon on the patio of the Kashmir Cottage.

To Nathan the discussion combined the rapid-fire question-and-answer style of yeshiva—and Tibetan debate. When she asked him questions, he had the feeling she was looking directly at his mind for answers. Having heard about Zalman Schachter's presentation, she wanted to know in what way Judaism was a path. It was the first time someone else had directed such Buddhist questions to him about Judaism—though he told me later, "I do that all the time in my own mind."

Borrowing from Rabbi Greenberg's lecture to the All Himalayan Conference, Nathan answered that in Judaism, studying Torah was a path. "At each meal we study, at Shabbas we study." He explained that the second part of the Jewish path was what Jonathan Omer-Man calls the vertical connection—prayer. Nathan explained "about life cycles, about seasons, about memory, loss, mourning, circumcision, the meaning of *brit*," or covenant. He told her as well about what Rabbi Omer-Man calls the horizontal direction—"acts of loving-kindness, ethics, repairing the world, *tzedakah*, the basic principle of *menschlichkeit*, and moral responsibility." He said, "That's our path, those three. Study, *tefilla*, acts of kindness or compassion."

But Chodron pressed him. "How does each of these aspects cultivate or transform the mind?" Nathan answered that question, but then, with geshe-like rapidity, she stumped him with another.

"Tell me," she asked, "your traditions, your teaching, your view on the origin, the arising, and the cessation of suffering. How is it that we suffer, and how do you ultimately overcome suffering?" He told Chodron, "I can't answer that, because I don't think my tradition explains suffering away. Or can explain suffering. I think my tradition holds that suffering is ultimately utterly inexplicable. And of course I'm of a post-Holocaust generation. So that the traditional answers to such questions are unacceptable to many Jews today. Also, we don't believe that suffering is ultimately overcome. Our tradition mediates how we suffer and thereby makes suffering sufferable through rituals, life cycles, passages, and so on. But it doesn't promise, doesn't really entertain the idea of ultimately overcoming suffering, except in a future universalist sense, the messianic hope."

In reply, she told him what as a student of Buddhism he already knew—that is, "how with great clarity and elegance the Buddha taught about the arising and cessation of suffering."

He said, "I know that. You've got me, I have to concede. My tradition does not answer that question as clearly as Buddha did, but nevertheless, I'm not sure it's a weakness of my system that it fails to explain suffering because I believe that's closer to the truth of suffering, that—medieval arguments about free will to the contrary—it remains inexplicable."

Nathan felt a lingering disquiet after this thorough scouring, which came out later that evening as he talked the day over with Zalman. The rabbi also had ambivalent feelings. He expressed some frustration—he called it a bellyache—born of admiration for Jewish Buddhists like Alex Berzin. "Why, if he knows where the action is, would he not come back to our vineyard?" To such Buddhists Zalman would want to say, "You're taking bodhisattva vows; who needs bodhisattvas more than Jews at this point? You guys have got something, so why the hell don't you come in and help us? Why have you abandoned us?"

It was interesting that even Zalman felt this ache so strongly. I understood a deeper psychological reason why Jews tend to dismiss Jewish Buddhists. Because getting close to them, and seeing how fine they really are, makes their loss even more painful. This encounter between Jews and JUBUs cut to the bone, very much as Yitz Greenberg had described all dialogue in an age of pluralism. "You meet these people with tremendous force and openness and they're not preselected, they're not prefiltered, or loaded in your favor."

I decided that when I returned to the United States I would try to meet more Jewish Buddhists and find out what they were thinking. The ones I'd met had broken down my old stereotypes of brainwashed zombies—these people were as lively and with-it as I could have wished. But while I'd been impressed by Alex and Ruth, by Chodron and Pemo, there was a slight note of superiority in their discourse that was the source of my own bellyache.

I wasn't so ready to declare Buddhism the hands-down winner in the all-round spirituality contest. I'd give Buddhism an A for meditation and Judaism an A for family values. But Buddhism gets a C– for boring poetry (too much hyperbole) and Judaism gets an A+ for great stand-up comics. And I thought kreplach and mo-mo were a dead heat, but lox and bagels a tiebreaker in the food category.

At a more serious level, I wondered if some of the kvetches JUBUs had about Judaism were based on a false comparison. There is a danger in comparing an idealized version of a new religion to the very gritty and lived version of one's birth religion. Was it a fair comparison—or were we looking at an idealized Buddhism, a Buddhism for export as Zalman called it? Though I didn't have his erudition, I agreed with Isaac Bentwich that Judaism is an ancient tradition as worthy of respect as any other. In fact, the Dalai Lama himself had taught me that.

But then Joy Levitt's point came to me with force: so many Jews had been turned off, not only to Judaism, but to any sort of spiritual experience. I was such a Jew. My own background was very similar to Chodron's and I could understand her impatience and dissatisfaction, especially if she brought any intellectual curiosity into her religious school class. It was clear, too, that if someone like Alex, who has mastered Tibetan and Sanskrit, passed through a Jewish childhood without being taught Hebrew, something was terribly wrong with Jewish education.

I was confused, caught between admiring the JUBUs and resenting them, feeling a little that they were putting Judaism under an indictment, though in a very friendly way that just made the inherent critique of Judaism that their lives represented more penetrating.

So I was grateful to Zalman, after all his bellyaching, and Nathan's and mine, when he reversed field and offered us a consoling vision to settle our stomachs before we retired that Saturday night.

"When you look at those dharma people," Zalman suggested to Nathan, "and look at the people who have made choices like you have made, they make a circle too. So there are people coming to Judaism from other, different religions, and there are those who remain with other traditions, and there are some people who started in Judaism and went to others, and then you have a line—on this side, you're Jewish, and on this side, you're not.

"Now imagine yourself drifting off in a rocket looking down at the group at the boundary you call Jewish and before long, what lights up on the map is the amount of awareness, like little pinpoints of light. You see the lights of awareness; it's night, so you can't see the boundary any-more. From that perspective all of us are in between."

All of us are in between. Given their presence that Sabbath morning, it's safe to say that applied to the JUBUs. They still feel Jewish in some way. For some the ties are bound with the hope of reconciliation with family members. Thubten Pemo, who seems to have a suffered a great deal in this regard, told me of a letter she received from an aunt. "Once, when I was in Nepal, she wrote me that she went to synagogue for Yom Kippur. She was reading the holy book and she realized that everyone just wants happiness. She wrote me, 'If you have found your way to obtain happiness, then that's all right with us.' Well, that's a high realization that His Holiness teaches wherever he goes. It's almost like she received a blessing that day in the temple."

Thubten Chodron also has hope for more reconciliation with her family. She told me, "I've been ordained thirteen years. My family sees I'm serious, stable, I'm happier, what I'm doing is useful to other people. Slowly, they are relaxing and opening up. They came to one talk I gave on Buddhism. They even brought some family friends. My real hopes and prayers are they will realize my choice was not a rejection of Judaism or them, but I was taking certain values from Judaism and expanding them in a way that made sense to me."

The Jewish value she mentioned so far was an awareness of suffering. I wondered what other Jewish values she'd been exposed to. It seemed to me that her main tie with Judaism was the old standby, family guilt.

On Sunday, just before we left Dharamsala, I tried to probe a little deeper. "Why is it," I asked her, "in spite of all you've gone through, this deep effort to free the self from attachments, why the curiosity, why still the draw, why the interest in meeting with us?"

She told me that she'd discussed this with Alex Berzin. For him, the visit of the Jews had been reaffirming: he is a Jew but he's also a Buddhist. "But for me, watching my mind and my reactions, I felt I had really come to terms with coming from a Jewish background and feeling comfortable with that, not feeling rebellious or hostile, but also knowing very clearly that I am not a Jew. I come from a Jewish background and I understand those people, I live in a Tibetan culture and I understand them, I live in a Chinese culture and I understand them, but I'm not any of them.

"I knew before I had left Judaism, I had some feelings why I left. Sometimes you're never sure if there's some hostility or resistance until you actually meet the situation. When you see you're calm in it, then there's been some progress. If you meet some hostility, if you can feel something inside of you shake, then you know there are some things to work on."

The difficulties with her family and with her Jewish background in general had themselves become objects of meditation, tests of her own spiritual development, just as she and what she represented had become a serious subject of contemplation for the Jewish visitors.

"I was excited the rabbis were coming, because I saw it as an opportunity to get in touch with things I'd lived before with other parts of myself and to check up from a different point of view, well, what is this religion? Do I still feel the same way about it? Do I still feel the same as the people? Because if you feel different, then maybe you could see that maybe you were being unnecessarily critical before. It just gives you a perspective. It's like meeting old friends from childhood. It gives you a perspective on yourself, how you've changed, how you've grown."

Before we parted, Chodron mentioned that she was making a teaching tour in the United States in the spring and I invited her to visit with me. I would get to know her better and learn more about the complexities of her spiritual life. Like Nathan Katz, or Marc Lieberman, she was not only a person, but a process, a living Jewish Buddhist dialogue all to herself.

Zalman's image of a circle came back to me, only this time with real faces: Chodron and Pemo and Alex Berzin and Ruth Sonam and Nathan Katz and Marc Lieberman all forming a circle. Where did one cross over and become a Jew, and where a Buddhist? Who had the more realistic idea of how to deal with suffering, or with anger? I loved the gentleness and equanimity of the Buddhists I'd met, their calm and their apparent freedom from anger. But I had been deeply moved, too, by the Jewish prayer, the dancing we'd done—Zalman and Yitz, our senior rabbis, leading the way arm in arm. I had seen, as Zalman had exulted on Friday night, "the sages of both traditions dancing."

I felt, though I couldn't really explain it, that there had to be a place, a very high place, where the circle of dancers was whole and the differences weren't differences anymore.

12

JUBUs in America

Finding that high place wouldn't be easy.

When I returned from Dharamsala, I interviewed a number of JUBUs, over the phone, through E-mail, and in person. I wanted to know what they'd found in Buddhism and why they'd left Judaism. I found myself conducting exit interviews for a generation of Jewish Buddhists.

When talking of Judaism, the JUBUs sometimes sounded ill-informed and harsh. But listening past the static, I heard a valuable critique of Jewish life today. Maybe Jews should consider adopting a formal exit procedure. We might learn more from the people who are leaving than from some who stay behind through sheer inertia.

The Dharamsala JUBUs had mainly stressed similarities, not differences. Alex Berzin had mentioned shared scholarly traditions, Ruth Sonam and Thubten Chodron that their awareness of Jewish history had led them to appreciate Buddhist ideas about suffering.

That was very diplomatic, but it didn't speak to the more visceral level where my Jewishness tends to operate. I knew there had to be more anger and pain involved with their leaving than that. Chodron as much as said so when she talked about looking to see if something in her encounter with Jews still made her shake. The JUBUs made me shake too.

They made me ask a question I'd never asked myself. What was I getting out of Judaism? What was I getting out of being Jewish?

And they threw out a challenge, implicit in Chodron's probing of Nathan Katz: Is Judaism a viable spiritual path today? That was Michael Sautman's question, too, after Zalman's presentation on kabbalah. While intrigued to learn about the rich mystical literature, he rightly wanted to know whether this stuff is available today.

Every JUBU I spoke to had found Jewish mysticism inaccessible. Most were as surprised as Rabbi Levitt that such teachings even existed. They certainly didn't know of any teachers. When, in the course of our conversations in May 1992, I mentioned the kabbalistic doctrines of *ain sof* to Allen Ginsberg, the poet responded with very practical questions. "What specific group with a lineage teaches that and has practices that lead to the understanding of that, the absorption of that? Who would be the contemporary teacher representing that tradition? What's available for students?" They were questions I could not readily answer.

Zalman Schachter had been born into Hasidism. And other Jews, such as Rabbi Jonathan Omer-Man, have found their own ways to authentic teachers of Jewish mysticism. But, as he later explained, he had taken a very private and idiosyncratic route, one that makes credible the JUBU complaint that such teachings have not generally been of easy access—especially compared to the very public dissemination of Buddhism in the past twenty years.

This inaccessibility was important, because the JUBUs' quest in turning away from Judaism was to seek direct contact with a teacher of wisdom. To meet a holy person. I could understand that—I had the same curiosity in meeting the Dalai Lama.

That personal contact changed their lives. Alex Berzin had come to Dharamsala as a scholar—but stayed because of the living masters he met there. In Tibetan Buddhism in particular, the guru becomes an overwhelming influence. I had seen close up the very special relationship of teacher to student, between Ruth Sonam and Geshe Sonam. I had felt it in the way Thubten Pemo spoke of her teacher, Lama Yeshe. "Lama was radiating love at everybody."

But just as important is the accessibility of the teachings. The early stages of the Buddhist path are experiential. You don't have to be converted to Buddhism to meditate. You don't have to sign up to a long list of beliefs or assertions about historical events or figures. The most basic meditations are as available as your next breath. And if they prove useful to an individual, beyond them are very systematic paths of spiritual development. The Tibetan pedagogy, *lam rim*, is, in fact, a graded path toward enlightenment.

Direct experience of meditation was key to Joseph Goldstein, one of the four JUBU founders of the Insight Meditation Society in Barre, Massachusetts. "A year or two into my practice I came back to the States and met with the rabbi who had bar mitzvahed me. He was very upset that I was leaving the Jewish fold, which is how he saw it. For me the real difference was that insofar as I understood it, the path of Judaism involved following the vision, the law, of someone else's experience. I used the Old Testament prophets as an example. I told him I was interested in having that experience. I wasn't interested in taking it on faith and trying to live up to it."

In the sixties and seventies some extremely skillful Tibetan teachers came to the West, among them Lama Thubten Yeshe, who taught Chodron and Pemo, and Kalu Rinpoche, a brilliant meditation master. But the best-known Tibetan teacher at that time was Chogyam Trungpa.

As befits a master poet, Allen Ginsberg explained Trungpa's great success with Jewish students as due to his language. "For the first time he expounded Buddhist dharma with a Yiddish accent. A lot of his students had been Jewish and he understood New Yorkese, Hymietown dialect." For instance, "the Buddhist notion of suffering—as in 'existence is suffering'—he could translate as *tzuris.*

"I had not until that time [1970] run across any wise men that completely penetrated my skull with their language and their insight and their humor." By contrast, Ginsberg found the Jewish esoteric to be relatively difficult to access. When I mentioned the outreach of the Lubavitcher rebbe, who lives across the river from him in Brooklyn, Ginsberg exploded, "He seems like a complete crank and a political reactionary on top of that. Who's going to go to him for wisdom?" I thought that was funny, because I could imagine a Hasid speaking just as harshly about Ginsberg's teacher for being a drunk and a sex maniac.

Maybe he thought better of it himself, because he added, less irritably, "What I'm getting at—there were no teachers who were clear. Or I didn't run into a teacher who was clear. There may have been some hidden teachers but I didn't know them. It was daunting to try and do it in English anyway when it should be in Hebrew, whereas it was less daunting to do the Tibetan in English because the teacher had by then found the English equivalents and did not have to rely on the Tibetan."

I asked Zalman Schachter why he thought so many had left Judaism for other traditions. He mentioned something obvious that had not been expressed by the JUBUs themselves—the appeal of the exotic. "First—it doesn't feel real if it comes from their own thing. If you come to shul on Yom Kippur—this is the gross level, yah?—and you know you're going to be hit for the United Jewish Appeal and the building fund, you can't take your own tradition seriously."

As to accessibility, Zalman pointed out that the mystical and esoteric were suppressed by the more liberal branches of Judaism, beginning with the German reform movement of the nineteenth century. "The early translators were very strong rationalists. Anything that smacked of mysticism they put down, as Graetz puts down kabbalah. Very ashamed that we Jews have such superstition. So the hunger is very great." This was, of course, exactly the climate Gershom Scholem had encountered in Berlin when he began his study of kabbalah.

With their own esoteric teachings inaccessible, most JUBUs grew up with a Judaism heavy on ethnic pride, obsessive about preserving itself, about maintaining Jewish identity at all costs. And Jewish pride, Jewish chauvinism, Jewish particularism—the idea that we are special, a chosen people—seems to contradict the very universalistic prophetic messages Judaism also teaches. Perhaps they wouldn't put it this way, but if examined closely, it appears that some JUBUs left Judaism *because* of their Jewish ideals.

Joseph Goldstein told me, "One reason I don't feel so connected, and this may be a totally exoteric dimension of Judaism, but I was never comfortable with its nonuniversal aspect. It seemed separatist to me. The whole notion of the chosen people. This is true of all Western religions. They are not so much talking about the universal nature of the mind, but rather a belief system. If you believe, you are part of a certain group. If you don't, you're outside of that."

Chodron told me, "I felt a very strong Jewish identity because I was one of four Jewish kids in the school. I was brought up, you're different. 'I'm not stupid like those people who believe in Jesus'—this kind of attitude. Though my parents weren't very religious, there was this ethnic feeling. When I was ten, I had a Christian girlfriend. We used to talk about God. I said I felt closer to God because I was Jewish." She laughed at the memory. "In high school I was already moving away from Judaism." She was disappointed in the whole idea of "this happened to the Jews five thousand years ago; therefore, this is what is important to you. I thought, hold on, that happened to people from a completely different society. What do I have to do with them?"

Chodron felt Jews emphasized their own suffering too much. "I felt very uncomfortable when I got into high school with Jewish paranoia. This whole feeling of unrelatedness to the rest of humanity because you're Jewish.

"I grew up in the time of the Watts riots, with black people saying they wanted equal rights. So were women and Chicanos. That made a lot more sense to me than this Jewish protectorate. I moved into the sphere of social action, taking what I learned about suffering from my Jewish background but going well beyond the narrow Jewish limit to which it was applied."

Allen Ginsberg remains very disturbed by Jewish particularism. He told me in our 1992 interview that he agreed with the former United Nations resolution stating that Zionism is racism. "And the fact that everybody is so screamingly angry Zionism can't be called that is even worse." The Israelis and Palestinians had both missed great opportunities for peace. He was equally hard on the Tibetans. He thought "the Dalai Lama's political group is partly responsible for the conflict with China, because the rather corrupt Office of Tibet asked for such a large chunk of territory that it offended the Chinese." He found the Tibetans "making the same mistake as the territorial overextension of the Zionists." Though there were hints of anti-Zionism among some of the Jewish Buddhists I spoke to, Ginsberg's expressions were the harshest.

When I asked him to define his Jewishness, he described himself as a "delicatessen intellectual." Yet despite that purely secular self-definition, there are many references to Jewish religion in his works. His powerful poem of outrage and mourning, "Kaddish," mimics the rhythms of the ancient Aramaic prayer. But as Ginsberg explained to me, both his parents and their family were completely secularized Jews. He said, "My family had a lot of the experience of the Orthodox and disliked it a great deal. My grandfather had shaved his beard and *payos* and had a job. My great-grandfather was Orthodox and I was exposed to him, briefly."

Like Allen Ginsberg, most Jewish Buddhists I spoke to came from secular backgrounds. In this they resemble the vast majority of two generations of American Jews. I'm convinced that the Judaism we were exposed to was primarily exoteric, preoccupied with social and political issues, and often embarrassed by expressions of spirituality.

There are many historical reasons for this. One has to do with the type of Jews who came to America during the massive wave of immigration at the turn of the century. Many had already dropped religion in the old country, some in favor of the Bund, Zionism, or Communism. Like Ginsberg's grandfather, most others quickly dropped the outer trappings of religious Judaism just to make it in American life. A New York rabbi once remarked that he would like to do some scuba diving around the Statue of Liberty. He was certain he would find hundreds of yarmulkes, prayer books, and *tallisim* that newly arrived immigrants tossed overboard.

American Reform Judaism—the kind both Chodron and I were exposed to—continued the process by streamlining religion. Though the Reform movement was born in Germany in the 1830s as a response to the emancipation of Jews from the ghetto, its success in America with the children and grandchildren of immigrant Jews had a lot to do with its elimination of old world religiosity. The more Reform synagogues resembled churches, the better.

The point is, the Reform Jewish strategy pretty much succeeded in assimilating Jews into American life. When JUBUs spoke against Jewish particularism, one could feel that Reform Judaism had succeeded all too well. An ethical ideal of universal justice, freed from the particulars of ritual, left many Jews free to leave the fold. We could be secular, or Buddhist, and still feel connected to these universal values.

At the deepest level, though, the JUBUs could never make a connection to God. "After all," as Allen Ginsberg told me, describing the

Naropa class of 1974, which included Joseph Goldstein, Jack Kornfield, and others, "most of us were nontheists, while Judaism finally does insist on a sacred personality to the universe." In that regard, Joseph Goldstein told me of "a real quest in my senior year in high school and first year in college: a pressing issue around the existence of God. I was grappling with it. It seems to me it had a lot of consequences: my life would be one way if there were and another way if there were not. I went to Columbia. For some weeks it was a very strong issue, but I don't recall what happened. I must have just gone on writing my papers. After college I went into the Peace Corps in Thailand and that's where I came into contact with Buddhism."

Many Jews, if pressed, could not say for sure that they believe in God. Although surveys show that a large majority of American Christians believe in God, a much lower percentage of Jews do. American Jews in general are more uncomfortable than their Christian neighbors with concepts of God, or heaven or hell.

Here the JUBUs are different. Spiritual issues grabbed them—they had a lot of consequences. God became a big issue to these folks at some point in their lives, a source of concern or conflict. And many JUBUs resolved this by concluding that God was a harmful concept, with disturbing effects on the personality of the believer.

This aroused my interest because I certainly could not claim to have had any direct experience of God. In fact, belief in God had not been much stressed either in my family or in my synagogue. God was a name we mumbled in our prayers, along with a lot of other Hebrew we didn't fully understand.

My Jewish attachment so dominated my thinking, I was even proud that Jews had invented God, or at least that most people seemed to worship the Jewish God, which I took to be the same thing. It never occurred to me that I should stop being a Jew just because I didn't have an experience of God.

Thubten Chodron's questioning began earlier in her life than Goldstein's, and she did arrive at some definitive conclusions. Yet she still has unanswered questions—which may account for her intense encounter with Joy and Nathan in Dharamsala.

She opened our conversations in the United States by telling me about her various efforts in recent years to meet with rabbis so that she could ask them about God. Their response to her was rather cold. As she had indicated to Joy Levitt during their encounter in Dharamsala, these questions go back to her Sunday School days, when she used to compare notes on the way home with a friend.

About "the Old Testament God," she said, "I didn't like his personality. He was vengeful, he had qualities I wouldn't want to develop, that my parents taught me were wrong. Harming others because they harm the people that you like. Smiting others because they criticize you or worship somebody else. When you're a kid on the playground, because somebody plays with somebody else, that doesn't give you the reason to jump in and assault. This kind of jealous, vengeful God—I can't worship that. I can't see that as holy, I don't want to become like that."

I tried to suggest that "people evolve different conceptions of God" and wondered if "the God and Judaism you rejected is one most Jews would reject also, if it isn't a very unsophisticated child's view of Judaism. As we mature, we realize that concepts of God as father, king, or ruler are baby steps toward some greater understanding."

Chodron answered, "Then they should teach that to people. If there are wider notions of God, that's what they should teach to the children—not that God is up there watching you and you be good or you'll get punished."

Likewise, Allen Ginsberg felt that "there doesn't seem to be a built-in security system against sneaking in an external deity" in the Jewish tradition.

The phrase "external deity" struck a chord with something Zalman had said to the Dalai Lama, about the kabbalistic notion of God. He had suggested "that the notion of creator who comes from outside who makes something happen is not the way kabbalah spoke about it. Kabbalah speaks about emanation. It comes out of God. There is nothing but God, so it all flows from God."

So I asked Allen Ginsberg if he was familiar with the mystical notions of God in the Jewish tradition, those that permitted the Dalai Lama to tell Zalman that he saw a point of similarity with the Buddhist concept of *shunyata,* or emptiness.

Then I quoted to him from the thirteenth-century Spanish kabbalist, Joseph Gikatilla, that *ain sof* is "called Ayin [Nothing] because of its concealment from all creatures." I quoted other Jewish mystical concepts of Nothingness from the Hasidic master, Dov Baer, and from the contemporary mystic, the late Rabbi Aryeh Kaplan. But though impressed by these quotations, Ginsberg became irritated with the suggestion that such ideas represent real Judaism. Ironically, he shared Yitz Greenberg's view that kabbalah is no more than a minority report.

"After all," he said, "what is the promised land, the special race, without a Bible that is the word of God of some sort, without all the literalism of the Old Testament?" He felt that there may be some eccentric kabbalistic definitions saying it's really nothing, but the mainstream seemed to be saying it is something, isn't it? By contrast, in Asian societies, he added, "they have the intelligence to realize there's no God."

This last remark seemed insulting, and I wondered at the wrath with which he denounced Judaism, God, the Lubavitcher rebbe, Zionism, and even the Office of Tibet. Why the vehemence, still? I was amused when he went on to explain to me in great detail the Buddhist methods of controlling anger.

He himself insisted, "I haven't left being a Jew. I'm there. But I don't feel I left anything because I didn't have anything to begin with, religiously."

I decided that in an important way he was correct. He hadn't left at all. Maybe I caught him at a bad time, but in our conversations, he sounded very much to me like what he condemned—a reactive, cranky, and very Jewish, prophet of Buddhism.

I don't mean to pose Allen Gisnberg as a model of all JUBUs or as a representative Buddhist. I tend to believe that at root, his real religion is poetry. I suspect that the rigors of the Tibetan Buddhist discipline—the prostrations and the advanced meditations—are not as interesting to him as the theory—and the language it engenders. (I happened to pass by him in the audience during a teaching by the Dalai Lama in New York. While others were dutifully chanting Tibetan syllables, Ginsberg was intoning "eenie meenie miney mo.")

Thubten Chodron represents almost the opposite pole in terms of commitment. From my own observation, she does spend hours a day on prostrations and prayers and, of course, she has gone all the way—shaving her head and putting on monastic robes.

But in our conversation, Chodron inadvertently threw a light on this persistence of the Jewish personality even after a Buddhist makeover when she mentioned how "God's preprogramming, intervening in the world," leads to a context of blame and punishment in our understanding of events. When she said that, I knew she had put her finger on an important aspect of Jewish, and Western, culture. The self-righteousness virus is a dangerous infection that easily follows from a belief in divine inspiration—or any transcendent spiritual experience.

Perhaps we are also close here to an answer to the question of Jewish particle physics—the gluons of Jewish identity that keep not only secular Jews such as me, but even JUBUs, still attached to their Jewishness.

I began to suspect that Jewish identity, as it has evolved in the West today, could be a real barrier to encountering the depths of Judaism. In other words, being Jewish could keep you from being a Jew.

In our secular times, the sense of chosenness has degenerated from theology to psychology to reflex—like the paranoia I felt in the Frankfurt airport. Just as some delis now serve kosher-style sandwiches that are no longer kosher, so one might have a prophetic-style ego—without the prophecy.

I see myself carrying around a sense of being special that has no content. I can also see it in some of the JUBUs—they have become Buddhists in part to get free of it. And as long as Jews make them shake, they haven't quite succeeded. Judaism is the wrathful divinity they must meditate upon until they are utterly calm.

In short, Chodron's disappointment with God and the rabbis is a very Jewish disappointment. And Allen Ginsberg's anger at God and Judaism is a very Jewish-style anger.

Zalman Schachter gave me a beautiful midrash on this subject. He told me, "Shlomo Carlebach said something that deserves attention. He quotes a Hasidic master, Rabbi Mordecai Joseph, the Izhbitzer Rebbe, who asks: 'Why is it that a *kohen* isn't supposed to go near a dead body?'" According to the law enunciated in Leviticus 21:1–3, 10–12, the *kohen* or Jewish priest, is forbidden to make contact with a corpse. Thus, a Jew today who knows he is a *kohen* cannot go to the cemetery except for the funeral of a close family member.

The Izhbitzer Rebbe, in his midrash, takes off from the text in Leviticus and uses it to find a spiritual message.

"So the short of it is," Zalman explained, "when you see a corpse, you can't help but be angry with God. 'Why did He have to make it that way? That that's the door you have to go through? It's terrible.' Now the *kohen* is supposed to be the gentle teacher of people, so if he is angry with God, he'll have a real bad time talking about God because what will show will be the anger.

"End of the Hasidic master, okay? Now Shlomo: Ever since the Holocaust we are all like priests who have become contaminated by death. It's hard for people who are looking for a loving, living God to find him among the angry voices. They go to people who at this point don't have any anger about God."

Yes, I thought, they didn't go to hear about God. And some of them, like Allen Ginsberg, are still angry and others, like Chodron, are seriously disappointed. It was clear that all the JUBUs dismissed out of hand the idea that God could be compelling or real. And I certainly couldn't condemn them—because there were only a few occasions in my own life where I had any intimation that God might be real.

That was the challenge Zalman had given me the morning he led davening in Dharamsala, when he touched me on the shoulder: Your God is a true God. That is, your God is real.

Long ago, Moses Maimonides commented on this verse from Jeremiah. To the great medieval Jewish philosopher it meant, "He alone is real, and nothing else has reality like His reality."

Between the faith of my ancestors and the challenge of the JUBUs I am caught in this dilemma: God is reality—or nothing.

Or are reality and nothing somehow the same?

Maybe where *shunyata* meets *ain sof*, I would find the high place where Jews and JUBUs and Buddhists could dance together again.

13

Tibetan Intellectuals, Tibetan Orphans

Saturday afternoon the Jewish delegation glimpsed the political tensions in the exile community. In the garden of Kashmir Cottage, we met with Lhasang Tsering, at that time president of the Tibetan Youth Congress (TYC), an organization that has played an opposition role in exile politics. In 1977 the group staged militant demonstrations at the Chinese embassy in New Delhi and made direct contacts with Indian political parties, which embarrassed the *Kashag*, or cabinet of the Dalai Lama. Since then, many TYC leaders have ended up working in the exile government's bureaucracy, including Tsering. At times, then, the Dalai Lama has managed to coopt the potential rebellion, believing "that a militant attitude is helpful for maintaining morale among our youth, but a military movement itself is not feasible. It would be suicidal."

When I met him, Lhasang Tsering appeared suave, sophisticated, very sharp in his sports jacket. A man in his mid-forties, he voiced his criticism of the government in mild terms. However, I could infer that greater political passion burned underneath. Later in 1990, after our meeting, he resigned from the TYC to pursue a more militant path of opposition. As an advocate of Tibetan independence, he has strongly criticized the Dalai Lama's peaceful approach to negotiation. That afternoon he told us, "When people are restless and unhappy in this land—as they should be—the challenge to our leadership is how to lead them into something constructive." Our friend, the monk and translator Laktor, replied that religious leaders faced a similar challenge. He admitted that westernized Tibetans in exile might get a feeling that "all this Buddhism is impractical" and added that "Buddhist education is confined to the monasteries, and we need to make it available to the people and let them judge if it is worthwhile or not. There is no need to change the truth but how to communicate it, so that other people can appreciate it." I wondered whether the problem didn't run deeper than packaging.

We did not discuss the situation in Tibet, but the problem of secularization is not confined to the exile. The Dalai Lama left Tibet in 1959, and an entire generation has grown up for whom he is a remote figure. And young Tibetans are not wholly isolated from popular culture, which has entered China through Taiwan and Hong Kong.

But the situation in the Tibetan and Jewish diaspora made for more immediate points of comparison. Like their American Jewish counterparts, Tibetan youth in India primarily attend public schools. Tsepak Rigzin, a translator for the library, told us, "Whether a nation survives depends on how well we preserve our tradition and culture. In Indian schools we are taught Tibetan one period a day for forty-five minutes. We blame the Indian educational system, but we ought to blame ourselves. We are allowed to teach in Tibetan but don't."

In response, several Jewish delegates praised Hebrew and Sunday School programs and offered them as a model. But Rabbi Levitt, a Sunday School principal herself, was less enthusiastic. She thought "part of the reason Jews aren't Jewish anymore has been the supplementary schools."

From my own experience, I wasn't quite as skeptical as Joy. I attended ten years of Sunday School and three or four of afternoon Hebrew school. Although I think I could have been taught better, and learned much more, the religious schooling did succeed in confirming my Jewish identity. Especially important was my confirmation class, which at a crucial time, ages fifteen and sixteen, planted me squarely within a Jewish social world. Somewhat providentially, I was also exposed in that setting to some truly iconoclastic Jewish intellectuals—one a rabbi without a pulpit who taught us existential philosophy with our Jewish history, and another a poet. Finally, our rabbi, Morris Lieberman—Marc Lieberman's uncle—challenged us to write down our conception of God. As I recall, my little essay was impudent and atheistic, so I was surprised when Rabbi Lieberman not only congratulated me for my honesty but also suggested I might consider the rabbinate as a vocation.

My experience may have been very unusual. I agree with Joy that too many Jewish kids find their time wasted in religious school. There's a lot of lip service in the Jewish world about the importance of education, but that's not where the money goes. After hours of boredom, week after week, a child could develop a real hatred for religion. Also, in terms of getting the basic tools—reading Hebrew, studying texts, or even learning the prayer service—my Jewish education had failed miserably. And in part to correct this failing, the more recent trend has been toward Jewish day schools. Hebrew literacy requires that kind of commitment.

But after talking to Pemo, Chodron, and Alex Berzin, I was also convinced there was a more fundamental problem: a defensive attitude. Young Jews growing up in America are intellectually curious and they demand a more open-minded approach to spirituality. The questions about God that Chodron had asked should have been answered—I gathered that instead they were ignored or suppressed.

Later, over dinner, Nathan Katz and others were peppered by the Tibetans with questions about Jewish communal institutions, "everything from burial societies to day schools to supplementary schools, the whole gamut, federations, how Jewish federations relate to each other." Nathan preferred this discussion to his encounters in the morning with the Jewish Buddhists and described it to me as "more an ethnic than interreligious dialogue and in that sense more direct and more honest, more concrete."

Paul Mendes-Flohr spoke fondly of his experiences at Camp Ramah, a Conservative summer camp that several of the Jewish delegates had once attended. The Tibetans wanted to learn more. The Jewish group promised to help bring Tibetans to observe a Jewish summer camp. This became one of the more concrete initiatives to emerge from the dialogue. It is remarkable, in fact, how many rabbis and Jewish leaders trace the origin of their commitment to summer camp.

But, in the same discussion, Zalman Schachter grew impatient with the nuts-and-bolts approach. He sensed that the secularized Tibetan intellectuals had turned their backs on the resources of their own tradition. "The Tibetan diaspora has not yet been done as a thought form," he told them. I believe what he meant was that they should use the mental development tools of the Buddhist tradition, such as visualization, to meditate on the exile situation, or as he put it, "use tantra to visualize their diaspora." This sounded a little like Zalman going to some secular Jewish community leaders and telling them they should don *tefillin* and daven before deciding how to allocate federation funds. Maybe that isn't a bad idea, but I have a feeling it is unlikely to happen.

Then Zalman scolded the monks as well, advising them to serve as "spiritual uncles" to Tibetan families. He suggested his pet idea of a Passover seder as a way of remembering the life of the Buddha. He also proposed that the monks create a new initiation of householders, "Empower them for household *puja*. The question of the householders has to be taken deeply into consideration. You have disenfranchised them."

I wondered if that criticism was fair. Perhaps Zalman was forgetting that there are major householder traditions alive and kicking in Tibetan Buddhism, in sects other than the Dalai Lama's. There are married lamas in the *kagyu* lineage—so not all teachers of Tibetan Buddhism are monks. Moreover, the problem may not be as simple as creating new prayers or rituals for the home, or household *puja*. The young people in exile, exposed to modern science and secular education, often feel that all religion is superstition.

I could see Yitz growing increasingly annoyed while Zalman was scolding. Finally he broke in, "We don't want to get a report that you are running for Dalai Lama!" It was the most open moment of tension among the Jews that week.

But Karma Gelek, who represented the official exile government, showed no sign of annoyance. "They are good ideas," he said, "but there is a lack of funds, or there are means but a lack of ideas. There is a brain drain," he added. Some Tibetans had complained to us that their best religious teachers were going to the West and teaching foreigners.

Karma Gelek spoke of a generation gap between those born in Tibet and those born in exile. "It's beautiful in this modern world, they think, so it's easy to forget your history because many people think you are born in this world, one life and that's it. We've been doing this for only thirty years. You are right," he said, addressing Zalman. "The family has a great responsibility. They used to be happy just to send them to any school. Now they ought to think differently. To save our Tibetan freedom by saving our culture. We may have a free Tibet back, but if it's totally different, then I personally would not want it back."

As for monks acting as spiritual uncles, Karma Gelek sounded defensive. Unlike, say, Catholic monks and nuns, there is very little tradition among Tibetan monks for doing social work. Still, Karma Gelek said, "There are many secular works. Whatever they are doing, it's a personal sacrifice. They could stay in the monastery and have a good life."

I came away with a better sense of the real divisions and tensions in the Tibetan exile community—the pressures the Dalai Lama faces on a day-to-day basis. It was one thing to maintain nonviolent ideals in the abstract, another when dealing with nitty-gritty politics and facing strong discontent. Yitz had raised the question of democratizing and renewing religion with the Dalai Lama, and now I was seeing how difficult that task might be. Many young Tibetans born in exile blamed their plight on the failures of the religious leadership.

The secular Tibetans in exile resemble my parents' generation in America, who grew up during the Depression. Both are children of immigrants, eager to assimilate into the prevailing culture. Their values include working hard and making it in the material world. Both generations embraced a modern, scientific worldview, turning away from anything that resembled superstition. They found their identity in the exoteric—politics and ethnicity, not inner religious experience.

For instance, I had occasion after my return from India to meet with a *geshe* living in Canada, who was sent to establish a Tibetan Buddhist temple there. He told me that most of his students were Westerners, that the local Tibetans were too involved with establishing themselves as immigrants to devote themselves to religion. They mainly came to the temple on special holidays, such as the Buddha's birthday. This reminded me of my parent's generation again: the shuls were full to bursting on Rosh Hashana and Yom Kippur, but empty the rest of the year.

Obviously, determinedly secular people are tough to reach in any case. But Zalman was asking Tibetan monks like Karma Gelek and Laktor to shoulder unaccustomed burdens at a time when they worried most about simply preserving the tradition.

Tibetans and Jews, and Hindus and Muslims for that matter, all face similar problems of preserving religious traditions in the contemporary world. The zeal to preserve could lead to conflict with others, to violence and war. That was brought home to us dramatically as soon as our meeting with the Tibetan intellectuals broke up.

Tsangpo, our travel guide, came to us with some bad news. While we'd been in dialogues about pluralism, India had plunged into crisis. A group of Hindu fundamentalists was marching on a mosque in Ayodha, in a bordering state southeast of Dharamsala. The Hindu militants claimed the site as the birthplace of Lord Rama. Rajiv Gandhi had predicted two weeks before our arrival that the issue would bring down the government of Prime Minister V. P. Singh, already under pressure due to the violent demonstrations over his affirmative action scheme. These new demonstrations touched on the fear of religious civil war that has hung over Indian politics since independence in 1947.

The demonstration was scheduled for Tuesday, the same day as our planned departure, and the Indian government planned a curfew and restrictions on travel for that day.

The history of Muslim-Hindu relations is full of both extremes: great mutual tolerance and fanaticism. The very recent development of a militant Hindu fundamentalist movement is especially dismaying, because Hinduism has traditionally been one of the most tolerant of world religions.

For me, the whole situation as we discussed it echoed an incident a few weeks earlier on the Temple Mount in Jerusalem. There, in a confrontation between Israeli police and Palestinian demonstrators, nineteen Arabs had been killed. That confrontation began when Palestinian worshipers at the Al-Aqsa mosque showered stones and rocks on Jews praying at the Western Wall below them. That stupidity was met by an overreaction on the part of the Israeli police.

Both Muslims and Jews consider the same site, the Temple Mount, to be sacred ground, just as now Muslims and Hindus were claiming the same temple site in Ayodha. The question is, what role should religion play in such conflicts? It seems to me that very often in Israel, religion exacerbates the conflict on both sides. Yet in the deeper, inner core of Judaism, there is a sweeter wisdom that knows better. For instance, Teddy Kollek, the former mayor of Jerusalem, is fond of citing the Orthodox belief that the Third Temple of Jerusalem is not something that can be built by a contractor. Rather, it floats in heaven and will not descend to earth until God is good and ready. That wisdom could temper the passions that would claim holy ground at the cost of human blood.

But a strong case can also be made that organized religion is the problem, not the solution. That in part was Yitz Greenberg's point, that if religion continues to exacerbate conflict and hatred in the world, then religion itself, in his words, "will go down the tubes, and good riddance."

Just to add a little more complexity to the argument, there is the current impasse between the Tibetans and Chinese. In this case there is currently no common religious ground. Once, long ago, when China was a Buddhist country, the Dalai Lama of Tibet was especially respected by the Chinese emperor, so that their relationship was known as "priest and patron." As a result, Chinese armies did not cross over into Tibet, nor Tibetan armies into China.

But since the Chinese Communist revolution in 1949, all that has gone by the board. The Chinese have completely abrogated seven hundred years of mutual respect by simply annexing Tibet militarily. Attempts at negotiation have proven fruitless. From their Marxist-Leninist perspective, the Dalai Lama is a feudal leader and the Chinese are simply bringing progress to a backward, superstitious land. The spiritual riches of Tibet are entirely invisible to them, and their concrete manifestation, including six thousand monasteries, have been reduced to rubble, or used as granaries and stables.

Recently, it is true, the Chinese have begun allowing Tibetans to rebuild a few of the monasteries—but mainly so they can be shown to tourists. The Chinese sell tickets for the visits, as in an amusement park, and administer the new monasteries under their department of antiquities. They continue to view Tibetan religion as backward superstition.

So on the one side there is a powerful empire with a purely materialistic ideology backed by an overwhelming military force, and on the other is the Dalai Lama, primarily relying on his spiritual principles and the support he can gain from international public opinion.

I think it is a difficult question whether the Dalai Lama's religious vision is truly adequate to the moment of history he finds himself in. If, for instance, one imagines that in 1947—when Israel was attacked by six Arab armies—that the young state had been led by a mystically minded rabbi, instead of a pragmatic secularist like David Ben-Gurion, the outcome might have been less favorable.

An interesting aside is that David Ben-Gurion studied Buddhism seriously. In 1961, during a visit to Burma, the Israeli leader spent two days in conversation with Burmese monks, and told a biographer that he "got some new insights in talks with U Nu, prime minister of Burma at that time, a scholarly and devout follower of Buddhist moral teachings." Elie Wiesel passed on to me further details, which he had on good authority. Ben-Gurion peppered U Nu with questions. Finally the Burmese leader said, "There is a man in Ceylon who is a great teacher, and he can answer your questions."

"What language will we speak?" Ben-Gurion asked.

"What else?" U Nu replied, "Yiddish."

It seems the guru in question was a Jew who had studied Buddhism in Sri Lanka. It's possible he was Nyanoponika Thera, a German Jewish refugee and author who is considered one of the most erudite monks in the Theravadan tradition—yet another major JUBU.

So maybe in exchange with Ben-Gurion, it might be a good idea for the Dalai Lama to study a little Zionism. It's not that I doubted the profundity of Tibetan Buddhism, or its deep consolations for the Dalai Lama's religious followers. Even having lost their land, their temples, and their monasteries, a thorough understanding that the nature of things is impermanence provides them with a powerful acceptance. Yes, Karma Gelek had told us with some pride at a dinner held the night after we'd arrived, "We have been able to reestablish two hundred monasteries in India, Nepal, and Bhutan, and because of the success of establishing monasteries, we don't worry about the disappearance of our culture from the surface of the earth." This intrigued Blu Greenberg, because it seemed to imply that the new could substitute for the old. She asked if the Tibetans had a concept of "holy space, sanctified space," like Jerusalem for the Jews or Rome for the Catholics.

To Karma Gelek, "holy spaces are symbols rather than the essence. We don't believe," he said, "in untransportable holy space."

Karma Gelek said the Dalai Lama had once told a refugee community that "you don't have to worry if everything is destroyed in Tibet—such as *thangka* paintings or statues of the Buddha—because if a person treasures the real holy thing in himself, he can reproduce the spiritual objects because they come from the spirit within the person."

This is very beautiful, but I can see where younger militants, such as Lhasang Tsering, might find this approach counterproductive, if the goal is to get back the actual land of Tibet. It's not the kind of religious philosophy that would encourage people to fight for their homeland.

This philosophy would seem to work against a Tibetan Zionism. Karma Gelek indicated that if people fail to stay with the essence of their religion, and instead cling to an exoteric identity, or if people mix up their religion with politics, they are themselves the greatest enemies to the survival of the inner meaning of their faith.

Jews have faced such choices again and again in their history, and I don't think there's any single lesson to draw. In the debate between pure idealism and impure action, sometimes the Maccabees have won, and sometimes the *hasids* or saints. For centuries in Europe accommodation and humility, and a focus on community spiritual life, helped Jews survive. Today the dominant reaction to the Holocaust has been that Jews must fight, must use violence, if necessary, to ensure survival. And now many thoughtful Israelis, such as Paul Mendes-Flohr, worry very much about the effect on young people raised in a life of constant conflict. But only a handful, and they would be considered marginal, would be willing to entrust the fate of Israel solely to God's hands.

As to our own more immediate fate, Tsangpo, our travel guide, helped us discuss travel alternatives. The railroad was out, too many terrorist attacks. As foreigners, we would be obvious targets. We might be stranded in Dharamsala for a week or so, unless we chartered a plane. Michael Sautman promised to look into it.

Nathan Katz found the political chaos astounding. This was not the India he knew and cherished. He felt there was "a vastly higher level of confrontation and violence, misery. It's a much angrier place than it was twenty years ago, much less charming, much uglier, much more crowded and, paradoxically, less poor."

For that evening, the Tibetans had invited us to dinner and a show in McLeod Ganj. Most declined, already exhausted by the intensity of the past twenty-four hours, but I was game. The buffet-style meal was served outdoors in a long tent. In chilly mountain air, I was able to sample delicacies like hard-boiled eggs cooked in pastry and Kentucky fried yak, as well as my favorite, *mo-mos*—Tibetan kreplach. Then, in a rather rough-hewn auditorium, I saw native Tibetan dances and music—very loud in the horn and cymbals department—with colorful red fringe hats, dragon costumes, and lots of stomping boots. The racket temporarily blasted away all worries and fears.

SUNDAY, OCTOBER 28, TIBETAN CHILDREN'S VILLAGE

After Sunday morning prayer and breakfast, we learned from Michael Sautman that a charter plane would not work out. We would leave Dharamsala Monday evening, right after our session with the Dalai Lama, and drive all night, hoping to slip into Delhi ahead of the curfew declared for Tuesday at 7 A.M.

With that settled, Paul Mendes-Flohr, representing the newly formed Israeli-Tibetan Friendship Society, and Yitz and Blu Greenberg, who serve on the board of the American Jewish World Service, an international relief agency, met with some Tibetan government officials to discuss how Israelis could assist the Tibetans. One possibility was sending Israeli technicians to help the Tibetans set up a cheese-making business. In a nation that reveres the cow, this technology was not highly developed, and the Tibetans might find a niche among hotels and restaurants that catered to foreigners. The strangeness and specificity of such a connection delighted me. The Tibetans, like the Jews, are able entrepreneurs. Apparently, for instance, because of the rug trade, the Tibetans have become the wealthiest people in Nepal. Some have joked that they are the Jews of the East.

After lunch we drove beyond McLeod Ganj to the Tibetan Children's Village, a large orphanage complex with a school and a handicrafts center. For many years the orphanage had been run under the watchful eye of the Dalai Lama's younger sister, Jetsun Pema. The kids live in crowded conditions, in small cottages sponsored by various international relief agencies. The Catholic charities have been especially helpful.

Each cottage houses twenty or more kids supervised by a Tibetan couple. We toured a group nursery for infants and toddlers, and Blu Greenberg, a Jewish mother to the core, fussed that all the children were not washing their hands after going to the bathroom.

But though the conditions were crowded and difficult and the Tibetans could certainly use more help, the children I saw were bright and cheerful. I'd brought a Polaroid camera and took several pictures of smiling groups in front of their cottages, which I gave to them for keepsakes. Especially in the early years of exile, many of the adults got sick due to the harsh conditions of life in India. Yet even thirty years later, a new generation of refugees continues to make its way to Dharamsala. Sometimes Tibetan mothers will make the arduous trip out of faith, to leave some of their children to be raised under the guidance of His Holiness. Some children make the trip themselves. I met a young man of sixteen working in the shipping department of the handicrafts center at TCV. As he wrapped a handmade Tibetan carpet in paper and tied it up, he told me of his journey by foot at the age of twelve over the Himalayas and into India. He had left with the blessing of his family. He told me he preferred life here in the orphanage under the care of the Dalai Lama to living under the Chinese. He hoped eventually to go on to college.

His cheerfulness, and the rather matter-of-fact way he related what must have been an incredibly arduous and dangerous journey, reminded me of my father's father—who as a young man left the Russian Pale for America.

That evening we were entertained by a show in the orphanage's auditorium. The pageantry combined East and West—a group of six-year-olds sang a patriotic song at the end of which a banner bearing an image of the Dalai Lama was unfurled and confetti was thrown. An adolescent girl gave an impressive recitation of a Gilbert and Sullivan number. The children at TCV study in Tibetan for grades one through five and then switch to English for secondary education, in order to prepare themselves for Indian society. There are no Tibetan universities in exile.

These young Tibetans face a formidable challenge, and for Jews, a familiar one: mastering Western culture while staying in touch with their traditional religious roots. That is why, in a nutshell, I think transmitting Tibetan Buddhism to this new generation will be difficult.

Yet leaving the village that evening, I felt more hopeful than I had all day. The tremendous energy, intelligence, and enthusiasm of these children was inspiring. For the near future, survival will continue to be the first priority. But those children are the hope of Tibet in exile, and feeling their energy gave me reason to hope too.

14

An Interview with the Oracle

I've always been intrigued by the oracle of Delphi, which plays such an important role in the myth of Oedipus and in the life story of Socrates. Though Delphi is in ruins and the oracle is no more, I like the idea of a terminal where messages can be received from realms beyond this one, a cosmic telephone.

Throughout the ancient world, oracles were a rather ordinary feature of most cults. Ancient Israel had an oracular tradition, too, associated with the functions of the high priest. The ancient oracles are no more, but the Tibetans have preserved the institution for the past thirteen hundred years. The Nechung is perhaps the world's last official state oracle.

In his recent autobiography, the Dalai Lama explains that "it has been traditional for the Dalai Lama and the Government to consult Nechung during the New Year festivals. I myself have dealings with him several times a year. This may sound far-fetched to twentieth-century Western readers. Even some Tibetans, mostly those who consider themselves progressive, have misgivings about my continued use of this ancient method of intelligence gathering. But I do so for the simple reason that as I look back over the many occasions when I have asked questions of the oracle, on each one of them time has proved that his answer was correct." The Dalai Lama describes the deities of the oracle as his upper house, while the *Kashag*, or exile cabinet, is his lower house. He likes to consult both for important government decisions. And, in fact, the oracle played a role in his decision to flee Tibet in 1959.

If Saturday afternoon and Sunday had been devoted to the pragmatics of exile—summer camp and children's schools and cheese making—our last morning in Dharamsala before meeting with the Dalai Lama was an intense reminder of all that is most exotic in Tibetan culture. Keeping in mind Nathan Katz's definition of history as what we *choose* to remember, we would soon remember the magical side of our own religion. In visiting a temple, a monastery, a library of ancient books—and, above all, in talking to the medium of an oracle—one had the sense of a living reality that contemporary Judaism has long repressed, the way a certain smell has the power to stir a memory from long ago.

A very pleasant smell, in fact, sifted through the courtyard of the Library of Tibetan Works and Archives, where an old peasant woman, in the traditional *chuba*, stood before a fire and heaped branches of pine needles upon it in some private devotion. (As I traveled up and down the narrow roads of Dharamsala, I often met groups of refugees, usually older people, dressed in traditional *chubas*, though a few details were distinctly Western, such as one older gentleman whirling a prayer wheel and wearing a Nike baseball cap and sneakers.) Quietly sitting under a street lamp, a monk in maroon robes studied a text and nodded as he read, deep in thought. He could have been a Jerusalem shopkeeper, studying a *daf* [page] of Talmud between customers. It reminded me that Dharamsala, as the home of the Dalai Lama, is a place of pilgrimage, a holy city. Yitz Greenberg had compared it to Yavneh, where the rabbis of the Roman era regrouped. But that morning as we entered the courtyard of the library, I thought more of Safed, the town in northern Israel where the great kabbalists of the Sephardic world took retreat after the expulsion from Spain. Safed is also on a mountain, a town of synagogues and prayer and study, and once the home of the great kabbalist Rabbi Isaac Luria, the master who infused the mainstream of Judaism with a mystical spirit.

I could almost imagine this old woman wearing a shawl and lighting Sabbath candles instead of pine branches. I tried to catch her eye, but she was intent on the fire. The blue smoke rose with a sweet smell, curling up into the mountain air. With her heavily lined face and intense devotion, she seemed an icon of the past.

We were met in the library by an icon of the present, a young assistant director in a sports jacket who guided us through an exhibit of religious artifacts: precious *thangkas,* beautiful gold-painted Buddhas with eleven heads facing in all directions. It was all art to us, but folded rupee notes and flowers left at various shrines reminded us that for the Buddhists this was not only a museum but a holy place of veneration as well.

Alex Berzin had joined us to serve as translator, and because we'd come to know him, our detailed questions about the Tibetan artifacts started going to him instead of to our official guide. The young Tibetan grew furious and said sharply, "Since you have him to answer, you don't need me" and turned on his heels. We were taken aback, but Alex simply paused and then continued to answer our questions.

Blu Greenberg told me later she thought the anger was healthy. "As a group the Buddhists are exceptionally low-anger people. But I was really happy for that little flash in the museum. That was a bit of normalcy that I'm sure exists under other layers, a normalcy of anger and pique. My reading of history and human nature, there's gotta be some anger. All love without any relief—although that's a very strange way to say it—is not realistic."

I suppose it depends on what you meant by realistic. Blu evidently saw anger as a natural emotion that ought not be suppressed. Tibetan Buddhism proposes that anger is a defilement and that what we in the West call "love" is the real nature of the mind. In that sense, love is realistic—not anger. Judaism traditionally does make more allowances for anger than Mahayana Buddhism. Still it's interesting to compare Maimonides, the great Jewish medieval thinker, to Shantideva, an eighth-century Hindu formulator of Mahayana who is revered by the Tibetans.

Shantideva, in his *Guide to the Bodhisattva's Way of Life,* writes, "Whatever wholesome deeds, such as venerating the Buddhas, and generosity / That have been amassed over a thousand aeons / Will all be destroyed in one moment of anger." Maimonides in his *Mishneh Torah* writes, "The ancient sages said, 'He who is angry—it is the same as if he worshiped idols.' They also said, 'One who yields to anger—if he is a sage, his wisdom departs from him; if he is a prophet, his prophetic gift departs from him.' Those of an irate disposition—their life is not worth living."

What had prompted the short outburst from the guide in the first place was Zalman Schachter's questions about a five-foot-high wooden model displayed in a glass case. Painstakingly constructed in the nearby craft workshops, this model was a three-dimensional version of the more familiar diagram, or mandala, used in Tibetan Buddhist meditation practices. The mandala, or "circle" in Sanskrit, is used to focus the mind and to visualize Buddhist deities and doctrines. Some mandalas represent in visual form the layout of the universe and the human position within it. For instance, a very familiar mandala represents the wheel of samsara, the cycle of events that lead to rebirth. In general, a mandala is a reality map, a visualization of the universe. The kabbalistic equivalent would be the four worlds Zalman had presented and the *sefirot* that form their substructure.

But if the more familiar two-dimensional mandalas are a map or blueprint of consciousness, this remarkable model in the museum was a very elaborate three-dimensional representation in the form of a temple. Courtyards surround a palace whose inner room contains a throne where the deity is imagined as sitting. In general practice the meditator, by focusing on a two-dimensional mandala, would be able to create this three-dimensional temple in his or her own imagination and walk through it. As Alex Berzin explained it, I could imagine the concentration and focus that would come from the visualization practice. For a thousand years, Tibetans have been perfecting such mental discipline, which in the West belongs mostly to the ancient world, such as the memory theaters of the Greek and Roman orators. Tibetan scholar and translator Robert Thurman, who would join us that afternoon, would characterize the Tibetan monasteries as "factories of consciousness."

To Zalman Schachter the 3-D mandala recalled the lost art of *merkavah* meditation, of "descending to the chariot"—the earliest technique of Jewish meditation we know anything about. Unfortunately, we don't know enough. It was believed to have been practiced by some rabbinic sages in the circle of Yochanan ben Zakkai, and later by the second-century sage and martyr Rabbi Akiva. The practice was based on a study of the Book of Ezekiel, a topic generally known as *maaseh merkavah* or "the work of the chariot." The text of Ezekiel was interpreted so as to provide instructions for others to have the same visionary experience as the prophet. The Talmud tells us that Yochanan ben Zakkai was asked to give a teaching on the *maaseh merkavah* and that he complied. Unfortunately, the teaching was not recorded. In fact such teaching was severely restricted. But apparently, through intense visualization and the repetition of Hebrew mantras, the meditator journeyed to heaven and God's throne—and received visions and revelations. Only fragments and traces of the technique are left, such as an intriguing warning in the Talmud, "When you come to the stones of pure marble, say not Water Water" (Babylonian Talmud Hagiga 14B). Gershom Scholem had interpreted this to mean that when traveling to the throne, one would eventually arrive at a place of glittering tiles, and that if one made the mistake of saying the wrong password— Water, Water—one would be flung from the heavens back down to earth. Indeed, the entire trip to the higher realms was fraught with danger, such as encounters with guardian demons. So much so that the abiding attitude in the Talmud was negative toward such meditation, as most often leading the meditator to apostasy, madness, and death— an attitude that still strongly marks the mainstream Jewish view of the esoteric.

But Zalman Schachter, an experienced Jewish meditator, was not afraid to speculate. He hoped a group of highly trained tantric meditators would collaborate with their Jewish counterparts in spiritual archaeology. The Tibetans, based on their own tradition, could help make sense of the scraps and fragments of the *merkavah* tradition that remain.

In Jewish life today, the mystical is either ignored or consigned to a distant superstitious past. And there is, at least popularly, a strongly felt dichotomy between what is considered the rational or reasonable aspects of religion and the mystical. This reflects the generally materialistic and scientistic worldview in the West.

As a result we tend to read our Jewish history as though the great rabbinic sages were pure rationalists, or dry legalists. While the rabbinic sages were cautious about esoteric experiences, that very caution shows they evidently viewed *merkavah* meditation as a very powerful, even if possibly dangerous, practice. The same Rabbi Akiva who was a great second-century Tanna, or codifier, of Talmud was also a practitioner of *merkavah* meditation. The two activities were intrinsic to each other because the rabbinic sages drew on their visionary experiences to interpret Torah.

Likewise, Rabbi Isaac Luria of sixteenth-century Safed, is considered by Orthodox Jews to be both a great Talmudic authority and a great kabbalist. So was another member of his circle, Rabbi Joseph Karo. He is known primarily today as the compiler of the *Shulkhan Arukh* (The set table)—the everyday practical handbook of Jewish law for the Orthodox. But this same Joseph Karo had regular communications with a *maggid*, or heavenly spirit, who produced automatic speech that came out of Karo's mouth. In other words, Joseph Karo was, in effect, both a codifier of Jewish law and an oracular medium—like the Tibetan monk we were going to visit later that morning. All of this history shows that the present gulf between rational and mystical, or between legalistic and magical, has not always been a feature of Jewish life. It is rather an artifact of an extreme rationalism.

These days, most of the research in Dharamsala involves preserving and translating texts, and this is where the Tibetan exile most resembles the activities of the *sopherim*, the scribes of the Jewish elite during the Babylonian exile. Jews like Alex Berzin and Ruth Sonam find this activity very congenial. They are among about a hundred resident scholars working at the library, which contains more than forty thousand original Tibetan books. The library has also published more than two hundred volumes of Tibetan works translated into English.

We visited a small office—a treasure house of rare Tibetan manuscripts, many carefully smuggled out of Tibet over the past thirty years and now lovingly preserved and studied by the scholars and monks. The Tibetan manuscripts, written on oblong parchment or palm leaves and wrapped in bright orange cloths, resemble loaves of bread on the shelves. An old monk showed us a precious manuscript from the eleventh century, its black parchment inscribed with alternating lines of gold and silver ink. Zalman Schachter noted that, as on Hebrew scrolls, very delicate guidelines were traced for the letters. The Jews and

Tibetans share a reverence for the ancient written word. Nathan Katz pointed out that, just as Jews distinguish between Torah and Talmud, the Tibetans wrapped those sutras taken as the authentic word of the Buddha in orange cloth, and the commentaries in yellow cloth. Marc Lieberman, a distinguished eye surgeon when not shepherding Jews through the lands of the Buddha, reminded us that the words *sutra* and *sutures* have the same root. The sutras are "threads" of discourse.

In the session held in New Jersey, the Dalai Lama had examined the Torah scroll very closely, remarking on how it was sewn together. The traditional Tibetan Buddhist book is a pile of palm leaves laid flat one on top of the other and tied in a loose bundle. These days, the texts are printed on slabs of orange paper—I'd bought one as a souvenir near Thekchen Choeling.

The Nechung monastery is a short walk away and before meeting with the *kuten*, the monk who currently serves as the medium of the Nechung oracle, we made a brief tour of the monastery temple, where young monks were busy practicing their rituals. The fruity aroma of Tibetan incense thickened the air and the young monks sat in facing rows in lotus positions, reciting in unison from a text in their laps, the whole time banging on drums and cymbals and blasting away on the *thugchen*, or long horns, which had the deep resonance of tugboats in mourning. I heard in them the continuous blast of the shofar on a Rosh Hashana morning—a mighty and extended *tekiah gedolah*—and the purpose was somehow the same, a spiritual wake-up call. At one level it worked: the young monks, cocooned in that sound, ignored us completely as we threaded through the shrine, examining the colorful butter sculptures of Buddhas and saints and miniature temples, beneath which heaps of bananas and other fruit were presented as offerings. (Later the young monks could eat them for lunch.)

In an adjacent shrine room we saw the fierce protector deities in all their multiskulled wrath, eyeballs bulging with the fierce rage of cutting through illusion with the diamond edge of the truth. I saw as well the sacred yabyum statuette, the union of Wisdom and Method represented daringly as sexual intercourse between a fierce deity and a lithe *dakini*, or goddess. It was hard to conceive what this might mean to a celibate monk, that the very highest mysteries of his religion would be portrayed in such a way. It struck me at first as outrageous and fantastic, but then I tried the trick of translating myself into a Tibetan and walking through the great churches and cathedrals of the West. There I would encounter, as the most common sacred symbol to meditate upon, the wounded and tortured body of a dying Jew. Was that any less strange? Having stabilized my thought with this mental exercise, my deepest layer remained strongly anti-idolatrous. To me, no image at all seems best. One of the holiest places I have ever been to is the Al Aqsa mosque on the Jerusalem Temple Mount—a very large temple completely devoid of symbols and representations.

We marched back through the temple, past the young chanting monks. They were mostly impassive, maybe bored, and reminded me of nothing so much as myself at the same age, getting through a late afternoon in Hebrew school.

The *kuten* was a different matter. He sat at the head of a conference table and received us with grace and aplomb, though with a certain reserve around the eyes that made it believable that he was occupied by other spirits and deities from time to time. *Kuten* means "physical basis"—his body is on sacred occasions the home of Dorje Drakden, a protector divinity of the Dalai Lama.

Yet that morning he was our genial host, serving us sugar cookies and tea in large white cups and politely answering our questions. I sensed, too, the somewhat uneasy position he held—in some ways one of immense authority—as an advisor to the Dalai Lama, and yet also a simple monk in the Nechung monastery, under the watchful eye of his abbot, an older man who sometimes answered on the monk's behalf.

The *kuten* explained that he had met with other Buddhists, with Hindus, Christians, and Muslims, but we were the first Jewish group to visit him and that we were very welcome. We got down to brass tacks quickly, and his answers were equally direct. Being possessed by a dragon-headed deity was simply a reality, like the tea in our cups.

Alex, serving as translator, told us that "the previous medium of the oracle passed away in 1984 and for three years there was no medium. Everybody was saying many prayers for the oracle to manifest. So prayers were said by His Holiness and people here and in various monasteries. Then in 1987 just automatically the oracle went into him."

Moshe Waldoks wanted more details. Alex continued to translate: "It was March 31, 1987, the second day of a Tibetan month, a special day each year when the abbots come together from Drepung monastery. There's always a special request for the oracle to appear on that day. All the abbots had come together, and as one of the monks here he was at the ceremony as well. Then, just all of a sudden, he had a very strong, electrical-like feeling within him. He passed out, had no consciousness. The oracle was speaking through him."

Zalman asked, "Is it one entity that comes through or different kinds of entities using him as a voice?"

"Actually the oracle is a set of five figures, the heads of the five Buddha families, and this group of figures has one figure within them which is the collection of the essence of them, and this is the main oracle that speaks through him."

Marc Lieberman asked if the oracle spoke in a special language. It was explained that "in older times the oracle mostly spoke in very elegant poetry. These days, he speaks more in a colloquial language."

With all that traffic coming through his body, I wondered what the physical effects were. I'd read descriptions of the moment of possession from the Dalai Lama's recent autobiography. "The *kuten*'s face transforms . . . puffing up to give him an altogether strange appearance, with bulging eyes and swollen cheeks. His breathing begins to shorten and he starts to hiss violently. Then, momentarily, his respiration stops. At this point the helmet is tied in place with a knot so tight that it would undoubtedly strangle the *kuten* if something very real were not happening." He leaps about, grabbing a ritual sword, bowing to the Dalai Lama until his heavy helmet touches the ground, then springs back up. "The volcanic energy of the deity can barely be contained within the earthly frailty of the *kuten,* who moves and gestures as if his body were made of rubber and driven by a coiled spring of enormous power."

The oracle is questioned and, as surprising as it may seem, the replies are "rarely vague." But as soon as Dorje Drakden has finished speaking, the *kuten* collapses into a "rigid and lifeless form."

I wondered if the physical effects of such trance states were long-lasting (because to me the *kuten* appeared somewhat haggard for his age). Alex translated his answer, "Physically it's very strenuous. Before the oracle enters into him, he feels a great deal of painful energy in his body, then he has no memory at all. When he's finished, he passes out and after that for several hours he has a great deal of pain in the chest."

To Zalman Schachter this called to mind the prophet Daniel,

> And I Daniel alone saw the vision . . . and there remained no strength in me; for my comeliness was turned in me into corruption . . . when I heard the voice of his words, then was I fallen into a deep sleep on my face, with my face toward the ground.

In his written report on the dialogue, Zalman would even suggest that we look into how to train a Jewish oracle. For now, he explained to the *kuten* that he had his counterpart in the high priest.

"In our tradition at one time the high priest would wear a breastplate. On it were twelve stones and in the stones the letters of the alphabet were engraved. When we had a question, not for private individuals, but for the welfare of the nation, under certain circumstances we asked the oracle and received an answer."

Precisely how the Jewish oracle worked is a matter of some question among rabbis and scholars. The first-century C.E. Jewish historian Josephus, writing in his *Antiquities of the Jews*, explained that "by those twelve stones which the high priest bare on his breast . . . inserted into his breastplate," God would declare beforehand when the Jews "should be victorious in battle: for so great a splendour shone forth from them before the army began to march, that all the people were sensible of God's being present for their assistance. . . . Now this breastplate, and this sardonyx, left off shining two hundred years before I composed this book. . . . "

In Talmudic accounts, the jewels on the breastplate are inscribed with the names of the tribes, and through a light shining on them, various combinations of letters are projected and combined. But also associated with the breastpiece are the *urim* and *thummim*—the mysterious Hebrew words inscribed today on the seal of Yale University and mentioned in Exodus 28:15–30 and Leviticus 8:8. According to scholars, the *urim* and *thummim* were lots—possibly marked sticks or stones—that were held in a pouch behind the breastpiece. Yes or no questions were answered by pulling out the objects—*urim* for no, *thummim* for yes.

All of this oracular technology, as Josephus remarks, was lost a long time ago—the last biblical mention of consultation of the oracle is at the time of King David. The oracular role passed on to the prophets of Israel. And when the line of the prophets died out, visions and revelations came through the rabbis, through *merkavah* meditation and other meditative practices.

The biblical references to the oracle are brief. When Joshua succeeds Moses, he is instructed to "stand before Eleazar the priest, who shall inquire for him by the judgment of the Urim before the Lord" (Num. 27:21). The last reference is 1 Samuel 23:9. David consults Abiathar the priest and receives helpful intelligence about an upcoming battle with King Saul.

Similarly, the Dalai Lama has received specific political intelligence and practical advice from the Nechung oracle. Two years before the Chinese invasion, the oracle warned that in 1950, the Year of the Iron Tiger, Tibet would face great danger. Later, Dorje Drakden, the oracular spirit, advised the Dalai Lama to go to India in 1956 and make his first contacts with Nehru, which proved to be an important political move. And in 1958 the oracle is said to have prophesied the Dalai Lama's flight: "In this great river where there is no ford, I, Spirit, have the method to place a wooden boat."

Neither biblical nor rabbinic Judaism ever denied the existence of oracles, prophecies, dream visions, or other communications. Rather, the rabbis applied a rather practical test for authenticity. A prophet is only real if his prophecies come true.

I think the Dalai Lama has a similar attitude. The Nechung oracle has always provided good advice, and therefore there is no reason not to consult him.

The *kuten* listened to Zalman's explanations of the Jewish oracle with a good deal of interest, nodding his large teardrop-shaped head and interjecting 'Ah . . . ah . . . ah . . .' as Alex gave the translation. Having established, however tenuously, an oracular connection, Paul Mendes-Flohr asked Alex gently, "Would he accept a question from us?"

"Yes."

"Should we go by plane or by car?" Yitz Greenberg interjected, and everyone laughed. A long conference between Alex and the *kuten* followed. "He says that it's okay to go by car this evening," Alex reported. "They will say prayers, ask for the protection of the Protector, you shouldn't worry. With the people here and His Holiness's request for protection, very naturally, there's no problem with traveling this evening."

However, to back that up, the *kuten* graciously offered us packets of barley seeds—bright orange—in plastic envelopes. The seeds, known as *chaynay*, had been blessed by Dorje Drakden. They were believed by Buddhists to have magical protective powers, and Nathan Katz took several packets of them for Buddhist temples in Tampa. But I noticed that we all lined up eagerly to accept them. Were we losing our rationalist edge, or were we just afraid? I figured it was a fair trade: we would be giving the Dalai Lama the Torah that had protected us on the way to Dharamsala. So the magical seeds seemed like the best possible substitute for our trip back.

While we were saying our good-byes and taking pictures, Blu Greenberg took the *kuten* aside and asked whether one of her sons, a nice Jewish boy over thirty, would get married soon. The oracle assured her he would. Soon I heard Yitz explain to Nathan Katz with wry casuistry as we walked to the Tibetan Astro-Medical Institute, that he was on perfectly good Orthodox ground accepting the blessed seeds, "As long as I don't think they work."

He added that "superstitious practices that belong to other religions are prohibited on the grounds that you are taking the superstition seriously. But if you don't take it seriously, then it's an act of gracious friendship that he's sharing it. That's my joke."

"Then it can work," Nathan said, "catch-22."

"Yes, blessings of good people do work, that's my catch. As long as you don't take it seriously, you do take it seriously."

But Yitz was thinking more seriously about the contact we'd been making that morning with the more exotic aspects of Tibetan Buddhism, trying in his careful way to fit it all into a pattern. He explained to Nathan and me how two very different religions might be compared, especially in regard to the attitude each took toward this world in the light of the ultimate goal of each religion. In short: the tension between everyday life and perfection.

He thought both religions start "with the equally utopian vision: that we'll overcome all sickness, all suffering, all death, all war—everything will be totally overcome." (In Judaism, this is the messianic vision; in Buddhism, the promise of nirvana.)

"But," he went on as we walked down a dusty path, "in Judaism the process along the way toward that final perfection works with imperfection and partial steps. So you combine the utopian vision with the pragmatic, in an unrelenting work toward perfection. That's *tikkun olam* [repair of the world]. 'That's the constant process of *tikkun*. You are as perfectionist as the Buddhists, but you define all the partial steps as having equal dignity" with the larger vision. In Jewish terms, then, the world "is not illusion, it's not lower, it's the very essence of achievement." He did not think that Buddhism honored the earthly steps toward perfection, because they viewed the ordinary world, the world of samsara, as *naarishkeit* [foolishness]. But he acknowledged that "in all religions you have a spectrum of 'perfection.' What happens is that each religion typically clusters around certain pieces of that spectrum, but it has a range of that spectrum and not infrequently the whole range, though the mainstream will be clustered around a certain place. If you look carefully, you will see that the other religion has the same theme, but it's not a major theme, it's a minor theme. The major theme is in another cluster. If you look even more carefully, if you can step back and see the whole spectrum, they actually have filled in those intermediate links in their minor traditions."

I remembered that during Zalman's presentation on the four worlds and reincarnation, Yitz had interjected the term "minority view" to describe—and downplay—the importance of these kabbalistic traditions. I suppose, broadly, what he meant was that although both Tibetan Buddhism and Judaism share beliefs in reincarnation, or angels/*devas*, these are major beliefs in Tibetan Buddhism and minor ones in Judaism.

Nathan Katz responded to Yitz's ideas enthusiastically. "Exactly, exactly. I was telling Chodron, both Judaism and Mahayana Buddhism are religions of transformation. Our transformation is dominantly of the world, but to transform the world means to transform ourselves too. Whereas their transformation is primarily of themselves, and by so doing they transform the world. And they do overlap."

"And if you look more carefully," Yitz suggested, "when the world is transformed it paves the way for the kind of spiritual perfection they are talking about anyway. So it's really not separable, and if you really are reaching out for that kind of spiritual transformation, it would be of this world as well."

In Yitz's wide view, the difference is finally, then, a matter of emphasis, of foreground and background. For Judaism the transformation is focused much more on "this world," but the aim is universal spiritual perfection. In Mahayana Buddhism, one begins with personal spiritual transformation with the hope of going on to transform this world.

Yitz's scheme also suggested to me another comparison: Judaism appears to be a very rationalistic religion, and Tibetan Buddhism much more mystical. Why is it that again and again in our history, the rational side of the Jewish mind has triumphed? Is Judaism inherently more rationalistic, or is our current view of the Jewish spectrum distorted by the last two centuries of Jewish experience, in which we have tried to assimilate to modern and Gentile expectations?

Just after World War I, when the great scholar Gershom Scholem began his studies of kabbalah, there was almost no one in the field. German-Jewish scholarship stressed the rational heritage of Judaism and dismissed Hasidism, kabbalah, and mysticism as superstition and nonsense.

Despite that rationalist climate, one that persists in many Jewish religious circles today, Scholem succeeded, almost single-handedly, in establishing kabbalah as an essential subject of Jewish scholarship. At the end of his career, he reflected on the impulses that drove his research. He explained that the questions that motivated him in 1917 were these: "Does halakhic Judaism have enough potency to survive? Is *halakhah* really possible without a mystical foundation?" Scholem felt he was trying to "arrive at an understanding of what kept Judaism alive."

He clearly felt that mysticism was an essential element of the Jewish spectrum. And now, through our visits with the oracle and the library, we could see and feel how preserving and transmitting their own esoteric tradition has been key to Tibetan exile survival, too.

I was also tasting, a little ruefully, some of the magic Judaism had lost. It was obvious, from the way we all lined up for the magical barley seeds, the *chaynay,* that Jews really enjoy the sense of play and wonder in religious life, which the Tibetans have preserved in great richness.

There has to be a way for Judaism to find the right emphasis between logic and mysticism, without one suppressing the other. I know that as we made our way back to Delhi, I would be very Jewish and this-worldly, but I would also carry my magical seeds, my *chaynay,* in my pocket, hoping they would keep us safe.

15

Secret Doors

Our last hours with the Dalai Lama were very rich. Doors were opened and secrets exchanged with an ease, frankness, and humor that came as one product of our week's immersion in a living Buddhist community. We had reached the stage Rabbi Jonathan Omer-Man had imagined upon leaving Delhi. He had quoted to several of us a Buddhist text stating that in pure dialogue you and I would become we and us. That had sounded purely visionary then. But when, during a brief press conference at the start of the session, Shoshana Edelberg from National Public Radio asked the Dalai Lama, "Why have you invited these Jews to Dharamsala?" he didn't hesitate, but laughed and said, "Because we are both chosen people."

The chosen people may be a red flag for some of the Jewish Buddhists I spoke to, but not for the Dalai Lama, who explained that the Tibetans also considered themselves chosen by Avalokiteshvara, the Buddha of Compassion. Then he grew reflective and answered seriously and with some feeling, "When we became refugees we knew our struggle was not easy, would take a long time, if not generations. Then we very often referred to the Jewish people. Through so many centuries, so many hardships, they never lost their culture and their faith. As a result, when other external conditions became ripe, they were ready to build their nation. So there are many things to learn from our Jewish brothers and sisters." I found this a very moving statement.

At this session, the Jewish sisters in the group, Blu Greenberg and Rabbi Joy Levitt, would explain the survival secrets of the synagogue and home. But I had a question about survival, too, which I put to the Dalai Lama just before Shoshana's.

"Your Holiness, all week long we've been meditating on the connection between the history of the Tibetan and Jewish peoples. With each of its crises, the Jewish people responded with spiritual crises and spiritual renewal. How has Tibetan Buddhism responded to its current national crisis, in particular, in relation to the concept of karma? What is national karma or group karma?"

I still had misgivings after my discussion Friday night with Geshe Sonam. I had been shocked, a little outraged, by what I'd heard about the Buddhist view of the Holocaust. I could not accept that the suffering of the Jews was somehow a result of their previous actions. Wasn't the knowledge of shared victimization the source of Jewish identification with the Tibetans? Weren't we fellow victims, fellow *innocent* victims? Yet I gathered from Geshe Sonam's response that in Buddhism, the whole notion of an innocent victim carried little weight in assessing how one responded to tragic circumstances.

So. Two peoples had gone through an analogous experience of destruction. The Jewish people had responded by becoming more militant, more aggressive, by armoring themselves psychologically and in Israel, militarily. Survival had become a key issue for Jews everywhere. In my view, a reflex of responding decisively to enemies had become part of the contemporary Jewish character.

He listened carefully to my lengthy question and, after a pause to absorb it, pronounced it "quite complicated," which brought down the house. Then he responded.

"Buddhism gives us a different attitude toward one's own enemy," he said, "since we believe a negative experience is due mainly to our own previous life, or the early part of this life's action. Due to that, unfortunate results happen. So therefore the so-called enemy, or the external factor, is something secondary. The main force is one's own, either the collective karma or individual karma. That is really helpful in the sense that it induces us never to feel negatively toward the external factor. Because negative things happen due to our own action, therefore, we have the potential to change that. Why not create a new action and it will bring positive results? So that I think is something relevant in our case."

That he calmly referred to the Chinese who had murdered his people and forced him out of his country as "the external factor" was breathtaking.

I understood one benefit of the Dalai Lama's thinking; namely, that by such clarity and lack of hatred toward the "so-called enemy," one could overcome any sense of despair and hopelessness. That was vital. Also, one could think more clearly and take more effective action when one is not burning with hatred and pain.

I wondered how the Dalai Lama's answer would apply to the current situation in the Middle East. One of the agonies of the conflict between Israelis and Palestinians has been the sense of entitlement that both groups derive from their history. Each side can claim with justice a history of victimhood and pain, and each side tends to blame the other for its misfortunes. So long as each side considers itself an injured party, there seems no way out of the impasse. Past grievances will justify continual mistrust and a sense on each side of righteous indignation. When, three years later, I saw Yasir Arafat and Yitzhak Rabin shake hands on the White House lawn, I remembered the Dalai Lama's response. It seems that through sheer exhaustion and disgust with the continual violence, important political elements on both sides have come to conclusions very similar to the Dalai Lama's viewpoint. I was moved when the old soldier, Rabin, called for an end to conflict. "We who come from a land where parents bury their children, we who have fought against you, the Palestinians—we say to you in a loud and clear voice: Enough of blood and tears. Enough!"

Still, letting go of self-righteousness is a very hard process, for Israelis and Palestinians, and for Jews, Muslims, and Christians in general. We are all caught up in the notion of justifiable violence—it is built into our political thinking and our law. In the West there is such a thing as righteous indignation and justifiable homicide. I gathered that these would be foreign concepts in Buddhist thought.

Jews in particular have always felt strongly about righting wrongs, whatever the cost. Deuteronomy warns us, "Justice, justice thou shalt pursue." It does not say being angry will damage you. And that sense of justifiable anger often filters down to everyday life, to the way we as Jews interact with one another, in our communities and families. Here Blu's comment about our angry Tibetan tour guide—that such anger is "realistic"—found its context.

The very Jewish secret of survival we'd brought to the Dalai Lama—memory—meant that Jews survived by keeping alive the joys, but also the enmities of the past. In fact two of our most joyous holidays, Passover and Purim, dwell on the triumph over our enemies. Other holidays mourn the losses and defeats in our past. In particular, the memory of the Holocaust, and the long history of European persecutions that preceded it, still conditions the way Jews respond to present conflicts. So it was plausible to many Jews when Menachem Begin compared Arafat to Hitler, a comparison that had nothing to recommend it in regard to historical clarity, or certainly in regard to improving the situation.

There is a Buddhist teaching that being angry at an enemy is like stabbing yourself through the stomach to hurt someone standing behind you with the tip of your sword. (And I had to consider that maybe Buddha had discovered here the origin of ulcers.) I thought back to the Frankfurt airport, to my feelings of anger at hearing German voices or just being on that soil. This was not clarity or wisdom—this was walking through a nightmare of my own projections, the ghosts of an experience I'd never had. When I mentioned those feelings to Zalman Schachter he had told me, "If you want to stay in prison all your life, become a jailer. Being vindictive, being angry at somebody, saying I'll never forgive that person—so the people who say I'll never forgive the Germans are still in a concentration camp."

Jews as a group , to a large extent, have been in a concentration camp for fifty years. Zalman had agreed, "Many many Jews haven't been able to make their way out of it. I want to say a lot of times, they aren't there. It's just that it's a cover, such an easy cover for everything you don't want to do. 'What? After the Holocaust—you want me to keep the Shabbos?—Where was God da da da . . . ' You can shoot down any serious challenge to your personal life with that terrible, terrible thing."

Anger over the Holocaust has paralyzed many Jews spiritually and emotionally, and as I learned more about the motivations for Jews leaving the tradition, I became increasingly aware of the high price that anger exacted.

On the other hand, especially after seeing the real conflict in the Tibetan exile community over how to handle the Chinese, I wasn't so sure that the Dalai Lama's position was, to use Blu's word again, realistic. So there was much to think about. Is Jewish anger, however damaging in some respects, essential to Jewish survival? Or will a Judaism that continues, in some ways, to dwell on and even nourish a sense of anger over past injustices prove to be an increasingly burdensome heritage to pass on to our children as we enter the twenty-first century?

Before the session was through we would get some illuminating answers from the delegates, and from the Dalai Lama himself. But first we came to satisfy the Dalai Lama's "very personal curiosity—to learn more about the inner experiences" of Jewish people. As he said that, he twisted his wrist, as if turning a doorknob.

The Dalai Lama's strong interest in the Jewish esoteric at the first session had already opened doors—and eyes—among the Jewish delegates. Moshe Waldoks thanked him for that. "You created a group of Jews that otherwise would never have gotten together and made our outlook broader and warmer." Moshe himself—through his prayers and humor—had done a lot to make that happen.

Moshe spoke about the four levels of interpretation—the Dalai Lama remarked that there were four as well in Buddhist tantric teachings. The first three were the literal, implicative, and midrashic; the fourth, and deepest, level is called secret. In Hebrew they are *pshat, remez, drash,* and *sod*—the first letters spell *pardes,* or paradise. For Jews, the journey to paradise is a journey of interpretation.

It is said in the *Zohar* that every new interpretation of Torah creates a new heaven. I had actually come to appreciate that saying in a very personal way during our stay in Dharamsala. All the days and nights we'd spent together studying the Torah and bringing out new meanings that fit our situation had created a new reality, a new heaven for me.

I recalled Zalman's comparing the Dalai Lama to Melchizedek. And I remembered another *drash* he'd done during the Shabbat weekend in London that had opened me up to the Torah in a new way.

That Saturday afternoon, about twenty of us sat around in our stocking feet in the living room of a London town home, where a Torah lay lovingly wrapped in a tallis. We had read the story of Noah. I wanted to know how God could have made such a botch of things that he had to wipe out his creation with a flood. Zalman answered with a midrash on the phrase of Abraham's, "God of my youth." It so happens the Hebrew can also be read, "God in his youth."

The midrash says that the flood happened because God used to be younger. When God was younger, he made mistakes.

With that twist, Zalman turned a point of doubt for me into a point of faith. "When God was younger" was a very liberating idea. It meant that God evolves in the Torah—and in our lives. A God who evolves, a God still evolving, a God whose evolution I had a stake in—this was a refreshment.

Zalman went on to show us that the Torah was much more open to interpretation than I'd ever thought. He pointed out that the first word of the Torah, in Hebrew, *bereshit,* is almost always mistranslated. *Bereshit* does not mean "in the beginning" but "in a beginning." (I later found that Rashi, the great Torah commentator, had pointed this out more than nine hundred years ago.)

It was stunning to me that the most familiar opening of any book in the West has basically been mistranslated. It's almost a metaphor for the whole way religious texts have been used and abused. If we can't get this right, what else have we been missing? As Rashi demonstrated through comparative Hebrew grammar, the first verse of Genesis should be read as a subordinate clause, not a sentence; "When God was beginning to create the heaven and earth, . . . "

This has more than grammatical interest. To Zalman "in a beginning" suggests that the biblical account of creation is not intended as a rigid recitation of God's plan, the way fundamentalists often argue, but something looser, more creative. "In a beginning" could mean something like, "one way of telling the story." This teaching liberated me from my own unconscious fundamentalism, my own rigidity about the Torah. It suggests that there is much more freedom to be found in its language than I'd thought, if only I would take another look.

This was just what Moshe Waldoks was explaining, in general terms, to the Dalai Lama: how midrash broadens the Torah and makes it relevant.

Midrash begins with the prophets, who come to the people quoting "a verse from the Bible. And they say, 'This is what it means for you today.'" Through their midrash, the Torah becomes again a living presence, a tree of life. Interpretation remains vital today, Moshe explained, because the life project of the Jew is to make the Torah a way of living. "Loving your neighbor in a book is easy; loving your neighbor in life is hard." Given the Hindu-Muslim conflict that hung over our departure, everyone could agree.

Moshe set the Sephardi Torah upright on the table in its hard-shell case. As the Buddhist leader examined the text, I thought of it bouncing along in Paul's lap: its strenuous journey from Israel to Frankfurt to Delhi to Dharamsala was now nearly complete. It would be left in the Dalai Lama's library—imagine in some distant centuries an archaeologist digging it up and wondering how it got there!

Now Moshe showed how the word Torah itself could be interpreted at the four levels. At *pshat*, the plain level, Torah is a book of stories and laws. That meaning is refined through *remez*, implication. Then through midrash, "the level that the rabbis developed, used today in every synagogue" comes "a freedom the Torah gives us. The word *drash* means . . . Seek me out, take me, stretch me, make me real to you. If this stays a book, it's dead. If you make it part of your life, it's a tree of life to all that will hold fast to it."

At the deepest secret level—"That's the esoteric," Moshe said. "This Torah is really the name of God, repeated again and again. It's made up into a narrative so people can understand it and you can teach it to children. But the reality is far deeper, and you spend a lifetime searching for the real meaning, the secret."

Further explanation of *sod* would be left to Rabbi Omer-Man. His legs paralyzed by polio, the rabbi had made his way through crowded airports, traveled rough roads, and walked on crutches up and down the rocky terrain of Dharamsala. There were no wheelchairs in town. Once, to reach the telephone at Kashmir Cottage, a few of us had to carry him up the stone steps in a wooden chair. He handled this moment with regal dignity. I later learned from Blu Greenberg that, as we departed Dharamsala, he left a donation with Rinchen for a wheelchair for the town's residents.

The Dalai Lama greeted him with special warmth. Jonathan is a very clear writer and thinker and spoke with enormous clarity now. If Zalman embodied some of the mad energy of the old Hasidim, Rabbi Omer-Man represented the other pole of mysticism, the quietist.

He began with the difficult situation of the mystic in contemporary Jewish life. "Many Jews who are not in the esoteric say we are wrong." Remembering Yitz Greenberg's previous comment about Zalman's presentation, he added, "The esoteric is perhaps a minority in the Jewish people."

The group had discussed Rabbi Greenberg's efforts at spin control after the first session. According to Moshe Waldoks, "We very clearly said to Yitz, 'Look, it's not our job to give the Dalai Lama a blow-by-blow of intra-Jewish politics. No one's asking you to sign on to everything everybody says, the way no one is necessarily signing on to everything you say.'"

Rabbi Omer-Man had been particularly disturbed and told the whole group he was going to be "more extreme than Zalman and I don't want to be told that I'm not in the mainstream." Jonathan later thought a difficult, but fascinating aspect of the dialogue was how the group represented a microcosm of intra-Jewish politics. He told me, "Defining one's Jewish religious experience is a profoundly political act that the leaders of certain movements and institutions do. People who have other experiences tend to be delegitimized. Sometimes there is a need to fight for space with those who would set the parameters for what Judaism is."

Rabbi Omer-Man traced briefly the history of the esoteric, alluding to its origin among the elite of the early Talmudists, its popularization through Hasidism, which made it much simpler and helped bring "the esoteric to ordinary Jews everywhere," and its present situation, "where in fact the esoteric is no longer in the middle of the Jewish people. . . . If today," he lamented, "a Jew wishes to discover the esoteric, they might go to their synagogue and their temple and there will be no way. The rabbi or the institution will not let that go any further."

I was sure Jonathan was right about that last point. In defense of the synagogue rabbis, very few of them would have time to study kabbalah. The demands of the job include everything from social work and pastoral counseling to bar and bat mitzvah lessons and public relations—in short, the exoteric.

Yet despite what he described as a peripheral position, "We believe, those of us in the esoteric, that we are the heart that keeps the entire organism alive." He added with quiet defiance, "The other Jews don't agree, but that doesn't matter."

The Dalai Lama asked about the provenance of Jewish mysticism. Rabbi Omer-Man explained that formerly it was in all countries, but the greatest number of followers had been killed in the Holocaust. A few teachers escaped to Israel and the United States. He himself had received two teachings, one Hasidic from Eastern Europe and the other "a North African teaching that came through Paris to Jerusalem." But he emphasized the fragility of transmission. "The esoteric is losing force in the Jewish world today." He mentioned the two young Jews from his hometown he'd met on the porch of the Dalai Lama's temple. "There are more Jews seeking the esoteric in Dharamsala than there are in my synagogue in Los Angeles."

Jonathan told me later, "All my work is among people who see the door slammed in their face when they seek the spiritual. On that balcony at Dharamsala, I accepted two students, people from Los Angeles who had no idea where to study the spiritual teachings of Judaism. For instance, you go to the temple on a spiritual quest and the rabbi may read a quote from books, but you will not find someone who will be ready to lead you on a path of spirituality."

The issue of the accessibility of the esoteric would come up again. For now, Rabbi Omer-Man wanted to say a few words about Jewish meditation.

He admitted to speaking with some embarrassment, first because it is an enormous field and his knowledge was limited, and second, because he considered the Buddhist tradition to be so highly developed in this area. He explained that there are two forms of Jewish meditation. One attempts to open a person up to greater insight, clarity, and vision. The other works on "purifying the vessel, changing the human being, making the human being more perfect." Though distinct, these two purposes to some extent overlap.

As an example of the first type, he spoke of doing meditation during prayer. "We examine ourselves during prayer, we focus on sounds." He described chanting the name of God, but using different vowel sounds with the consonants *yod he vov he.* (In ordinary Jewish prayer, the sacred name of God is not vocalized at all. Instead, it is read as *adonai,* Lord.) Rabbi Omer-Man called this "a very powerful, enlightening, opening meditation."

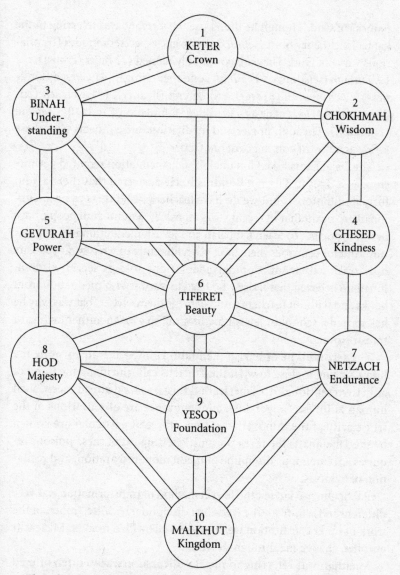

The *sefirot* arranged in a traditional pattern.

Through this meditation different vowel sounds are joined with colors and organs of the body. Jonathan described such meditation as working "on different parts of who we are, different powers in different names" of God. Though he didn't use the term, he was referring to the kabbalistic theory of the *sefirot*, ten powers, aspects, or grades (translations vary) of God. They are commonly named (1) *Keter* (crown), (2) *Chokhmah* (wisdom), (3) *Binah* (understanding), (4) *Chesed* (kindness), (5) *Gevurah* (power), (6) *Tiferet* (beauty), (7) *Netzach* (endurance), (8) *Hod* (majesty), (9) *Yesod* (foundation), and (10) *Malkhut* (kingdom). Through prayer and meditation one connects with these *sefirot* as a way of coming closer to God.

The Dalai Lama asked Jonathan if such meditation required permission, as it does in Tibetan Buddhism. He answered that there are no formal initiations, "but we do have teachers—and this is a problem." Jonathan meant that in recent years especially, a number of people have been purporting to teach kabbalah and Jewish meditation in a popular way. And for centuries there has been a literature of what some scholars call "trash kabbalah," popular adaptations sold as secret wisdom. Jonathan believed that those who tried to learn Jewish meditation from books and without teachers could damage themselves. That was why he has started a school of Jewish meditation, to give an authentic line of transmission.

The second type of Jewish meditation aimed at transforming the human being is close to what the Tibetans call "purifying the mind of afflictive emotions." To Tibetan Buddhists, as we'd already seen, such human failings as anger, lust, and ignorance are obscurations of the true clarity of the mind. (In fact, these three in particular are known by the Tibetans as the three poisons.) Getting rid of these poisons requires a tremendous discipline of meditation, prostration, and recitation of mantras.

Rabbi Omer-Man felt the Jewish method of transformation was very different in form from the Buddhist discipline, because "much of the work of inner clarification we do in dialogue with a teacher. My teachers often change me through stories."

Jonathan was referring to the Hasidic masters, who often offered counseling to their followers in the form of parables or tales. The stories the masters told, and the stories about the masters themselves, were compiled by their followers. They are probably best known in the general Jewish world through Martin Buber's well-known collections, *Tales of the Hasidim*. But, as Jonathan intimated, the stories were not intended as literature but as ways for teachers to change students. Hasidic counseling is usually one-on-one and includes the delicate art of picking the right story for the right student at the right time.

Jonathan then explained some specific Jewish meditations. One he thought "very unlike Buddhist meditations was screaming—going alone to a place and shouting and crying to God . . . 'God, I'm afraid. God, I'm alone. God, I need you.' For a whole hour, once a night for a year or two. What this does is to take away all the surface and after you finish, very subtle things emerge." Jonathan had learned this meditation from a teacher influenced by the Bratzlaver Hasidim.

We had done a little screaming ourselves, as part of an emptying out meditation Jonathan led outside Kashmir Cottage just before the first dialogue session. One participant found that exercise frightening. The harshness of our voices calling out sounded too intense. The expression of vulnerability Jonathan described is not customary in mainstream Judaism. But the Dalai Lama had no problem with it. He remarked that the calling out to God resembled taking vows of refuge in the Buddha.

Jonathan Omer-Man described two more paths. In the path of joy one "forces oneself at all times to discover a place of joy, with singing, with laughter and wine. It's very difficult. The nonesoteric says you pursue joy with all your heart, all your being, with a great deal of self but in the esoteric path, when you pursue joy you have to be transparent."

There is also a path of tears. "One does not weep from one's own pain. One weeps for the pain of the Jewish people, for the pain of exile. There is a wall in Jerusalem called the Wailing Wall. They don't weep for their own problems. They weep because the world is broken."

The Dalai Lama commented that the path of tears resembled the meditation for the initiation of the altruistic mind, or *bodhichitta*. For instance, the Buddhist practitioner visualizes in great detail the suffering of all sentient beings. Then the practitioner visualizes all of this suffering as taking the form of black smoke, which enters into the heart and is there dissolved. This sort of mental self-programming can be a very powerful way of transforming an individual.

While the Jewish path of tears, as Jonathan described it, is very emotional and expressive, and the Tibetan visualization much quieter, both practices move past individual feelings of depression by helping the practitioner conceive of the much larger weight of sadness in the world.

Both open up the heart. Jonathan Omer-Man had demonstrated that the Jewish tradition also has techniques of mental transformation. But he told the Dalai Lama, "We have a very big problem in the West. The work of transformation has been stolen from us by the psychiatrists. The work of transformation, for us, is a holy path. But more and more people who seek transformation, and who are stopped, don't go to a rabbi or a priest. They go to a psychiatrist, who will teach them not enlightenment, but self-satisfaction."

The Dalai Lama smiled broadly and said, "Very good."

Jonathan concluded his presentation by discussing his personal path, *keter malkhut,* or the crown of sovereignty. It meant "to be a sovereign human being, to be a king, to be not reactive, but active, to know one's place in the world, to be conscious. And it is extremely hard work. The ego always gets in the way, all the needs get in the way; it is a long, long path. But the path is very specific."

He added, "King doesn't mean the boss. The person who sweeps the floor could be king and very often is, more than the person at the top." Although there were no formal stages or initiations toward being a king as in Buddhist paths, "we do have pictures of what the end is like, what is a complete human being, a person who has got there. He may be described as a knower of God. And we say for the person who has reached the level of knowing God, the knower, the knowing, and the known are one. Another picture is the lover of God, in which the lover, the beloved, and the love are one."

Then, perhaps in part to demonstrate the power of Jewish story-telling, Jonathan concluded with a story directed to the Dalai Lama's situation. "Moses was not allowed to enter the land of Israel. He made some mistake on the way that could not be corrected. There are many attempts to understand what was his sin. The answer given by my greatest teacher, Rabbi Nachman of Bratslav, is that Moses had reached the level where he could exist twenty-four hours a day knowing God, in communion meditation with God. But he had to serve the people. The people down there needed his help over boundaries, over laws, over many things. And Moses went down, but Rabbi Nachman of Bratslav says that his sin is that for a moment—he resented having to go down. Because he resented having to break off his communion with God, he could not enter the land of Israel.

"This teaches us a great deal about the Jewish esoteric tradition. You must always stay in the world of service. We can never seek completion outside the world, even the human being who has reached the level of being a knower of God or a lover of God."

"You must always stay in the world." The Dalai Lama lived that lesson every day. I recalled the intensity of Lhasang Tsering and other Tibetan intellectuals we'd met with and the inevitable jealousies and petty intrigues the Dalai Lama would have to contend with as the leader of an exile community. It reminded me of the stories in Exodus where Moses is called upon to settle every little quarrel and dispute. It is why, perhaps, the Tibetan leader has sometimes stated that he will be the last Dalai Lama. Moreover, should he return to Tibet, the country will become a democracy, and secular and religious realms will be separated.

For Rabbi Omer-Man indirectly to compare the Dalai Lama and Moses was a great compliment from a committed Jew. The Dalai Lama made his own connection. The story reminded him of the bodhisattva who "does not long for just nirvana or his peace alone. He comes back into the service of human beings."

That was the end of the formal part of Jonathan's presentation. What followed was a close question-and-answer session, which took a surprising turn toward the topic of sex and the esoteric.

16

Tantra and Kabbalah

Now the two teachers, rabbi and Buddhist master, compared notes on admission policy. First the Dalai Lama asked about age limits. Jonathan explained a law that you should not learn kabbalah "until the age of forty. The truth is," he added, "all the greatest kabbalists were dead by the time they were forty."

"Which proves the point!" Moshe Waldoks joked.

The Dalai Lama wondered if the neophyte kabbalist is tested as a monk is before entering the monastery. Jonathan replied that very often there was a pushing away. His own teacher told him, "not now, come back next year." The Buddhist leader asked about limits on the numbers of students. "Like we say, you cannot teach more than ten." Jonathan answered, "There used to be limits. Now we welcome anybody, there are so few. There are empty seats in the academies" in part because of the Holocaust. Rabbi Greenberg explained that we lost 30 percent of the Jewish people during the war, but more than 80 percent of the scholars, mystics, and teachers who could pass on ancient traditions.

The Dalai Lama asked about the qualities necessary for the student to be initiated into the teaching. Rabbi Omer-Man answered that "some very old esoteric schools look at the lines on the forehead . . . but normally it is at the discretion of the teacher." Although "there used to be a law that you had to study the first three levels of Torah first"—that is, *pshat*, *remez* and *drash*—"in fact, some of the greatest kabbalists did not know the first three levels."

Jonathan Omer-Man mentioned another qualification: the student must be married. "There is a lot of discussion of sexuality and sexual energy in the meditations," he explained, "and we say this is only appropriate for someone whose blood is not boiling."

The Dalai Lama was curious. "When you relate this esoteric teaching and focus on the relationship with sexual energy," he asked, "do you lay emphasis on the importance of the channels and drops?" He was alluding to concepts from traditional Tibetan physiology that are used in meditation. We would learn more about the channels and drops as the dialogue continued.

Rabbi Omer-Man answered softly, "I cannot open that door." But he stated that "there is most definitely an attempt to connect the inner tree of life with the outer tree of life in order to find a better balance within, and by so doing, align ourselves with the tree of life that is beyond."

In his answer, Rabbi Omer-Man alluded to an analogous kabbalistic physiology, in which the *sefirot* are mapped onto body parts. The array of *sefirot* is visualized as a tree.

Moshe Waldoks had already explained the traditional Jewish image of the Torah as a tree of life. This derives from Proverbs 3:18 where the reference is to wisdom. Wisdom "is a tree of life to them that hold fast to it and its supporters are happy." In kabbalah, the tree is turned upside down. The cosmic tree grows with its roots in heaven, and spreads out through its *sefirot* into trunk, and main branches. The tree is an array of the ten *sefirot*, each *sefirah* being an aspect of the infinite. (The etymology of *sefirah* is the Hebrew for sapphire and suggests the glow of supernal light.)

But in addition to this picture, as the scholar Gershom Scholem notes, "we have the more common image of the *sefirot* in the form of a man." (The tree is turned right side up again!) The kabbalists interpreted the phrase that God created man in his own image to mean that the human body is a cosmic map of divine energies, much in the spirit of John Donne's poem "I am a little world made cunningly."

In the interior tree, the ten *sefirot* are arranged and mapped out on the body. "The first *sefirot* represent the head, and in the *Zohar*, the three cavities of the brain; the fourth and the fifth, the arms, the sixth, the torso, the seventh and eighth, the legs, the ninth the sexual organ, and the tenth refers either to the all-embracing totality of the image or . . . to the female as companion to the male, since both together are needed to constitute a perfect man" (Scholem, *Kabbalah*, pp. 106–7).

The mapping is quite complex, and the whole system as used in Jewish meditation and prayer exceedingly difficult. That alone could account for Rabbi Omer-Man's reluctance to take the discussion of sexual energies much further. There were other reasons he would reveal to me later.

After Jonathan's demurral, Rabbi Zalman Schachter offered a few more specifics, based on Hasidic prayer. He showed how the body parts corresponded to various *sefirot*, as well as to vowel sounds that the practitioner would take a breath through. For instance, "the right hand represents generosity and the sound of 'ehh' is connected to that." Similarly, the heart is represented by a long *o*, and the *sefirah* of *tiferet*, or beauty, resides there. This whole meditation, combining breathing and visualization, "was suggested by the *Zohar* and worked into the prayer book by Rabbi Yitzhak Luria. It is not pronounced with the mouth; it is heard on the inside and the body goes with it."

He explained a second system, which he believed close to tantra, in which each month and letter of the alphabet is associated with eyes, ears, and inner organs "so that in the twelve months of the year each of the organs is purified."

All the energies of the body are enlisted in the service of this meditation, including sexual. But like Jonathan, Zalman appeared cautious about opening this door. However, the Buddhist master apparently had heard enough to come to a conclusion, for after intently following the details of Zalman's explanation, he leaned back and shook his head with amazement, smiling. He spoke rapidly in Tibetan to Laktor, who reported back his comment, "It's interesting to find that there are very striking similarities."

These similarities soon became even more apparent. While tea was served, Michael Sautman introduced Charles Halpern from the Nathan Cummings Foundation. Halpern asked the Dalai Lama to "share with us the Buddhist approach to esoteric practices."

Over a hot cup of tea, the Buddhist master explained that through tantric meditation one learned "how to actualize concentration."

"One important method is to bring the twin practice of method and wisdom together, or the integration of the practice of method and wisdom. For that it is important to block the ordinary appearances as we are.

"First you visualize that everything is dissolving into the nature of emptiness and from that emptiness you visualize a purified state of existence, like a purified deity. And then you focus on that purity and see that deity as having a level of inherent existence. In other words, through that visualization you bring the practice of method and wisdom together."

In Jewish thought, wisdom is equated with Torah. In Buddha tantra, wisdom is defined as a consciousness that realizes emptiness, or the lack of inherent existence of every phenomena. Uniting method and wisdom means generating a mind that, as scholar Daniel Cozort explains, "realizes emptiness at the same time it compassionately appears as a deity." To one unfamiliar with tantra, it sounds like doing a handstand with no hands. The Buddhists, however, use even more daring imagery—sexual union.

That was the significance of the yabyum statuette I'd glimpsed in the Drepung Temple during our visit to the oracle. In tantric meditation, wisdom is the female figure and method the male. We did not go into specifics, but Professor Robert Thurman—a scholar and translator of Tibetan Buddhist texts who sat in on this session as an auxiliary translator and observer—told us, "You employ the energies of the body when the mind is in meditation. You empower the meditations of the mind to mobilize the energies of the body." The Dalai Lama added— probably enigmatically for most of his Jewish listeners—"With respect to that we do meditation on the channels, winds, and drops."

As scholar Daniel Cozort has written, these winds or vital energies "cause all movement by and within the body. The winds move in a system of 72,000 subtle 'channels.' The white and red drops are the pure essence of the essential fluids of the male and female, having evolved from the original white drop of the father and red drop of the mother that combined to become the original physical basis for the human body at the time of conception." The white and red drops are found everywhere in human bodies, "where they coat the inside of the channels 'like frost.'" Tantric meditation melts these drops, thereby releasing the energies of winds dissolved in them. It then controls and directs the movement of winds into various channels of the body. Coarse and subtle winds correspond to different levels of consciousness.

The Dalai Lama told us, "We divide consciousness, or inner energy, into three levels. Grosser level, more subtle level, innermost subtle level, or subtle state. Now to utilize the innermost subtle consciousness or subtle energy, the first two levels of consciousness energy should be reduced, should cease." Because in ordinary life, too much energy comes from sense organs and mental consciousness, "the subtle consciousness remains inactive and very weak." For ordinary people, subtle consciousness is only apprehended at the moment of death. But in tantric meditation, the activities or energy of the grosser levels are reduced, "then," the Dalai Lama explained, "subtle consciousness becomes more active. For this to occur, we first should control the sense faculty. So the power of the external sense faculties can be brought down or reduced through visualizing or meditating on the seven important physical points, like channels and drops." Robert Thurman added, "especially on the red and white elements inside the body. By bringing them up, that brings the sense down."

Moshe Waldoks thought this practice sounded "like sublimation." Zalman Schachter quoted a relevant passage in the Talmud. "It says the mother gives the red, the father gives the white, but God gives the sight to the eyes, the hearing to the ears."

I suppose before coming to Dharamsala, I might have dismissed the whole business of drops, channels, and winds as nonsense, *mishegos*. But I was beginning to see that this was highly useful *mishegos*. There was no doubt in my mind that the Dalai Lama and many of the other practitioners had a very clear understanding of the subtle levels of consciousness. I now saw this elaborate physiology as a way of guiding thought—a steering mechanism. It allowed the meditator to get past the bumps in the road, the distractions to concentrated thought. And one of the biggest bumps was lust.

Tibetan Buddhist tantra was largely derived from Hindu tantric texts and practices. ("Tantra" is the name for both the philosophy and its texts; at root the word means web.) Though some deny it, Hindu tantra was a frankly sexual yoga, according to the Buddhist scholar David Snellgrove, with its texts written in "outspoken and deliberately scandalous language and in the unorthodox terminology which one might well expect of wandering tantric yogins, who claim to have no allegiance anywhere except to their own revered teacher." It was a different matter when they came over into Buddhism. According to Snellgrove, it was possible for the tantric texts to be "accepted into the mainstream of the Indian Buddhist tradition by interpreting them [tantras] in accordance with the theory of enigmatic meanings. This is what the commentators set out to do." He gives as an example the *Guhyasamaja Tantra*. Its literal interpretation was still a cause of anxiety some two centuries after its introduction to Tibet, as shown by the ordinance of eleventh-century King Yeshesod of western Tibet:

> As retribution for indulging your lust in your so-called ritual
>   embrace
> Alas! You will surely be born as a uterine worm
> You worship the Three Jewels with flesh, blood and urine.
> In ignorance of enigmatic terminology you perform the rite literally

Tsongkhapa, the founder of the Dalai Lama's *gelukpa* sect, wrote that only those on lower stages of the tantric path would require an actual consort, known as a "knowledge woman" to practice deity yoga, whereas those further along could achieve the same ends, a union of bliss and emptiness, purely through the power of meditation.

Certainly, as the Buddhist leader explained his practices to the Jewish group, tantric yoga is sublimely psychological. A visualization of the sexual union of deities generates subtle states of consciousness. In the *gelukpa* sect, the practice, as the *geshes* had explained to some of us Saturday night, was reserved for those who were extremely well schooled in Buddhist philosophy and dialectics, and only after many years of training. (This may be why Zalman Schachter's suggestion to the *geshes* to speed up the training might not be well received.)

On the other hand, the meditation was not simply a fantasy, because at the highest level, one simultaneously believed in the deities invoked and recognized them as empty. Snellgrove writes, "It would be useless to invoke any form of divinity, higher or lower, without believing in such a being. The practitioner is certainly taught that the divine forms are also emanations of his own mind, but they are not arbitrary imaginings and they are far more real than his own transitory personality, which is a mere flow of nonsubstantial elements. In learning to produce mentally such higher forms of emanation and eventually identifying himself with them, the practitioner gradually transforms his evanescent personality into that higher state of being."

As the Dalai Lama told us, the goal is clarity. The noise coming out of the sense organs has to be quieted, including the powerful sexual impulses. In the puritanical religions, this is done through suppression, denial, hatred of the body. As D. H. Lawrence defined it memorably, religion is bad sex. The daring of Buddhist tantra is to work with the energy, rather than suppressing, denying, or opposing it.

Constraints of time did not allow the discussions to go much further or into greater detail, but enough similarities between tantra and kabbalah had been noted to make it seem worthwhile to continue the comparisons, perhaps in smaller and more intimate working groups.

The whole issue of what to do with sexual energy, or how to accommodate it in religious contexts, goes to the core of life today. The highly moralistic and rigid approaches of some religious denominations to sexuality has led to schizophrenia and denial. In his discussions with the *geshe*s, Zalman Schachter had touched on the Hasidic approach of the Baal Shem Tov and his doctrine of "strange thoughts"—namely, that even thoughts of lust come to the mind begging to be raised up. This is probably something Jimmy Swaggart has never thought of. And reflecting on the Dalai Lama's explanation that the whole purpose of tantric meditation was to "actualize concentration," I thought again of how distracting our culture's obsession with sexuality is, and how dealing effectively with such energy is crucial in having a spiritual life. (This was also true in the time of the Baal Shem Tov, when in order to continue their studies, the best students had to put off marriage.) So I delighted to discover that in both kabbalah and tantra there are attempts to recognize the whole human being and all of our impulses, lovely and unlovely, body and soul.

Within Tibetan Buddhism there are various attitudes toward tantric practice. The *gelukpa* sect is the most highly philosophical and scholarly of the Tibetan Buddhist lineages and gives tantric teachings a strong intellectual framework. In this sense, the *gelukpa*s resembled the rabbis who also carefully embedded mysticism within a rational framework. Thus the conversation about strictures with Jonathan had a certain resonance. Likewise, the Chabad Lubavitch were the *geluk-*

pas of the Hasidim, the most philosophical and intellectual of the Hasidic sects.

We did not discuss in Dharamsala what might be called Jewish tantra. But, in an utterly different context—the marriage bed—Jewish mysticism also teaches certain techniques for raising sexual energy to celestial realms. The very first written description of Jewish meditation is found in a marriage manual, *The Holy Letter*, attributed to the kabbalist Joseph Gikatilla.

As described in Rabbi Aryeh Kaplan's *Jewish Meditation*, the partners meditate throughout the sexual act, becoming "aware of the spark of the Divine in the pleasure itself and elevat[ing] it to its source." According to a contemporary Hasidic description by Yitzhak Buxbaum in *Jewish Spiritual Practices*, "The *Zohar* teaches that when man and woman in sex are both directed to the Divine presence (*Shekhinah*), the Divine Presence rests on their bed. . . . [It is taught that] a man should make his house a Temple and his bedroom a Holy of Holies."

In Jewish mystical thought, then, there is a sacralization of the erotic and an eroticization of the sacred. But this mixture of the erotic and the holy, though very salient in kabbalah, is highly suppressed in mainstream Judaism. It emerges, rather, in hidden forms, such as the Shabbat hymn "Lekha Dodi"—"Welcome to the Bride." Samuel Alkabez wrote it in sixteenth-century Safed, under the influence of the great kabbalist Rabbi Isaac Luria. At one time in Safed, the men would dress in white and await the Shabbat bride as night fell, greeting her with "Lekha Dodi." For Isaac Luria and his followers, this amounted to a "visualization" of the *Shekhinah* arriving like a mother with a troupe of Shabbat souls.

In fact, as expounded in kabbalistic texts such as *Sod Ha-Shabbat* (Secret of the Sabbath), the entire mystical Shabbat was organized in anticipation of the sexual union between husband and wife, timed to coincide with a celestial coupling, the "union of the Bride with Her Beloved." The physical union would produce a new body and the celestial union a new soul. "During the six days of the week *Shekhinah* is a folded rose, but on Shabbat and holy days, She opens to receive fragrance and spices [from Her husband] and to give souls and joy to Her children. . . . "

"This discovery of a feminine element in God," Gershom Scholem notes, "is of course one of the most significant steps they took. Often regarded with the utmost misgiving by strictly Rabbinical, non-Kabbalistic

Jews, this mythical conception of the feminine principle of the *Shekhinah* as a providential guide of Creation achieved enormous popularity among the masses of the Jewish people, so showing that here the Kabbalists had uncovered one of the primordial religious impulses still latent in Judaism."

In Hasidic prayer, attention is constantly directed toward the union of the heart *sefirah* (*Tiferet*) with the *Shekhinah* (*Malkhut*), also visualized as the union of *Yod He* and *Vov He* in the name of God. According to Gershom Scholem, "The Kabbalists held that every religious act should be accompanied by the formula: this is done 'for the sake of the reunion of God and His *Shekhinah*.' And indeed, under Kabbalistic influence, this formula was employed in all subsequent liturgical texts and books of later Judaism, down to the nineteenth century, when rationalistic Jews, horrified at a conception they no longer understood, deleted it from the prayer books destined for the use of Westernized minds."

In general, Scholem explains, the kabbalists aimed at "the transformation of essentially profane acts into ritual," especially eating and sexual activity. "These acts are closely bound up with the sacral sphere." At one point in the discussion, Jonathan Omer-Man described a group of kabbalists in Jerusalem who spent six hours a day just on morning prayers and hours reciting blessings over every activity. He used this example to suggest that to the Jewish mystic, every act, no matter how mundane, was part of an ongoing meditation.

In the same vein, Scholem cites the story of the patriarch Enoch, "who according to an old tradition was taken from the earth by God and transformed into the angel Metatron" and "was said to have been a cobbler. At every stitch of his awl he not only joined the upper leather with the sole, but all upper things with all lower things. . . . He accompanied his work at every step with meditations which drew the stream of emanation down from the upper to the lower (so transforming profane action into ritual action) until he himself was transfigured from the earthly Enoch into the transcendent Metatron who had been the object of his meditations." Scholem points out "that a very similar legend is to be found in a Tibetan tantric text, the 'Tales of the Eighty-Four Magicians' (translated by A. Grunwedel in Bassler-Archiv, V, [1916], p. 159.) Here . . . the *guru* Camara (which means shoemaker) receives instruction from a yogi concerning the leather, the awl, the thread, and the shoe. . . . For twelve years he meditates day and night over this shoemaking, until he attains perfect enlightenment and is borne aloft" (Scholem, *On the Kabbalah and Its Symbolism*, p. 132).

Clearly, then, even down to legends, there are "striking similarities" between kabbalah and tantra, as the Dalai Lama exclaimed.

Strikingly similar too is the meditation on complex body maps that align physical and spiritual energies. Both systems work past the famous contradiction in the West between the mind and the body. Ever since Descartes Westerners have been stuck with a soul in a machine, a disembodied body seen as a purely spiritless mechanical construction.

Yet our everyday language teaches us differently. The mechanical body of science, with its circulatory systems for blood lymph, its nervous systems, skeleton, and organs, is rarely the body we "have in mind." Rather, we construct our own mental map, our own imaginal body: emotions in the heart, hunger in the stomach, lust in the genitals, thought in the brain. To that picture we add our own overlay—a private map of our feelings and fantasies. Perhaps that is why a look in the mirror always brings a slight shock.

The subtle physiology of tantra can be seen as a highly elaborate and systematic development of the imaginal body. The tantric practitioner visualizes a very complex and elaborate physiology of seventy-two thousand channels, as well as winds and drops. What's fascinating is how this "subtle physiology" creates a workable interface between the mind and the body that allows for an extraordinary control of autonomic systems.

Many in the West are familiar with biofeedback, which has been used successfully to gain control of blood pressure and heart rate. Dr. Herbert Benson of the Harvard Medical School, a leading researcher on using meditation to lower stress for heart attack patients, came to Dharamsala in February 1981 to study tantric practitioners, longtime solitary monks who practice "inner heat," or *Tum-mo*, meditation. It is said that the monks are able to sit all night meditating in the snow without ill effect. Dr. Benson was able to document, using electronic measures, that the monks were capable of raising the temperature of their extremities up to 8.3 degrees centigrade, an extraordinary feat.

In Dharamsala, the rabbis could not provide a detailed explanation of the use of the interior tree in kabbalistic meditation that would permit a fuller comparison to tantra. But the leading scholar of kabbalah today, Moshe Idel, speculates that precisely here kabbalah, by way of Sufism, was "infiltrated" by Hindu concepts. He sees a marked resemblance between Hindu mandalas and the kabbalistic inner tree, or body maps. Since Buddhist tantra is also derived from Hindu texts and teachings, there may even be a point of common origin for both esoteric systems.

Supposing that is true, still the same concepts would have encountered very different environments and therefore manifested in very different ways. Tantrayana is practiced in both householder and celibate contexts within Tibetan Buddhism. Marpa, a great eleventh-century teacher and guru of the *kagyu* lineage, was married, and his student, the poet and saint Milarepa, had many consorts. Up through 1959, many of the great Tibetan tantric practitioners or yogins were householders, and some were women.

However, in the dominant *gelukpa* sect of Tibetan Buddhism, tantra was set into a celibate, monastic system. The mysteries of higher tantric meditation are reserved for those who have spent years refining themselves through study, debate, and meditation practice—it is very unlikely that such a trainee would fall into a merely vulgar interpretation.

Judaism is definitively a householder religion. Historically, its experiments with monasticism were brief, the Essenes being the best-known group. (It's not clear that all Essene groups were celibate.) Even the holy man, the *tzaddik* or prophet, must be part of "this world" as Jonathan had stressed. Therefore, in the Jewish context, the practice of sexual yoga—if one can borrow the term from tantra—is exclusively between husband and wife.

Another major difference today is that the Tibetans have a well-preserved, complete, and highly developed path of meditation, which they are willing to teach to qualified Westerners. For many historical reasons, the doors to the Jewish esoteric remain shut to most Jews.

After the session, I asked Jonathan why, when asked about sexual energies, he had replied, "I cannot open that door." He said, "There are some things that have to be held back, taught one-on-one. I don't know how else to do it. The moment it becomes public, it becomes so open to misunderstanding and the wrong kind of visualization—seeing it as an exciting image and not part of a discipline for very advanced people."

Moreover, Jonathan felt that the use of sexual energy had been abused in both the Jewish world and the tantric. Among some Hasidim, for instance, "it became an object of obsession, of doing it the right way—a negative abuse." He referred to kabbalistic texts and folklore, which concentrate on how to avoid getting semen on the sheets, whether due to masturbation or marital sex. There was a medieval belief that Lilith, the first wife of Adam, would make use of the spilled semen to create demonic creatures, the *shovavim,* or "ill-bred" creatures of man's desire. In Jonathan's view, this sort of superstition "is an extremely negative development of it when it became popularized." Therefore, these Jewish teachings should only be given to major adepts, people who are deeply involved. "That's one level—it's dangerous or it can be abused. The other level is, when one aligns oneself with the ultimate reality—the divine world—then it's more appropriate. But when one sees oneself as the ultimate reality, when one is looking for reinforcement of oneself, of one's momentary ego, one's sexuality, then it becomes dangerous—a perversion, a distortion."

That did not mean he would refuse to speak about sexual energies in Jewish meditation. "When I speak about it publicly or avoid it, it's also an invitation for people to come one-on-one to discuss it." The teaching is available, "but it's information you don't get for free."

Jonathan added, "One of the major themes of our entire encounter there, from my perspective, was the relation between the two, between the esoteric and the public. It's something the Tibetan Buddhists face because of people like Chogyam Trungpa and others who made things public that shouldn't have been public." But if the teachings remained private, how were most Jews supposed to learn about them? Jonathan himself had not been born into kabbalah like Zalman Schachter. I asked him how he'd learned it.

He'd grown up in England in what he described as a not very observant Orthodox family, in a country where "Orthodoxy was the only club in town." As a young man he'd come to Israel for Zionist reasons. He felt he was fighting against his religious impulses—"just saying no for a long time before I said yes." He worked as a cowboy on a kibbutz until he had the misfortune of contracting polio in the winter of 1956.

After that he came to Jerusalem and found work in publishing. He collaborated with the distinguished Talmudic scholar and mystic Rabbi Adin Steinsaltz for four years as his personal editor and edited *Shefa Quarterly.* The magazine brought to attention a number of important scholars and mystical Jewish texts. He also worked with Gershom

Scholem, editing for the *Encyclopedia Judaica* his articles on kabbalah, which touched Jonathan very deeply.

Personally, Jonathan found Scholem "a very impenetrable person who sometimes gave a glimpse beyond." Following that glimpse, he enrolled in Hebrew University to study kabbalah, but "I realized that wasn't the place. It gave me some useful tools, but I sought out more traditional teachers after that." Like Alex Berzin, Omer-Man wanted the practice and wanted to learn from living teachers, not just from a text. Jonathan did not belong to the ultra-Orthodox communities in Jerusalem where kabbalah was taught at that time. But his two most important teachers "were trying to communicate to people who were not in the direct sociological lineage." One came from a Hasidic, Bratzlaver-influenced community; the other brought teachings from an extant kabbalistic community in Tangiers. "The Hasidic teacher knew I wasn't going to join his community but even so taught me. In some ways I took this as a challenge from him to transmit it elsewhere."

After many years of study, Jonathan personally received ordination (*semikha*) from Zalman Schachter. Recently he conferred his own first *semikha* upon Rabbi Judith Halevy. So the mystical transmission continues outside its original closed circles and has been passed on to a woman.

Still, Jonathan's story is more exception than rule. Accessibility is still quite difficult—the door still mostly closed. For instance, even now Jonathan declined to publicly name his teachers. "When ultra-Orthodox people teach less Orthodox people, they can get into deep problems in their own community," especially if the less Orthodox reveal this to the world at large. After all, as Jonathan had explained, the Talmud greatly restricts who can receive such teachings. To pass them on outside of a given community might seem a betrayal to its members.

Jonathan's presentation to the Dalai Lama also made clear that, in the past, women rarely received instruction in kabbalah. That gave Joy Levitt's joke an unintended irony. "Some of us are hearing this for the first time as well," she'd said. As long as the transmission of kabbalah is confined to ultra-Orthodox circles, women are unlikely to receive it.

The question and challenge of gender, and the role of women in Judaism—and Buddhism—would be raised implicitly by the last two Jewish speakers, Joy Levitt and Blu Greenberg.

17

Survival Strategies

Rabbi Joy Levitt spoke first of the synagogue—an institution so familiar in the West that it is difficult to appreciate how original it is. The Tibetans currently have nothing to correspond to it. At the preliminary session in New Jersey, the Dalai Lama had been impressed by what he heard. He'd commented, in the light and joking tone he often used in referring to his own tradition, that perhaps the Buddhist temple services were too long and boring. Some of the rabbis joked back that their congregants made the same complaint.

But in her formal presentation, Rabbi Joy Levitt stressed that the Hebrew word *beth knesset* meant "more than just a place of worship; it is a house of assembling, a gathering place." A synagogue is a focus for the community, a place to study and learn, and a place to share happy occasions. She gave some familiar examples such as a naming ceremony for a baby, held in the synagogue, because "that child doesn't just belong to the parents but to the whole congregation." Ultimately the synagogue is a focus of Jewish identity in the diaspora, "among many peoples who are not Jewish, the central place to affirm that you are Jewish."

She went on to explain that the synagogue developed in response to the loss of the Temple. In exile, "we needed local places to worship. We needed a place to console each other after the great tragedy. We needed a place to teach one another, because the level of ignorance as we dispersed, grew."

In America, where so much emphasis is placed on individualism, the synagogue helps to reinforce the Jewish value of community responsibility. Joy Levitt gave examples such as the charity box (the tzedekah box, or *pushke*) found in many Jewish households. The Dalai Lama wanted to know if the sense of collective responsibility derived from a religious teaching. Joy answered that it was "deeply embedded in our religious tradition but also derives from our experience."

Before leaving for India, Joy had told the story of the Tibetan exile to her Hebrew school children. She asked them to prepare an album of letters and drawings, "their attempt to sum up what is important about Jewish life." As she presented it, she quoted from the letter of a twelve-year-old girl. "I know that you are probably looking for information on Jews, but did you know that Jews all over the world stick together? Whenever other Jews are in trouble people pray for them or try to help them in some ways." The letter ended with some advice for the Dalai Lama. "The main purpose of my letter was just to tell your Holiness that no matter what, your people should stick together." The child's advice sounded remarkably like the Nechung oracle's.

The Tibetan leader took a few minutes to page through the album. I noticed that he often took time—cleared a space—to contemplate and absorb something new. He seemed genuinely delighted by this contact with Jewish children.

I thought how he himself had been deprived of a childhood to a large extent. As a *tulku* he had been taken from his home at age three. Yet Buddhist monks have mothers; Dalai Lamas have mothers. I had been touched by his autobiography. "Of course I was very sad at my mother's death," he writes. He explained that although they had been physically apart in recent years, spiritually they had been close so that "I experienced a great sense of loss—just as I always do when any old member of my entourage dies." That last part might sound rather cold, but I knew it reflected instead the depth of his commitment to Buddhism and the difficulty of the path. The need to explain any sense of personal loss, and to so temper it, was as foreign to my way of thinking as perhaps my very Jewish attachment to my family would be to his.

Joy asked him for his thoughts, wondering "what institutions you've developed or ways you've found to maintain Tibetan culture and religion."

Jews, while disagreeing among themselves about the proper proportions, tend to cook Jewish religion and Jewish culture into one identity. But the Dalai Lama distinguished between the Tibetan culture and the religion. He mentioned that in the Tibetan community there were "a few thousand Muslims, very few Christians, and a few hundred thousand who follow the ancient Tibetan religion," Bon. Moreover, there were Tibetans "who joined the Chinese Communist party as early as the fifties. Later some of them became very good friends of mine . . . very good people—very good Tibetans." And the Tibetan Muslims "kept, I think, the best part of Tibetan culture. Emphasis on cultural identity is not laying emphasis on the importance of religion."

But this point met with "respectful disagreement" from Professor Robert Thurman. A large and garrulous man, with a ready laugh and a commanding presence, Thurman reminded the Dalai Lama, in mildly scolding terms, that "Your Holiness works day and night so that the doctrine doesn't decline. This is very important preservative work that you do, in keeping the dharma from disappearing in the world." Then Thurman turned toward the Jewish delegates. "He's saying, 'Oh, we don't do much for religion, do we?'" Then, turning to the Dalai Lama, he said, "You're doing tremendous work for the Buddhist religion."

The Dalai Lama listened to this animated outburst with a smile on his face but countered that "it seems in the sixties and early seventies and a little bit today" that "especially younger people" were "skeptical about religion." (Perhaps he was referring to movements like the Tibetan Youth Congress.) They felt that "because of too much concentration on religious matters, we neglected other fields, other work, so we lost our country."

But the Dalai Lama admitted that since the mid-seventies, and then eighties, interest in Buddhism has been much stronger. Ironically, this return was in part because many "Europeans and Americans are showing genuine interest in Tibetan Buddhism." He felt that, overall, "since exile—more than one hundred thousand Tibetans are in exile now—for thirty-one years—comparatively, we are a quite successful refugee community. If this situation remains another fifty or one hundred years, then I think [we will be] OK. After that, nobody knows. Sometimes I'm afraid I may not be able to keep up, like our Jewish friends."

Joy Levitt reassured him, "I don't think you have anything to worry about."

"One way," the Dalai Lama added, "[that we survive is] Tibetans quite easily adapt to new situations: their mental attitude is quite flexible. . . . Maybe we've gotten too flexible, I don't know." He asked Thurman what he thought.

"I think the contemporary system itself is falling apart pretty fast so that the Tibetans won't get too comfortable if they try to become totally modern. . . . Then perhaps Tibetans will find more to be proud of in making their own contribution to the modern culture.

"But, as I say, Your Holiness is underestimating, out of humility, the contribution to Tibetan identity of the desire—the sense of responsibility—to preserve the Buddha dharma—because, after all, Tibet has been the country that has most preserved so many Buddhist traditions. Your Holiness has taken years of retreats, you get up at four in the morning and say hours and hours of prayers—you're almost like a rabbi!" At that the Dalai Lama laughed and gestured to Jonathan, "Certainly much less than your teachers."

To Thurman, preserving dharma or Buddhist teaching is the glue that holds most Tibetans together. "So many young Tibetans, who in Tibet have been brainwashed by materialism and communism, when they have a chance, go into a monastery and rebuild it. They want to come to India to study in a monastery."

In recent years, the Chinese have allowed the rebuilding of some of the ruined monasteries in Tibet and have allowed a limited number of monks to study there. There is a strict quota and no financial support is provided. Unfortunately, due to the previous actions of the Chinese, there are few qualified teachers. It is estimated that one-fourth of the male population in Tibet in 1959 were monks. Today fewer than 1 percent are monks.

Thus, the major propagation of Buddha dharma rests with the exiled Tibetans. The Dalai Lama has been actively teaching Buddhism worldwide. He has presented the Kalachakra tantra to several large audiences in Los Angeles, New York, and Wisconsin. These Kalachakra teachings are events unprecedented in the history of Buddhism—and may well represent a unique moment in which previously unavailable ancient teachings are passed over to the world at large.

Alex Berzin added that the Dalai Lama has also transformed the traditional monasteries in their new settings in exile, by stressing modern education such as studying mathematics and science. "In this way," he said, "the young monks feel that modern studies and religious studies can go together."

Obviously, the Dalai Lama's efforts at both preservation and adaptation are very important. But in Jewish life, much of the day-to-day task of preservation has fallen on women. The active site has not been the temple, but the home. It was Blu Greenberg's turn to speak. She is not only a Jewish mother and grandmother but also the author of *How to Run a Traditional Jewish Household*, an excellent guide to the subject.

Blu began by praising all the efforts and achievements of the Tibetans over the last thirty years, "the planning ahead and looking forward," but added in a homely way that brought the discussion down to earth, "nevertheless, exile is exile." She wanted to talk about what she feels has been the most significant institution for helping the Jews through a very long exile, the family. And she wanted "to know from Your Holiness what role you see the Tibetan Buddhist family playing in the years ahead."

Our contact Saturday afternoon with the Tibetan secularists had convinced Blu the topic was important, and more so after hearing through Nathan Katz of an urgent plea from Alex Berzin. The "Dalai Lama's rabbi" had cornered Nathan after the first dialogue session. "You've got to tell them more about the home," he said, "they don't understand that, they don't know about that. Unless you Jews tell them about how to observe religion in the home, the Tibetans won't be able to do it."

But how to explain the role of the family to a group of celibate monks? In Judaism, Blu said, "it wasn't just the exile that created the centrality of the family. This is a fundamental principle of Jewish theology. The very first commandment in the Torah is 'be fruitful and multiply,' create the family." Moreover, "the family is the carrier of the covenant. To maintain the partnership with God and fulfill the responsibility in the covenant, we have to have children and pass the message and the tasks on. What you can't do in your own lifetime you expect the future generations to do." She concluded that "the family is our wheel of life, as compared to the wheel of rebirth" in Tibetan Buddhism.

These were foreign concepts to the Dalai Lama and the abbots and monks, firm believers in rebirth. In the Tibetan view, the spiritual mission of highly enlightened people is carried on from lifetime to lifetime through various bodily frames. Through rebirth, Buddhism stresses a connection between all beings. Every sentient being has at one time or another been one's mother.

To get to a similar idea, Judaism takes a very different route. Blu Greenberg cited a midrash on Genesis. "We are all the children of one couple," Adam and Eve. Why? So no one can feel superior to another in being close to God.

Although Blu admitted that in recent years the Jewish family has begun to have problems, she stressed that divorce is still lower among Jews than the general American population. Family remains a vital metaphor in Jewish life. "The notion of the family is so deeply ingrained in us, that it is not just the immediate family, our first cousins, the extended family, but the whole family of the Jewish people." She pointed to the ongoing resettlement of Ethiopian and Soviet Jews in Israel as examples of this broadened sense of family. Ultimately, it extends to all humanity, "because we are all cousins. And part of the power of this week is that we have been reminded of our Tibetan cousins."

To Blu Greenberg this commitment involves prayer. That morning, in fact, we had finished our prayers by shouting, "next year in Jerusalem" and then, "next year in Lhasa." But it also meant concrete political action. She promised solidarity with Tibetan women and a protest by Jewish women's organizations against the Chinese policy of forced sterilization. "We know in our bones what it is like to have life cut off at its source."

In stressing household, family, and, ultimately, the Jewish mother that afternoon to a group of celibate monks, there were many paradoxes and echoes. In their own lives, Joy and Blu had found an accommodation between traditional roles for Jewish women and feminism. Blu describes herself as an Orthodox feminist, and Blu and Joy are devoted mothers who are also highly active professionally—Blu as an author and Joy as a rabbi and editor. On the Tibetan side, Rinchen Choegyal, who combined roles as diverse as guest house manager and head of the Tibetan Women's Association, was also showing a new status for women.

At the first session with the Dalai Lama, Blu Greenberg and Zalman Schachter had commented on the influence of women's consciousness on contemporary Jewish thinking. Blu had asked the Dalai Lama if any similar discussions were going on in the Tibetan context. The Dalai Lama did affirm the possibility of women's high spiritual achievement, citing the story of the goddess Tara, who upon achieving enlightenment asked to be perpetually reincarnated in a woman's body. He also explained that the mother is considered the symbol of compassion and affection, while at the level of practice, without the female side, without wisdom, you can't develop.

Furthermore, at least in the abstract, there was no justification in Buddhism for distinguishing men and women, each having equal spiritual potential. "From the Buddhist viewpoint, all sentient beings are the same," the Dalai Lama affirmed. However, it was clear from his explanation that historically Buddhism had accepted social inequality between the sexes without trying to change it. It wasn't hard to see anyway—there were no female counterparts for Joy and Blu on the Tibetan side.

The Dalai Lama's explanation for this seemed somewhat strained, in my view. "In order to serve humanity," he explained, "if in a certain social system the male is more influential, then at that time more preference is given for the male. If under certain circumstances in certain situations the female is more influential, more useful, then initially—automatically, the preference will go to the female." The actual social result is that in Tibetan and other Buddhist cultures, such as Burma and Thailand, the inferiority of women is a widespread assumption. For instance, in Tibet it is common for religious women to pray to be reborn as men. On the American scene, Judaism has often been attacked as a patriarchal religion, in which women are relegated to diminished roles in spiritual life. Blu's amplification of the importance of the home and family in Jewish spiritual life added an important correction to that image. Jewish women have given Judaism enormous strength. Any condemnation of Judaism as purely patriarchal overlooks the contribution of countless Jewish women who have found their spiritual needs satisfied through their roles as wives and mothers. Today Jewish women work hard to combine such roles with careers as Jewish educators, rabbis, and cantors.

Still, as Rabbi Levitt had admitted to Chodron on Shabbat morning, Jewish religion remains patriarchal. After listening to the life stories of Chodron and Pemo, I knew that the Buddhist nuns had sought a much more individual and free spiritual path than the traditional roles of Jewish wife and mother could have provided them. The Judaism they had left behind did not seem to offer women an independent spiritual path.

However, despite the broad-minded view the Dalai Lama presented, the actual Buddhism the women encountered is not an egalitarian paradise. I already had an intimation of that from Rinchen Choegyal's work: the Tibetan nuns needed special support because they weren't getting it the way the monks were. Westerners had to be completely self-supporting.

In Dharamsala, Western Buddhist women have had to struggle with the social customs of the traditions they have adopted. For instance, Thubten Pemo made it clear in our interview that Western nuns in particular were often treated like second-class citizens, and this seems to parallel the treatment of Tibetan Buddhist nuns. The very name for nun, *ani*, means something like "auntie"—hardly a term of respect. And the Tibetan word for woman means "lowborn." It is clear that the egalitarian theory of the Dalai Lama has not infiltrated Tibetan customs.

Thubten Chodron has found that Tibetan women are very self-effacing, and that this social relationship continues when they become nuns. All of this is made even more complicated because the lineage for Tibetan nuns has been broken, so that to be ordained, vows must be taken through an order of Mahayana nuns in Taiwan.

Joseph Goldstein, a leading American meditation teacher, later confirmed for me that there are similar problems for Western Theravadan Buddhists. "One of the big influences of the dharma coming to the West is the equalizing of role between men and women. There was never a difference in the actual practice and attainment. But certainly the way people related to one another was quite sexist. I see it reflecting cultures at the time of the Buddha and Asian cultures since.

"In Burma when I was at one of the monasteries, you go into the dining room in file. The monks would go first, then the laymen, then the nuns, then the laywomen. Which is just indicative of how they saw things."

In her *Meetings with Remarkable Women*, an account of Buddhist teachers in America, Lenore Friedman concludes that, "At best, then, Buddhism historically encompasses a grand ambivalence toward women. The dharma itself is beyond ambivalence, resting nowhere, shattering concepts. The *teaching* of the dharma is another matter, since it arises from minds and from language conditioned by history and personal experience. This is true of all religions—how could it be otherwise? The more they become 'solid,' the more they betray their original transcendent inspiration or mystical core. . . . For many women practicing today, one of the greatest obstacles remains the absence of clear female role models and foremothers in Buddhist literature and scripture. It is still a truism that all major teachers, lineage holders, and masters down the ages have been men."

In Western Buddhism the solution to this discrimination seems to be coming about in part by women practitioners insisting on changes in language and teaching styles. There is also an active effort at rediscovering Buddhist "foremothers"—as well as honoring Buddhist women teachers today.

Something similar has been happening in Judaism. One chief complaint, which cropped up among us in Dharamsala, has been the separation of men and women in prayer. Egalitarian prayer is commonplace in the liberal branches of Judaism and is gaining in popularity in conservative circles. Moreover, Marcia Falk and other Jewish scholars have pioneered in revising the language of prayer to avoid strictly masculine formulations of God, or to include feminine ones, all the while making use of traditional sources.

Yet much of the focus has been on the more formal exoteric factors, such as the movement in the more liberal branches of Judaism to ordain women rabbis and cantors. Some emphasis has been given to creating new life cycle rituals, such as the bat mitzvah and naming ceremonies for baby girls, to correspond to the traditional bar mitzvah and bris.

These are all welcome developments in mainstream Judaism, and they show a creative appropriation of traditional practices. But such gestures sometimes seem merely substitutive, without truly acknowledging the uniqueness of women. They are in effect "disembodied"; what's missing is a deeper acknowledgment of the body, and also of the body of literature in Judaism that might deepen the change.

This is why an opening to the esoteric could be very important in correcting the impression that Judaism is strictly patriarchal, or that its imagery of God is strictly masculine. For the door closed by mainstream Judaism on the esoteric is also a door closed to the body, and to the feminine. For instance, it's interesting to read the Zoharic commentary on the verse in Genesis, "male and female He created them." In Daniel Matt's translation, "From here we learn: Any image that does not embrace male and female is not a high and true image. . . . Come and see: The Blessed Holy One does not place His abode in any place where male and female are not found together. Blessings are found only in a place where male and female are found, as it is written: He blessed them and called their name Adam on the day they were created. It is not written: He blessed him and called his name Adam. A human being is only called Adam when male and female are as one."

On paper, at least, there are very fine things in kabbalah emphasizing the importance of women, the recognition of the feminine aspect of God, the spiritual importance of sexuality in the context of marriage, the recognition of women's needs. But the problem for most Jewish women today is that all of this is very theoretical. On the fringes, in the Jewish renewal movement, there is a strong recognition of the power of the *Shekhinah,* and even an acknowledgment of what Zalman Schachter calls "prepatriarchal Judaism"—that is, the goddess worship of the Canaanites. But as a whole, Jews are very far from coming to terms with a feminine God, or its thoroughgoing implications.

Yet just below the surface are hints of new directions. Before reading the Torah, Jews pray to "*Av Harakhamim,*" the "Merciful Father." The root of *rakhamim,* or mercy, is *rekhem*—womb. Av Harakhamim could be translated, our Wombly Father, our Motherly Father.

That phrase came back to me when to my surprise, I saw a *thangka* depicting a *dakini,* or goddess, dancing next to a large Jewish star. In tantric Buddhism, the six-pointed star is a symbol of the cervix. This is a coincidence worth meditating on. In Judaism, the star is proudly displayed on the flag of Israel. It represents the *magen david*, the shield of King David. A shield is the outermost layer of protection, what one thrusts out to the world as a mark of identity and a sign of God's protection. A cervix is in a sense an esoteric part of the body, hidden within, a mystery, the neck of the womb, the channel through which all life emerges. It is purely and uniquely feminine.

In part, this coincidence shows once again that Jewish and Tibetan culture have common historical influences. The six-pointed star originated in ancient Mesopotamia as a symbol of fertility. It did not become a specifically Jewish symbol until the late Middle Ages. The same symbol came into India with the Aryans, where it represented Shakti, the Mother. It entered Tibet along with the teachings of the Hindu tantric tradition.

The shield of David was not always a symbol of Judaism, nor was it always Jewish, nor is it solely Jewish now. Perhaps Judaism can put down its defensive shield and reflect more on its inner mysteries. There, at the heart of revelation, one finds female images of God. That indeed is what the *Zohar* makes explicit in its commentary on the revelation at Sinai. "It was the *Shekhinah* who manifested Herself at the giving of the Law."

The conversation Blu Greenberg had with the Dalai Lama did not touch on these esoteric matters, but she did show the importance of women in preserving Jewish values through family life. The Dalai Lama thanked her for her presentation. He had some questions of his own—actually very familiar questions that Jews often hear from those who know just a little bit about us—flattering questions, though stereotyped. He understood better now how synagogue and the family helped Jews to survive in exile in different countries where there were many obstacles to religious practice. But Jews have done more than merely survive, they have thrived, competed, and excelled. Why, he wanted to know, are Jews leaders in "economy, education, scientific research, and other fields?"

Several answers were offered to this familiar question, though the religious one—that God had blessed the Jewish people—was omitted. Moshe Waldoks stressed that Jews lived on the edge and were risk takers. Zalman Schachter answered with genetics. "The people who are studying and practicing are also marrying and having children." He added pointedly—and I saw Yitz turn red—that "where the best people of the society don't get married, then the factors that contribute to excellence don't get transmitted genetically."

Blu Greenberg thought Jews have excelled in the Diaspora because they are intelligent, a quality she also found among the Tibetans. "All the people we have met this week have such an extremely high level of intelligence and forethought that I kept having this feeling during every conversation, these are just like Jews."

Robert Thurman also commented. "If I can make a suggestion as a Gentile," he said, "there is something very famous in America—the Jewish Mother." Alex Berzin, swept up in a burst of Jewish pride, added that "in Judaism there is great deal of emphasis on the creativity of life and the joy of life. This gives a great inspiration to people to be creative—in education and upbringing, everyone is encouraged to come up with new ideas."

Yitz Greenberg added a footnote, which continued the conversation we'd had after seeing the *kuten*, about the spectra of the two religions. He said one reason for the appeal of modernity at the expense of traditional religions was "that it affirmed life and improved the conditions of life. To the extent that traditional Judaism resisted this, it lost ground."

Therefore, the challenge for modern Judaism is to stress something already in the Torah—the religious significance of daily life—while making sure this emphasis doesn't become a materialism for its own sake. Jews have achieved because they consider secular achievement a religious excellence. Rabbi Greenberg turned the question back to the Dalai Lama. "How would you propose to deal with this? Because in some ways Buddhism, even more than Judaism, has tried to move people beyond their daily lives to a higher plane. But then how do we manage to give religious purpose and achievement to daily life?"

The Dalai Lama found Yitz's question complicated. I suspect this is because we were in an area where the spectra of the two religions did not match up very well. The Torah, with its admixture of homely narrative and specific law, is deeply rooted in daily life, and the Talmud even more so. Because the Jewish covenant was made through a family and a nation, Jewish religion is Jewish culture is Jewish family is Jewish history. In contrast, the Dalai Lama continually stressed a separation between culture and religion, between religion and nationalism, and between religion and daily life.

He mentioned some individuals who concentrate solely on individual practice. "For example, a few practitioners on these mountains," he gestured out the window, "are almost like hermits, completely withdrawn." They spend most of their time on meditation. In that case, he felt that this was one time Chairman Mao Zedong had a point when he compared religion to opium, because if Buddhist faith is utilized in the wrong way, sometimes it could become a hindrance to the development of people.

Therefore, he advises the general Tibetan public to be "half half"; that is, "They should spend only 50 percent of their time on religious practice, and 50 percent on their own life. Because this is concerned with national survival. If every Tibetan went to the mountain [like the hermits], we would starve."

The Buddhist leader made a distinction between long-term and temporary benefits. He said religious practice is necessary for achieving the long-term benefit of nirvana. But to achieve the temporary benefit of worldly life pleasure, it is equally necessary to work. With this distinction in benefits kept in mind, there is no reason to be negative toward worldly progress or development.

"So," Yitz concluded, "you are able to give religious meaning and responsibility to worldly work?"

"Yes," the Dalai Lama answered and explained through Laktor that although usually in presenting religious discourses it was stressed "that in order to be a successful practitioner you have to renounce life, there were other teachings, which lay emphasis on the possibility of combining practice with practical involvement."

Returning us to the original topic, Blu Greenberg wanted to know if there might be a different level of practice for the Tibetan Buddhist family in exile, as opposed to previously?

He thought a moment and said, "I don't know." The Dalai Lama felt it was too soon to tell. He commented that the Tibetans were holding on to their practices because of the Chinese persecution. "The Chinese activities are so negative. So it makes a tremendous reaction."

The Jewish experience was analogous. Yitz Greenberg pointed out that persecution makes a stronger Jew, to which Moshe Waldoks added, "It's a terrible way to be strong."

Rabbi Greenberg rejoined that modern cultures are more difficult to resist, because they are so kind and accepting. "Because of persecution you get stubborn, but when you are kissed and hugged, you relax."

This recalled to Nathan Katz the situation of the Jews in China. "That community went out of existence because the Chinese never practiced discrimination against the Jewish people. The Jewish people would take examinations and enter into the service of the emperor. As a result they vanished."

To which the Dalai Lama, laughing, commented, "That is *ancient* China. Not this."

Robert Thurman made clear that the "Tibetans have not accepted that they will be for long outside of Tibet. So the thought is not how to settle down and survive for, say, five hundred years in exile. They expect to return."

Instead, most of the Dalai Lama's creative thinking has to do with how to change things in Tibet. "He has adopted democracy and a constitution. He told me once he had a very clever, devilish idea—to have monks in monasteries in Tibet learn to make electronic things, to do some kind of skillful production. I can see thousands of monks sitting there making computers in His Holiness' Monastic Computer Factory."

However, if exile would be of a longer duration, the Tibetans would turn their attention to family and then—addressing Blu—"your kind of strategies would be very valuable." Thurman imagined the Dalai Lama composing a poem of grace for lay families to say at meals, or that a book of ceremonies might be published in Dharamsala for families to use in India or Switzerland. "Don't you think?" he asked, turning to the Dalai Lama.

"Yes," he said, and through Laktor added that "for example, His Holiness has composed a prayer called the Word of the Truth, on the fate of the Tibetans, the need for the development of the Tibetan situation, the progress of the dharma."

"When the *geshes* were with us Friday night, they recited this prayer," Zalman noted. Clearly, the Dalai Lama's hope for a brighter day is very strong. He is inspired by Jewish persistence in the face of an unimaginably long exile—nearly two thousand years—but for his own part, he hopes to see the Tibetans return in his lifetime.

Blu had raised the issue of the family very directly, but it was clear from the response that not a great deal of thought had yet gone into it on the Tibetan side. The issues of simple survival are still too pressing.

But at least, through Joy and Blu, the Jews had broached the subject and communicated the importance of family and children to Jewish survival. In the last minutes of our encounter, we also asked for and received a secret of survival from the Dalai Lama. It was a dramatic moment of the exchange.

18

One Last Question

Ever since Saturday night, Nathan Katz had come down with a serious case of the JUBU blues. Despite Zalman's comforting vision of a dancing circle of Jews and JUBUs and Buddhists, Katz still felt troubled. His intense dialogue with Chodron and his respect for her and Alex Berzin made him feel acutely the quality of loss to the Jewish community they represented. He consulted with Yitz and Blu Greenberg. They encouraged him to address his concerns to the Dalai Lama. When Nathan Katz spoke, it was heartfelt, direct, and sincere—a dramatic moment of the dialogue.

In reconnecting with dharma people, Katz was encountering the road not taken. Like Alex Berzin, whom he'd met fifteen years earlier, Nathan had been seriously attracted to Buddhism as an academic and personal path. He had participated in the latest chapter of the fitful history of Buddhism in the West, one in which Jews have played a significant and disproportionate role.

When I started asking why this was so, I heard a lot of stereotypes at first. In Dharamsala, for instance, both Tibetans and Jewish Buddhists assured me that Jews are a highly intelligent group who, therefore, could learn and appreciate the teachings of Buddhism. This struck me as self-serving flattery. Another explanation: Jews tend to be affluent and "dharma is a rich man's game." A third is that Jews are "spiritually minded people." These stereotypes don't run very deep. After all, there are plenty of intelligent, affluent, and spiritually minded *goyim* running around.

I offered myself the consolation that in raw numbers, at least, the loss to the Jewish people is not great. But then again, since fewer than 5 percent of American Jews define themselves at all religiously, Jewish Buddhists do represent an abnormally large percentage of a precious pool of energetic, talented, and spiritually committed Jews.

To Moshe Waldoks, the loss is very real. He told me, "People who have a good experience from a meditative life or the life of insight have a lot to offer to the Jewish community. We have done so little to develop that side of life. It's a double loss. Not only are these people not part of the Jewish community, but all they've learned they're not giving back."

But though Nathan Katz had come back to Judaism, he knew most other Jewish Buddhists wouldn't. So when he turned to face the Dalai Lama, after Blu's presentation on Jewish family, this loss was on his mind.

"Your Holiness," he began, "this is not an easy point to raise. But in this dialogue, which we take so much to heart, we must be totally frank about our feelings. There is one issue, in terms of relations between our peoples, that for some of us causes pain.

"You see our sense of family. We are connected to each other in very deep ways. And when someone might leave our family, we feel pain. I can see very clearly that Jewish people who adopt the Tibetan path benefit greatly as individuals. Their practices, their peace, their intellect, are elevated greatly.

"But we suffer something of a brain drain. Because, as Rabbi Omer-Man was saying, our mystical esoteric teachings are not so accessible—and that's our fault—many of our finest people are leaving our family.

"I have no question. I have no request. But this issue is in the heart of everyone in the delegation. I know it's in my heart, and with the encouragement of my co-religionists, I felt compelled to put this issue before you."

The Dalai Lama listened quite intently and paused to reflect. The room grew quiet—I could hear the magpies whistling outside.

"According to the Buddhist tradition," he began, "there is no sort of conversion or missionary work. It is not good to ask someone to follow a different faith. Yet, because there are so many different mental dispositions, one religion simply cannot serve, cannot satisfy all people.

"Religion knows no national boundary. For example, among Tibetans, the majority are Buddhist, but nobody says, 'Since you are Tibetan, you should be Buddhist.'

"Likewise, among the millions and millions of Westerners, a few find Buddhist teachings more suitable" than Judaism or Christianity. "So when someone comes to us to learn Tibetan Buddhism, then we consider it our responsibility to explain—that's our basic attitude. . . . Since Tibetan culture and Buddhism are two separate things, I feel also that some Jewish people remain mainly attached to Jewish culture, heritage, while their personal religion could be Buddhism or some other religion.

"Since you told me we are family," he said, looking to Nathan, who nodded in agreement "the response should be very frank, no?" The Jewish delegates agreed.

The Dalai Lama felt he understood from Paul Mendes-Flohr's presentation on secular Jews that it is possible to keep the Jewish tradition as a culture without necessarily being a believer. "So, among the Jewish community there are several millions. If some of them are attracted to Buddhism, we cannot stop it. Among Tibetans, also, some are taking an interest in new religions. We cannot stop it. No use in stopping it."

Though expressed in necessarily simple diction, I thought the Dalai Lama was offering us a very sophisticated, and very Buddhist, take on the problem. In the long run, tolerance and maintaining contacts are more likely to keep Jews connected to other Jews than rejection or guilt-mongering. I wondered, though, if many rabbis or committed Jews would be able to restrain themselves and follow this helpful advice.

Rabbi Greenberg, for one, thought that the Dalai Lama's response made a lot of sense. But he also suggested that when a Jewish student comes seeking, "Say to them that their first search should be to discover the depth or significance of their birth religion—and that even this spiritual discipline you open up for them might well be found in their own tradition." This is the traditional Jewish attitude toward converts—to refuse them at first and only respond if the request is repeated.

The Dalai Lama answered, "I do like that. In my public teaching I always tell people who are interested that changing religions is not an easy task. So therefore it's better not to change, better to follow one's own traditional religion, since basically the same message, the same potential is there." Further, after a conversion, "there is no point in looking negatively toward your previous religion." As for a nonbeliever or "extreme atheist"—the Dalai Lama said he uses that term because "sometimes people call Buddhism also a kind of atheism"—for such people, "taking a new religion doesn't matter."

Michael Sautman, who had up to now mainly served as an MC, felt the urge to speak.

"Your Holiness," Michael said, glancing quickly at his parents, "as someone who this issue might be directed to, let me just say, and maybe Alex Berzin might agree, that although the fruit of our religious activities might lie within the Buddha dharma, the roots of our tradition and heritage will always lie with the Jewish people. So in that way I don't think there is any worry."

Robert Thurman agreed. Raised a secularist Protestant, he felt that if his Buddhist teachers had told him go back to his church first and ask them three times how to meditate, "I would have been just annoyed." But through years of studying Buddhism, "I finally found a way to appreciate Christianity, and His Holiness is actually my best Christian teacher—though I didn't convert back." Thurman felt that "it may be impossible to lose someone. If they convert to being a good human being through whatever process, you haven't lost them in the real sense that counts."

Marc Lieberman spoke up next. He summarized the results of the dialogue as raising the level of Jewish awareness about Tibetans. He promised action on plans for an academic exchange, so that Tibetans could learn about Judaism formally, and on bringing Tibetan observers to Jewish summer camps. He saw the meetings with Jewish Buddhists as "a challenge to prepare the ground in the Jewish community so that spirituality will be recognized and appreciated." He hoped "some of these wonderful Western Buddhists will take the bodhisattva vow very specifically and help their co-religionists learn new spiritual pathways in the Jewish path so that spiritual renewal can go on from both directions." Then he thanked the Dalai Lama for being a gracious host.

But the Dalai Lama was still thinking about Nathan's question. "I have something more to say." He explained that among those who follow various different religions, there are two types, or two levels. The first follows mainly with faith, "not much is questioned. They say, my family background is in such and such religious faith, so I take this faith without much question." The second, skeptical type asks more questions and carries out research and experiment. He or she will do the meditations or try the prayers, or observe whatever rules the religion requires. But the skeptic will only accept the faith if that person finds some benefit from its practices. If in the course of study or experiment such skeptics do not find the religion satisfying in their lives, then they will reject that religion.

The Dalai Lama explained that from the Buddhist viewpoint, unquestioning faith is not very profound. "The second is much better. So generally the Buddhist approach is first to be skeptical and examine and find some meaning, some answer to your own life, your own problems." Only then is it worthwhile to accept a religion.

In other words, try it, and only stick with it if you like it. I found this empirical approach very attractive. It harmonizes well with the scientific spirit. Also, Buddhism offers portions of its practices and teachings for a person to experiment with. You do not have to believe in Buddha or Buddhism to meditate on the breath—you merely have to give it a try. This is the charm of Buddhism's open door.

Now the Dalai Lama offered the Jews advice. Open the doors and open them wide. In learning about Jewish mystical teachings, he confessed that he had "developed more respect toward Judaism because I found much sophistication there." He thought that what he had learned about the four levels of interpretation and Jewish meditation is very important and should be made available for everyone, especially to the sharp-minded. He gave a parallel from Buddhist history. Like kabbalah, traditionally Buddhist tantra as taught in India had been very secretive, very confidential, and given only very selectively to very few students. "Public teaching never happened." But if there is too much secrecy, sometimes there is a danger that the tradition will discontinue and that many qualified persons will miss the teaching and the practice.

Therefore, when Buddhist tantra later came to Tibet, the teaching became more flexible and available. He advised the Jewish group to adopt the same flexible attitude and avoid too much secrecy about esoteric teachings.

"As I mentioned earlier, during Rabbi Omer-Man's presentation, I found many similarities between kabbalah and tantra. If that is the case, then why would your people want Buddhist tantra?" He smiled at Zalman, teasing him, "You yourself say you have your own tantra!"

"Then a second thing," he said. "I myself have tried to openly accept that all different religions have some value. At the same time, I always think that other people also should be open." He did not think it good to force someone to follow a religion. "Although your motivation may be sincere, the result may not be positive if you limit the right to choose and explore." Again, referring now to Zalman Schachter's presentation, "Provide them all the material of the four spiritual realms. If despite that, someone is still attracted to a different religion, then they are right. This is my experience."

Now he turned to address Yitz Greenberg. "Previously we referred to more traditional, more conservative ways. And you said modernity creates new problems. Due to that, if we try to isolate ourselves from modernity, this is self-destruction. You have to face reality. If you have reason, sufficient reason to practice a religion, sufficient value in that religion, there is no need to fear. If you have no sufficient reason, no value—then there's no need to hold on to it. Really. I feel that." He added that if a faith cannot provide satisfaction for someone, to insist on that person holding on to it is foolish.

"So you see, the time is changing. Nobody can stop it. Whether God created it—or nature is behind it, nobody knows. It is fact, it is reality. So we have to follow the time, and live according to reality. What we need, ourselves, as religious leaders, is to do more research, find more practices to make tradition something more beneficial in today's life" and more open to people. "Then they will choose which is more valuable, more useful." Either the modernity of the secular world or else traditional teachings.

The session ended with Rabbi Levitt leading us in a traditional prayer for "our teachers and their students"—with one phrase amended to "for those who study Torah Dharma." The Dalai Lama and his fellow monks offered a brief dedication. Then we waited in line as he received each of us individually for a last farewell. I was just brimming with emotion.

I'd come to Dharamsala as one of the skeptics the Dalai Lama referred to: a cultural Jew, a Jew by birth, though very fierce about it, even angry. As I found in the Frankfurt airport, nervous was my religion, nervous and defensive.

In Dharamsala I encountered a holy community that lived in horror of the expression of anger. Formerly, I would have associated this with emasculation. I would have considered such people to be lobotomized zombies with fake smiles. In my thinking, anger was an essential part of a natural person. It was, as Blu had put it, realistic.

But the monks I met were witty, had a sense of humor—and an enormous clarity. Laktor, who'd spent some time in Israel, joked around with me and, because of the Indiana Jones hat I wore, called me "cowboy." My parting gift to him was a red yarmulke that matched his monk's robe perfectly. I also valued Karma Gelek's wry and very dry sense of humor, his patience and calm when we were confused and worried.

The lamas I spoke to on Friday night were shining—the sweet, wise old men in robes one dreams about, but never imagines meeting. I especially remember Geshe Sonam's dignity and warmth. The Western Buddhists, such as Alex Berzin or Thubten Chodron, were impressive in their own right. Despite my initial prejudices, I saw they had not lost their strength or personality through Buddhist practice. I found them to be very creative, intelligent, engaged human beings with distinctive personalities. The loss of anger had not meant loss of personality, but liberation and clear thinking.

As the Dalai Lama suggested, to a skeptic, results speak for themselves. I had in the past encountered enthusiasts in various cults and self-help groups and had come away from the encounter with my initial skepticism undimmed. But these encounters in Dharamsala were different. I knew nothing about techniques of meditation. But I could see that this stuff worked. These people and the community they shared had succeeded, largely, in overcoming a demon I had struggled with in vain. They did not make anger, or any other emotion, the boss of their lives. As the late Geshe Khenrab, a lama from Montreal whom I met later, once told me, "You doubt everything else. Why not doubt anger?" That is a beautiful challenge that expresses in brief the Buddhist perspective.

The Dalai Lama is leading his people through their most difficult period in history, in a situation where anger is a very predictable response. So how he handles anger is not just a personal, but a political challenge. After being driven into exile along with 115,000 of his countrymen, after years of reports of torture and destruction in his homeland, after fruitless and frustrating negotiations with the perpetrators, after being relentlessly hounded all over the world by the Chinese government, that he could still refer to the Chinese as his "so-called enemy" and "the external factor" is a rare and inspiring example of a religious perspective carried over into the political world of conflict and violence. My only prayer is that somehow, against all odds, with this stance he will succeed in freeing Tibet.

At the personal level, I had said that in observing the Dalai Lama, I went in the spirit of the Hasidic student who wanted to see how the master tied his shoes. At the end, I knew I had. His presence from moment to moment was a constant teaching. His ready humor, his wit, his engagement with ideas, his deep receptivity—his simple ability to stop for a moment and take things in—were all elements of his power.

I learned that humility can be powerful, that receptivity can be dominating, and that kindness can be challenging. I learned the power of what the Buddhists call "a quiet mind."

For Tibetan Buddhists, the Dalai Lama is an aspect of the Bodhisattva of Compassion, a being with extraordinary knowledge and power, who can see you not only in this life but in your previous ones. Though I do not believe this personally, I still felt a power in his glance.

So often we say about someone, he's not worth a glance. This was the opposite—a benevolent feeling that each individual is worth a very deep regard. It was kindness, but almost a scientific kindness, like a doctor's light shining into your eyes. So strong, that at the first session, when I saw him face to face, I turned away. This time, I promised myself I would meet his eyes. As my turn approached, I heard him laughing. He was shaking a Purim *grager* Paul Mendes-Flohr had given him. He was completely open, eager for any new experience. Charlie Halpern, from the Nathan Cummings Foundation, was next ahead of me. He bowed slightly to the Dalai Lama and smiled—very suave and New York in his demeanor. But not me. I stooped down to look into the Dalai Lama's eyes and to have his eyes search mine.

There is a beautiful Hasidic teaching, that before every human being comes a retinue of angels, announcing, "Make way for an image of the Holy One, Blessed be He." How rarely do we listen for those angels when we encounter another human being. How rarely do we see in another human being's eyes an image of everything we hold most dear.

For the Tibetans perhaps, and for many Western Buddhists, the Dalai Lama's powers are magical and other-worldly, but I found they were even more beautiful for being so human and closer at hand.

The Dalai Lama laughed and grabbed me by the shoulder. In that brief moment, he'd understood what I was after—a deeper human contact—and he had given it. But he had given that to each of us.

Especially, in response to Nathan Katz's question, the Dalai Lama had offered Jews extraordinary advice—and a challenge. Could we make Judaism more beneficial—instead of just asking Jews to hold on out of guilt?

For some it reinforced the work they were already doing, such as Rabbi Greenberg's efforts to promote Jewish unity through dialogue, Zalman Schachter's work for Jewish renewal, and Rabbi Omer-Man's school of Jewish meditation. For others, such as Rabbi Levitt, it was a challenge to rethink the role of spirituality and the esoteric in the synagogue and Jewish community. Paul Mendes-Flohr came away with an increased awareness of the roots of group anger in individual consciousness.

As for Professor Katz, he was thrilled by the Dalai Lama's response. To Nathan, "Being Jewish means to struggle against either enemies who threaten you with gentleness or harshness, with persecution or assimilation. Unless you feel you're called to be Jewish, or that karma works and you're supposed to be Jewish, unless you feel that deeply, the system doesn't work very well.

"I can very well understand people who say I'd rather cash in my chips, drop my Jewishness, and assimilate with society at large. The danger is, if we don't transmit to people the utter joy and transcendence the tradition offers, if we transmit to them only that you should be on guard all the time, then we are going to lose them. The danger is failing to transmit the beauty, the joy, the profundity. If we fail to do that, that's what the Dalai Lama told us, then we're not going to survive."

"Then that was the secret he gave back to us?" I asked him.

"Yes. To me that was the moment. If you have nothing to offer them, there's no sense holding on to them. And if you have something to offer them, there's no reason for them to leave. Boy, does every Jew in the world need to hear that."

19

A Buddhist Jew— The Allen Ginsberg Story

The dialogue with the Dalai Lama gave me a glimpse of what Judaism might be, but my conversation with JUBUs in America after my return told me about the Judaism they'd encountered. They weren't very happy about it, and Allen Ginsberg especially.

As the main spokesperson of the Beat generation, Ginsberg had been an early herald of the whole opening up of consciousness that led many Jews in the 1960s and 1970s to explore Eastern religions. So I asked the poet to tell the story of his own personal spiritual quest and how it led him ultimately to Tibetan Buddhism. On the surface, his turn to Buddhism might be seen as a surprising development. After all, when Ginsberg emerged into public attention in 1956, he was widely seen as a Jewish poet. His great energetic poem "Howl" burst on the scene as an outrageous, angry, and powerful social statement, in the mode of the Hebrew prophets.

And in his next major work, "Kaddish," Ginsberg sought explicitly Jewish language for his deepest emotional experiences. There is a poignant anecdote told about his searching for a synagogue to say kaddish for his mother upon learning of her death. It says a lot to me that this was his primary impulse at that time—and it's certainly not uncommon for highly secular Jews, undergoing bereavement, to turn back to religious forms and observances they otherwise have rejected.

The poem, one of his most deeply moving, not only uses the kaddish as its framework but also employs the rhythm of the ancient Aramaic prayer to undergird its sound.

YIS-bo-RACH v'YISH-tab-BACH, v'YIS-po-AR, v'Yis-ro-MAM,
   v'YIS-nas-SEH . . .
MagNIFiCENT, MOURNED no MORE, MARRED of HEART,
   MIND beHIND, MARried DREAMED, MORtal CHANGED . . .

This shows a deep assimilation of Jewish religious experience in spite of Ginsberg's own self-declared identity as a "delicatessen intellectual." They don't say kaddish in the delicatessen.

In general, Ginsberg definitely fits the prophetic Hebrew modes: the angry prophet demanding society's attention and denouncing its hypocrisies—whether the issue is the CIA or nuclear waste; the anguished prophet keening and mourning for lost Edens of kindness and brotherly love; and the comic prophet exploding with humor and rage. He has been crucial in opening up our awareness of human suffering and bringing to focus those previously at the margins—and I see this activity as well in the prophetic tradition.

Again, like some of the prophets, such as Isaiah and Ezekiel, Ginsberg sought and cultivated visionary experiences. He saw visions. He heard voices. And he clung to these visions with tremendous courage and at high personal cost. Because, in our society, to be obsessed with a vision about how to make a better automobile makes you a genius, but to be obsessed with a vision about the nature of reality makes you a nut.

In the avant-garde literary circles of his time, such prophetic obsessions were viewed, at best, wryly. In a 1959 poem, the essential New York poet Frank O'Hara has a line, "And Allen's back in town talking about god a lot."

The actual visionary event has been retold many times by Ginsberg. It took place in a tenement building in Harlem in 1948. He heard the voice of the English mystical poet, William Blake, and saw a tremendous order, coherence, purposiveness—intentionality—in the universe. The vision unsettled him, especially since, at the time, Ginsberg's mother, Naomi, had been recently hospitalized for paranoid delusions.

He went around to leading intellectual and literary figures recounting his vision. He was advised to see a psychiatrist. The vision itself did not return. In part to recapture it, Ginsberg experimented repeatedly with LSD. All he had to show for himself after a string of bad acid trips was a bad case of writer's block. So, in 1962 he traveled to the East, looking for a language, "babbling to all the holy men I could find about consciousness expansion."

But the first holy man he babbled to was Martin Buber. On the way to India, he stopped off in Jerusalem and asked the great Jewish thinker how to handle bad acid trips. "He had a beautiful white beard and was friendly; his nature was slightly austere but benevolent." As a result of taking drugs, Ginsberg had been frightened by a nightmare vision of writhing insect forms in a nonhuman universe. As Ginsberg recounted it to me in 1992, "Buber said, 'Mark my words young man, our business is with the human, not the nonhuman. You'll remember my words years from hence.'"

Since Buber was a leading authority on the wisdom of the Hasidim, it's possible to conceive that this answer might have been satisfying, and the encounter might have led Ginsberg toward exploring Hasidism and Jewish mystical texts. Based on his poetry and his whole approach to life, Ginsberg's natural spiritual home would appear to be Jewish. But although Ginsberg did mark Buber's words, he told me—"That was a very good answer, but it wasn't quite good enough. It didn't explain the experience. I wanted to see how to absorb it and integrate it.

"Whereas the Buddhist view from Dudjom Rinpoche, in that same year, 1963, was if you see something horrible, don't cling to it. If you see something beautiful, don't cling to it. In a sense Buber was saying cling to a certain aspect of life."

Ginsberg now feels he "fell into a theistic trap because I couldn't find any words for it, so I began to refer to it as a divine vision or God and so forth, but that solidified the experience into a concept, and once it became a concept I became very totalitarian about it and aggressive and nuts."

As a result, Ginsberg continues to be critical, even vituperative, about Jewish religious language—what he calls "Jehovic" conceptions, feeling that "sooner or later, where you have the Jewish thing, one tries to sneak in a central intelligence agency . . . a central divinity" and this leads to spiritual and political problems.

Here is where the crux of the JUBUs' quarrel with Judaism comes in: the language about God. Because within Judaism there's certainly plenty of authoritarian, masculine, and even paranoid language: God is a father, God is a king, God is a source of wrath and punishment—there's plenty to back up Ginsberg's claim about "the Jewish thing."

It's fascinating, then, that had Ginsberg explored Hasidism, he would have encountered a very different language about God, one that would have been far less likely to have made him "aggressive and nuts."

In fact, in that same seminal summer at Naropa, 1974, he came very close to encountering it, in the person of Zalman Schachter, who was also teaching there.

Zalman's father died that summer, and being rather isolated—as the only religious Jew on the faculty—he asked Ginsberg to help him organize a minyan, so he could recite kaddish. And remembering the power of Ginsberg's own "Kaddish," he asked the poet to read Psalm 49. The whole experience in Boulder was deeply moving to Zalman—he told me Ginsberg read the psalm as if he'd written it himself.

And at that emotional moment, gathered around him were all the Jews who were teaching there—"out of the woodwork," Zalman described it: Joseph Goldstein, Jack Kornfield, and others. It hit Zalman with tremendous force how Jews and Buddhists might learn a common language.

As Zalman tells it, "I said the kaddish and then we said *aleinu* [prayers of reverence]. In the middle of *aleinu* it was like lightning hit me. There's a line that goes, 'For they bow down to emptiness and void and we bow down to the king of kings, the holy one blessed be he.' Now usually it means, they bow down to *gornisht mit gornisht* [Yiddish: nothing with nothing], emptiness, void, stupid . . . But *there*, I read it: They bow down to Emptiness . . . and Void . . . and we bow down to the King of kings . . . and both of these are legitimate ways. You can imagine how that hit me. That's a story I tell people who are involved in Buddhism. If you do meditation and you see deep in meditation what this is all about, you see that emptiness and void is just one look and king of kings is the other look."

I know from our conversations that Allen Ginsberg would not agree. *King of kings* could lead to a real ego trip. *King of kings* is a look that has also put off many Jewish women, who simply cannot identify with the male imagery. And underlying these spiritual struggles is a deep Jewish family problem: women and homosexuals often feel excluded from Jewish spiritual life.

What Zalman's anecdote does tell me is that, at least theoretically, Ginsberg might have found answers within a Jewish context. Because Jewish prayer and Buddhist meditation can both be seen as visualizations. Just as a tantric Buddhist might contemplate an image of a deity, so a Jew in deep prayer might contemplate the image of king of kings. But in the depth of that contemplation, one is not identifying one's ego with the divinity: this is a key point.

Jonathan Omer-Man had already insisted on this in his conversation with me about sexuality in Jewish mysticism. If one comes to the sexual experience as an ego, then the identification with God and *Shekhinah* is dangerous.

Likewise in regard to king of kings: Here is where Jonathan Omer-Man's explanation of thought transformation through Hasidic prayer fits in. He had explained to the Dalai Lama his own path as *keter malkhut*, the crown of sovereignty—an intense meditation on the kingly nature of God. But king does not mean boss—the janitor sweeping the floor could be on the path.

The Jewish mystical encounter with God is definitely not supposed to be an ego trip. That's why in fact the path requires very careful preparation, and very careful training, and a specific teacher. It isn't something you do on your own, or do out of a book. If an experience of closeness to God makes you egotistical and angry, then you aren't doing it right, at least as the Hasidim describe it.

More than a century ago, the Hasidim had struggled with Ginsberg's problem of "totalitarian" ego. They'd written treatises about it. One of the most influential was written by Dov Baer of Lubavitch, the son of Reb Shneur Zalman, the founder of Lubavitch Hasidism.

In his tract on ecstasy (*Qunteros Ha-Hithpa'aluth*), Dov Baer describes the problem of the ego—what he calls the *yesh*—the "thereness" of the human self and of the material world in general. The higher one rises in contemplation, the more the *yesh* dissolves. One becomes transparent through clinging to God. The closer one gets—through prayer, meditation, and vision—the less ego one has. The highest level is only reached when the *yesh* has been utterly dissolved, a process known as "the losing of self in the divine *ayin*, the divine Nothingness."

In Zalman's language, the king of kings is one look, and emptiness and nothing is another look. They are in fact the same look, and the paradox of the highest Jewish contemplation is that the closer one gets to an experience of unity with God, the less relevant the traditional images and languages become. The imagery of father, king, and judge that so deeply concern many JUBUs—and obviously create a barrier—dissolve in the contemplation.

But Ginsberg looked to Buddhism for his answers. Back in 1962, the Tibetan *dzog chen* master Dudjom Rinpoche had advised Ginsberg not to cling to visions, whether horrible or beautiful. Instead, as Ginsberg explained it, "the Buddhist notion is not to look for a vision. In ordinary mind, you don't collect experiences, you don't collect visions. If they come, you let go of them. There's no sense cultivating them."

Today Ginsberg no longer regards his Blake experience, which once so preoccupied him, as a vision. Rather, "as time goes by it seems more like it came from within me as a projection of my own." He finds a helpful analogy in the Buddhist concept of deity. "In most Buddhist practice if you have a *deva* or a *yidam* or a meditation divinity, it begins with emptiness meditation, and you visualize the divinity in practices and then you dissolve it into yourself—dissolve the divinity completely and go back to *shunyata*, so there's a built-in definition that this is a creation of your own imagination, that it does not exist outside your own projection. Whereas there doesn't seem to be that built-in security system against sneaking in an external deity in the Judeo-Christian-Islamic tradition."

Ironically, as mentioned, there *is* such a built-in security system, certainly in the Hasidic tradition, and also in the great mystical traditions of Christianity and Islam.

I don't say that Ginsberg should have known this. Given the situation of Judaism, I don't blame him or anyone for looking elsewhere at the time. I am not mad at people for leaving the fold—they are perhaps the scouts for the big anthill of Judaism.

But in the long run, there is no need for anger on the scouts' part either. And I think it arrogant for JUBUs to assume that Judaism is somehow inherently inferior to other religions. I just don't buy that. If there'd been a brief pause in persecuting and murdering Jews in history, maybe I would look at it differently. But our picture of Judaism today, fifty years after the Holocaust, is just that—a picture. Judaism is so old and has so many contradictory currents and elements that two things can be said: it is likely to survive, and it is unlikely to survive in its present form. So the question is, what shape will it take as we move forward, post-Holocaust and with a modern state of Israel?

I have a sense that everything happened for the best, that it was necessary for some Jews, led by Ginsberg and others, to seek answers where they were available in a language, and in a setting they found compelling. The Hasidim represented everything Ginsberg's family in particular had run screaming from for two generations. It would have been absurd to say to him, "Look, you've got it wrong. Leave your apartment on Fourth Street and go to a Lubavitcher Hasid and he will explain *Tanya* and Dov Baer's tract on ecstasy to you. Sit in a yeshiva and learn Hebrew, daven with us, and it will all come clear to you."

Ginsberg and the other JUBUs were starving, and the Buddhists fed them. So there is no point in Jews being angry about it.

My hope is that perhaps some day he and others will see there's also no point in being contemptuous of or angry at Jews, Judaism, or God. If nothing else, Buddhist practice should tell us that.

But the issue today is different. The job for Judaism is to make sure that the very powerful esoteric language of Judaism does become more widely available—so that when the next strong wave of spirituality occurs among Jews, it takes place *within* Judaism. This, in essence, is what the Dalai Lama told us when he advised us to open the doors of our esoteric teachings.

As my conversation with the poet makes clear, this represents a formidable problem of translation. And a major task of Jewish renewal.

20

A Synagogue in Delhi

MONDAY, OCTOBER 29, 1990—DHARAMSALA—
TUESDAY, OCTOBER 30, 1990, DELHI

At three in the morning I woke to the sound of our broken tire rapping against the curb. Our cars clumped together—and a tired collection of Jews milled around disconsolately in a small Punjabi town, which came increasingly alive as we loitered. First some figures rose from cots on the shoulder—a string-bed motel where they'd been sleeping. Then a car repair shop opened—or had it ever closed?—followed by an outdoor restaurant. While our flat was fixed, some flat bread was patted on a stove, *chai* was served, sweet with cloves, anesthetizing lips and tongue.

Zalman and Jonathan had been nonstop yakking Jewish and Buddhist metaphysics, trailing a bright stream through the Punjab. I worried about beating the curfew. After our repair, our car lost touch with the caravan. In Harayana, we entered a low white fog, thick as wool. Mr. Singh pressed ahead, guided by Sikh internal radar. I fell asleep, woke with a jolt to the sway of the vehicle. The windshield filled with the cab of a giant truck. I heard *Shema* muttered in the back seat. My life was over. Mr. Singh swerved into oblivion and the moment passed. I blinked and fell asleep. We stopped again just outside of Delhi. Tire trouble again. Mr. Singh went for help. I unfolded my body. I watched an old harijan, wrapped in a long white rag like a winding cloth, shoveling a house-high heap of manure into an ox cart with the side of his bare foot, a ghost worker in hell.

It was the hour of the metaphysical hangover, the descent from the holy mountain to the world of dung.

Singh patched the flat and we rolled away, my head pounding, my belly full of phlegm, my eyes bleared and sandy. I muttered OM MANI PADME HUM to the rhythm of the throbbing veins in my temples. The jewel in the lotus. The Jew in the lotus. I babbled the *Shema* and felt for the little orange barley seeds in my pocket. I was a living confusion, a messy dialogue. But I had no use for talking. The car was silent as we rolled into Delhi. The fog lifted in tatters with the first gray sun. We'd beaten the curfew, though as we turned toward Connaught Circle and our hotel, I saw a truckload of men all dressed in white tunics and caps, packed tightly against the slats of an open truck, *kar sevaks*—Hindu fundamentalists—on their way to Ayodha. That day there would be several more deaths in the ancient battle between Allah and Ram.

We'd left the bright hopes of dialogue behind in Dharamsala. That was the dream, and the intent eyes of the fundamentalists were the reality. These eyes were Hindu, but I'd seen Jews, Muslims, and Christians with that same fixed stare. The light changed. Their truck lurched away.

We'd left Dharamsala in a rush. At Kashmir Cottage, Chodron and Alex Berzin said good-bye and exchanged addresses; Richard Gere had left the afternoon before. We had tried to be cool around him all week. But at the last moment, the Greenbergs persuaded the actor to pose for a farewell snapshot. We all came running, waving our cameras. Gere took one look and bolted. He seemed to have very long legs.

We had a more dignified farewell with Rinchen-la, thanking her for her hospitality with a small gift. In the fumes of Delhi, I recalled the rose gardens around Kashmir Cottage and our time there with Laktor, Karma Gelek, and the Western Buddhists as a sacred precinct of a brighter, greener world.

But there were sacred precincts in Delhi too, as I would find out the next morning.

I saw Ram Dass in the hotel lobby, dressed in white pants and sandals. The old shaggy beard was gone; he looked like a retired tennis star, very handsome and trim, with short white hair and blue eyes. I remembered him from my college years as Richard Alpert, a Harvard professor fired, along with Timothy Leary, for his experiments with LSD. After that he went to India, studied with a guru, and became one himself. He wrote a bestselling book—*Be Here Now*—and more since then. I'd lost track of his spiritual evolutions, so my first question was, "What religion do you follow these days?"

"I worship a monkey."

I laughed—though I was a little taken aback, as I suspect he wanted me to be. He explained that the monkey in question, Hanuman, is a servant to Ram, and that his devotees likewise stress service to others. Specifically, Ram Dass helped start the Seva Foundation, which funds charitable projects in South India. Now this Jewish Hindu was on his way to Dharamsala to meet with the Dalai Lama, another dancer in the circle Zalman had visualized for us Saturday night. Strangely, the next time I would see him would be in shul.

Zalman, Nathan, Blu, and I left the hotel with our driver, Ran, a tall Sikh in a blue turban. We headed for the shrine of Nizamuddin Auliya, a fourteenth-century Sufi saint.

Nizamuddin is credited with attracting many Hindu followers to Islam with his gentle ideals of "all-embracing love and great affection for the poor and needy." Today his shrine is the Sufi Jewish Community Center and Associated for a very poor section of town, with a mosque, public kitchen, and bath.

Ran parked at the end of a narrow street, and we threaded our way through a crowded bazaar where merchants sell carpets, tapestries, books, and religious items. A row of goats perched on the mud wall that lined one side of the street. Children enjoyed a hand-cranked ferris wheel, a four-seater. Threading through a maze of indoor booths, I purchased garlands of orange geraniums and rose petals wrapped in a broad leaf. The custom of visiting Sufi saints' tombs is widespread in India. Miraculous powers are said to reside near the bones of the holy dead. Some Sufi saints cure leprosy, others the bites of mad dogs. Dust from another tomb is sprinkled on the foreheads of schoolchildren to lift their IQs. For most, the shrines provide a moment of intense communion with a spirit still held to be alive. But we Jews have the same custom. In Tiberias, I'd once visited the grave of the Rambam, Rabbi Moses Maimonides, a dazzlingly white loaf of cement. In the Talmud, it is said that on fast days people go to the graveyard and ask the holy dead to pray on their behalf. The whole notion of saints (in Hebrew, *hasidim*) is not much thought of in mainstream Judaism. But in Meron, near Safed, at Lag B'omer, Sephardim, kabbalists, and Hasidim make an annual pilgrimage to the tomb of the holy rabbi Shimon bar Yochai, the reputed author of the *Zohar*.

So with some sense of familiarity, and wearing newly acquired Muslim yarmulkes, we removed our shoes at the threshold to an open courtyard. I was embarrassed to find holes in my socks. Near the marble edifice of the saint's tomb, we were greeted by the *duago*, or caretaker, Haji Mubarak Nizami, who later would write to me for contributions in a charmingly obscure letter, asking for help during "Ramzan" for the "large number of saints, Durwaishes, Devotees and poors" who gather at the dargah "from and near to offer prayers."

When we reentered the teeming bazaar, Blu got into a price dispute with a Muslim yarmulke vendor. In the joy of haggling, which Jews and Muslims share, she didn't notice the crowd she was drawing. I took her by the arm and as we rushed to our car, we were mobbed. We slammed the doors shut as Ran gunned the engine and the beggars beat their palms on the sides of the car. Now I knew how Richard Gere felt.

Nathan Katz had worried with some affection about exposing Blu to the raw poverty of this poor section of Delhi. Personally, on that day of unrest, I just didn't want to get killed. A Jew could get in trouble in the Muslim part of town. Later we would visit the grave of one who had.

But there were also peaceful precincts to be found. Zalman led us to the nearby shrine of Hazrat Inayat Khan, a contemporary structure of clean white marble oblongs and traceried latticework. As we entered, an ancient doorkeeper in a filthy white tunic and his young granddaughter, holding her little baby brother, stared at us with beautiful, solemn, intense eyes and said not a word.

In 1926, the year before his death, Inayat Khan brought Sufism to the West. A musician and prolific poet, his poems praising God, Allah, Christ, Ram, Krishna, and Buddha covered the far wall, welcoming all.

I felt very welcome in this syncretic shrine. I personally appreciate any religion that honors poetry. Also, the simplicity of the architecture and its harmony with nature was powerful. A flourishing tree that had long grown near the tomb pierced the roof, adding a lively green touch. Inayat Khan's tomb was profligate with flowers and I heaped on a few more garlands.

That morning, Zalman and Nathan had davened in their hotel with *tefillin*. But Rabbi Schachter told Nathan to stop before *Shema*, and Nathan knew Reb Zalman had something special in mind now. He asked Nathan and me to join hands with him, and this expert in davenology led us in chanting a familiar prayer. (In English, "The Lord is King, the Lord was King, the Lord will be King, forever and ever.") We repeated it in the style of Sufi *dhikr* and, following Zalman, tossed our heads in the four directions of time: left—the past, right—the present, down—the future, and for eternity—lifted high. The three of us became an elaborate human prayer machine—an organic vehicle, a chariot, chanting until our necks were loose and our spirits light. It was about joy finally, the practice behind Zalman's theory of four worlds, uniting the motions of the body, the words of the mouth, and the meditations of the heart. Especially with Blu there, even with her standing apart as a witness, it seemed we all had come a long way together since the evening in Karnal when Zalman had davened in a Sikh temple.

Blu had been deeply moved by Dharamsala. She now felt sufficiently relaxed that she could have integrity as an Orthodox Jew but still understand the joy of other religions. Though still guarding her traditional boundaries, she understood "those boundaries were a little larger" than she had come to India thinking.

To Nathan, our prayer in Inayat Khan's dargha was a meditation. In our freshly purchased, white, lacy Muslim yarmulkes, I thought so too. There was nothing in our prayer a Muslim could not affirm. With so much pain between Jews and Muslims in recent years, I felt a certain release now. I saw as I left the precincts of the dargha that the sculpture on the outer wall was a heart with wings . . .

So there was my Jewish predicament in a nutshell: one minute, fear and paranoia, mobbed in a Muslim marketplace; the next, praying Jewish Sufi *dhikr*. But my depression of the day before was lifting, I was coming up on the side of hope. Maybe our encounter with the Dalai

Lama could provide a model for a dialogue between Jews and Muslims. During our visit, the Dalai Lama reaffirmed to Michael Sautman his long-held desire to come to Jerusalem to convene a world conference of religions. That would be a dialogue of dialogues.

Since our trip to India, Zalman Schachter, at a gathering sponsored by the Jewish renewal group, P'nai Or, has made public several practical proposals for increasing dialogue with Muslims.

He mentioned a custom of Jews in Arab lands of providing their neighbors a meal at *Eid al Fidr* at the end of the Muslim fast at Ramadan. He described a *bris* where Muslims were invited as honored guests. Since both groups share the rite of circumcision, this would be a good point of contact.

There is an ancient dialogue between Islam and Judaism, but we have forgotten it in the West. For six centuries, Jews and Muslims interacted, and the tenth to twelfth centuries marked a Golden Age for Jews in Muslim Spain, which some have compared to the situation for Jews in America today. In that period, Jewish religion and culture flourished under unusually tolerant Muslim rule. The Jewish poet Judah Halevi borrowed forms and techniques from Arabic poetry and composed his great philosophical work, *The Kuzari,* in Arabic. The great Spanish kabbalists, such as Moses de Leon and Joseph Gikatilla, also borrowed from Islamic mysticism. Most of the very complex angelology in Jewish mysticism came through Islamic teachings, so that perhaps some of the lore Zalman had given to the Dalai Lama was Islamic in origin.

In these days of continued Arab-Israeli conflict, it would be of benefit to reconciliation if the degree of interpenetration were known more widely—and talked about more in the Jewish community. It seems to me that every time a rabbi gets on a pulpit and denounces an Arab leader, he ought to spend at least some time remembering the great harmony and richness of Jewish-Islamic contact, at least during certain periods in certain countries. History is what we choose to remember, but I think as Jews we are big enough to acknowledge all of our history.

For instance, we had spent hours wondering if we could call the Dalai Lama His Holiness. Our visits to Sufi tombs threw a whole new light on that discussion, because although external influences on Judaism are almost never acknowledged, there is particular evidence that

Sufism influenced Jewish concepts of holiness. To this day, yeshiva students study Bahya ibn Pakudah's *Duties of the Heart*, an eleventh-century devotional masterpiece written in Arabic during the Golden Age by a *dayan*, or judge, in the rabbinic court. It is the most influential Jewish guide to the inward quality of Jewish religious conduct. Yet, as the scholar Louis Jacobs points out, throughout the text ibn Pakudah quotes numerous illustrative tales of "a certain *hasid*" who, in fact, was a Sufi saint.

The Golden Age for Jews ended abruptly with the rise of more fanatical Muslims, which forced the greatest medieval Jewish philosopher, Moses Maimonides, to flee Spain for Egypt. Maimonides's great works, such as *The Guide to the Perplexed*, were written in Arabic and show that he was certainly aware of Sufism. His son, Abraham ben Moses ben Maimon (1186–1237), succeeded his father as *nagid,* the temporal and spiritual head—in effect the Dalai Lama—of Jewish Cairo. Outside the synagogue, Abraham practiced Sufi-style meditative prayer in his home, with a small group of like-minded Jews. It was very much a *chavurah* group and makes Abraham ben Moses ben Maimon a pioneer in Jewish renewal.

In Dharamsala, mystic to mystic proved to be the warmest connection between Judaism and Tibetan Buddhism. Perhaps a similar opening can be found for Jewish-Islamic dialogue in encounters between Sufis and kabbalists.

After stopping off at the Bahai Temple, marble shaped into an immense white lotus, we ate lunch in Bangla Market, vegetarian plates and fresh-squeezed pomegranate juice. Now we were ready for Sarmad.

Like the Taj Mahal, the grand mosque of Delhi, Jama Masjid is a symbol of the splendor of the Moghul rulers of India.

A quarter mile of pavement stretched before us, bordered by park land, the fences lined with vendors selling carpets, baskets, and tapestries. Two young boys and their father sold shish kebab on a huge metal tray garnished with red onions and bright yellow lemons. Musicians squatted on the steps to the mosque playing drums. A young girl of twelve in a ragged green dress tugged at my sleeve. She told me her name was Janet. She insisted I take her picture, then demanded ten rupees for the privilege. Well, she was worth it.

Zalman guided us unerringly to the dargha. We found above the roof of the tomb a weather-beaten red sign telling the story in "English"— "GRAVE (MAZAR) HOLY HAZRAT SARMAD His Holiness was executed in the year 1650 by the orders of Emperor Aurangzeb. When his head was chopped he took his head in his hand and climbed stairs of jama masjid and a voice was coming from his head and from that day onward Emperor Aurangzeb could not get peace for a moment."

Sarmad lived in the time of Shah Jehan, the great Moghul ruler, builder of the Taj Mahal, the Red Fort, and the Jama Masjid mosque. He taught in the court of Shah Jehan's son, Dara Shikoh, a mystic whose conflict with his more orthodox brother, Aurangzeb, ended in his death. To scholar Annemarie Schimmel, their conflict expresses "those trends which were to result in the partition of the subcontinent in 1947."

Caught in the middle was Sarmad, a Persian or Armenian Jew, who came to India as a merchant, but like many other visitors before and since, fell under the spell of mysticism. His reputation as a poet and mystic spread to Dara Shikoh, who summoned him to court.

Though nominally a convert to Islam, there's evidence Sarmad remained a Jew. He encouraged the first translation of the Torah into Persian and contributed the Jewish chapter to an extraordinary work of comparative religion commissioned by Dara Shikoh, the Dabistan. The scholar Walter Fishel notes, "Through the medium of the 'Dabistan' Sarmad thus became the channel through which Jewish ideas, though with a Sufic blending, penetrated into the religious fabric of the India of his time."

When I looked at the text, I discovered to my delight that the chapters on "Tabitians" and "Yahuds"—Tibetans and Jews—follow one upon the other. Since Dara Shikoh frequently staged religious debates, it seems very possible that in the Muslim ruler's court, Sarmad had preceded us in Tibetan-Jewish dialogue three centuries ago. But religious dialogue was not to the taste of Dara Shikoh's younger brother Aurangzeb. He was offended by his brother's association with infidels. In 1657, Aurangzeb seized power and executed his brother. Then he rounded up his associates.

The "atheist Jew" Sarmad was brought before the new emperor for a theological trial of a kind sickeningly familiar to students of Jewish history. He was asked for a profession of Islamic faith—the traditional *Shahadah,* which resembles the *Shema,* "There is no God but God." Sarmad stopped with, "There is no God . . . " When the emperor demanded that he continue, Sarmad replied, "Forgive me, but I am so caught up in the negative, that I can not yet come up to the positive. I cannot tell a lie."

To my ears, this echoes the kabbalistic conception of God as *ain sof,* about which nothing can be stated.

Sarmad means everlasting. That day I thought of another meaning as well. Sarmad is nearly an anagram—for Ram Dass. They had much in common: wandering Jews, spiritual seekers in India, an everlasting type of the syncretic Jew, the polar opposite of the particularist—the spark that flies off the wheel.

Zalman, Blu, Nathan, and I entered his dargha with garlands of flowers. The tomb was fenced by bright red, low walls, and its roof was supported by red and white tiled columns. A bare incandescent bulb poked rudely from a receptacle above the headstone.

Zalman and Nathan said kaddish. It all felt quite right, a recognition of our predecessor in dialogue—or a martyr to intolerance, take your pick. That there was such a thing as a Jewish Muslim saint opened yet another door.

Our last stop was the Sikh temple complex. We were getting tired, but Ran, our Sikh driver, would have been insulted had we not visited *his* "shul." It was quite a beauty. A golden onion dome capped a white marble building set in a huge courtyard paved in shining marble tiles. Inside, shiny silver columns supported a pavilion under which the guru sat, a black bearded man in a cobalt blue turban. Three musicians in turbans to his right played hand drums and electric keyboards.

Blu Greenberg told me later, "I didn't want to leave that place. I loved watching. My eyes were bulging." With the music going constantly, Blu said she was "taken up in the life of it. What on earth is a nice Orthodox girl doing in a Sikh temple and enjoying herself? I wasn't praying and yet I wasn't just standing there coldly and observing. It wasn't a religious experience for me in the Sikh sense, but it was a religious experience."

I understood what she meant. My contact with Buddhism had opened me up. In Delhi, facing the multiplicity of religious expressions, and the obvious quality of devotion in several of them, I could feel the pressure of competing identities burst and melt—it was an emotional confrontation with pluralism that stripped away the need to feel one way was better than another.

Paradoxically, this did not make me feel less a Jew. Rather, I had gained a much broader view of the power of all religions, including my own. As Sarmad had written, "Only when being has been left behind/ Canst thou the only source of Being find." That sounded a lot like the *Shema* to me. If the source of being is one, then despite the apparent contradictions, this was the One others are worshiping, the One behind the whole sacred whirl.

But who or what was this One?

Before I left on this trip, I was basically an unthinking agnostic—I neither believed nor disbelieved in God. Now I was haunted by Zalman's challenge, "Your God is a true God," which seemed to give me both enormous freedom and responsibility.

What experience did I have of God?—that's what I didn't understand. There was just—nothing. And a terrible sense often that the world was empty of meaning.

During the Shabbat with the Jewish renewal people in London, Zalman had retold the parable of a Hasidic master. The Kotzker Rebbe explains the seeming absence of God. God is like a child who plays hide and seek. He hides, but sadly, no one comes to look for him.

Then Zalman extended the image. He asked us to picture a God who was not only playing a game that no one else wanted to play, but who feels very lonely sitting in a kind of prison of isolation. This God is lonely because God has no peer, God has no God.

In fact, God is an atheist; when Zalman said that, it hit me right where I live and doubt. A God who is an atheist was something I could relate to.

I am sure that part of the impact was that I did feel rather lonely and apart in the presence of this very warm group of Jews who had formed their own special community.

When our discussion ended, the London *chavurah* formed a circle. As I prayed arm in arm with these strangers who had received me so warmly, I was embarrassed to find big tears rolling down my cheeks. I had no such group myself to return to. I was feeling sorry for myself, and in a funny way, feeling sorry for God.

I knew that the feeling of emptiness, of lack of meaning, of absence, which I'd often encountered in my life, was connected to this lonely God Zalman had conjured up. And I realized that at some very deep level, which I had never even allowed myself to express, I had felt lonely for God myself for many years.

Perhaps at some essential level this is a difference between Jews and Buddhists. Both may experience a profound sense of emptiness in the universe: the meaningless swirl of samsara, the spilled and scattered light of our fragmented lives. For the Buddhist this emptiness is open space. For the Jew it is an absence. And from there the paths diverge.

Quite appropriately, the last temple we visited that day was a synagogue. The architecture looked very familiar, too, like my old temple in Baltimore built in the fifties. There was a nice courtyard garden and the obligatory plaque with its list of donors on the outer wall. As we passed into the prayer hall, six Jewish stars were framed overhead in the glass transom.

We were met by a short, energetic man. Ezekiel Isaac Malecar is extraordinarily proud of his temple and keeps it going as *shammas* and *chazzan*. Nathan Katz, who had arranged our visit, called him "Judaism's flickering candle in India's capital."

I was impressed by the variety of our hats. Tsangpo, our Tibetan travel guide, joined us, smiling broadly, glad our trip was nearly over. He wore a yellow sateen yarmulke. I wore my Indiana Jones. Marc Lieberman, sporting an orange Hindu cap from the Tibetan market, sat next to his wife, Nancy Garfield, who'd spent most of the time we were in Dharamsala in England recuperating from an asthma attack. Zalman, learning we were going to do a kiddush, ran out to get the drivers, a very sweet gesture. The handy Mr. Singh joined us and so did Ran, in a powder-blue turban.

Meanwhile, Isaac's seven-year-old daughter was being grilled by two experienced Jewish mothers.

"Do you know what *shalom* means?" Joy asked her. The little girl with dark brown eyes smiled shyly. Then Blu, "Do you know what *Shabbat Shalom* means?" She nodded vigorously.

Yitz, adjusting his glasses, stood beside Isaac at the prayer stand and led a brief service. We sat on metal folding chairs. I saw Moshe Waldoks, and next to him, Ram Dass, the yellow yarmulke looking pretty natural on his head. He was very carefully studying the prayer book, his finger creasing his temple.

21

Buddha's Jews

Ram Dass remembers that moment in Delhi as a kind of epiphany. As he leafed through the Jewish prayer book in the Judah Hyam synagogue, he felt himself to be "in a very tender state."

He told me later, "I was reading the prayers and feeling that they were coming out of a time and place and wording that made it very difficult to connect to the essence of Judaism.

"But I was also remembering sentimental feelings of my bar mitzvah and high holidays. I was feeling a distance from the whole process and at the same time somewhere touched very deeply in my being. That was an interesting moment in time—part of a sequence that's been going on for many years. I mean, to be a Jew and then feel alien in your own religious situation is a strange feeling. Because of the nature of Hebrew and of Judaism, the closed circle quality—you're either in or out in a certain way—the feeling I had at that moment, I was outside of it. And yet I was there, and there as a Jew. So I had that interesting feeling I've had before: I don't belong and yet I'm there—what many Jews feel who have gone into Eastern religions."

Ram Dass's mixed feelings testify to the strength of Jewish roots, no matter how attenuated. Allen Ginsberg, who defines himself strictly as a cultural Jew, can reel off the blessing over bread at the drop of a hat.

Thubten Chodron and Alex Berzin maintain an ongoing correspondence—Dear Sadie, Dear Melvin—full of Jewish jokes and Yiddish words. These scraps and remnants of Jewishness made me wonder if JUBUs from strong Jewish backgrounds might be evolving a blend of Judaism and Buddhism.

Clearly, the whole venture to Dharamsala expressed Dr. Marc Lieberman's personal struggle to have the two traditions meet with love and respect. He had spent at least ten years as an observant Jew, in Israel and the United States, was fluent in Hebrew, and is knowledgeable about Jewish texts. When he came to Buddhism, he made an audacious decision.

"I'd shed identities before, and there was a real superficiality to that. If anything I was learning in meditation was true, it was true at the level of integration, not disintegration." He felt no compulsion to fragment into another identity, or to be angry at Judaism. "I asked myself, are you running away from being Jewish? Though there was no role model to integrate the two, I decided, it won't make sense, but I'll be Jewish and Buddhist.

"After all, when you're on your *zafu* [meditation cushion], you're just meditating. So if lighting candles feels right, honor that too. Even if intellectually it's in conflict. It still feels awkward. My son asks me, 'Dad, are you Jewish or are you Buddhist?' And I answer, 'I've got Jewish roots and Buddhist wings.' I'm honoring my tribe. Jews in general have tremendous resonance with other tribes, with Indians, and blacks. So why not with our own? I'm from the Jewish tribe, but Buddhism speaks to my heart."

On Friday evenings, Lieberman observes Shabbat; his wife, Nancy, lights candles, he says kiddush. He makes the traditional blessing of his son, and then with Mahayana expansiveness, she extends the blessing to all children everywhere. That same evening may also be spent in Buddhist meditation, or studying abidhamma, Buddhist philosophical texts. Through a private foundation, Nama Rupa, the Liebermans raise money for Tibetan monasteries in India and help Tibetan orphans. They also promote Jewish-Buddhist dialogue.

I asked Marc how he combines elements of a monastic tradition with the Jewish emphasis on family life. Lieberman sighed. "I went to an interesting meeting three or four years ago at the Zen Center with Jews and Buddhists. A strongly identified Jew familiar with Buddhism said, 'Look, Buddhism is a universalist religion. Its central metaphor is choosing a path that is homeless and walking out in thin air. Judaism is the exact opposite. The home is the central shrine and the heart of all being. When those of us are attracted, is it to Buddhism or do we simply want to leave home?'

"In my experience, as one profoundly realizes the nature of the way things are, Buddha is someone who is awake, the rest of us are dulled by sleep. If someone is awake and sees the way things are, it's like a lining you can put into various gloves. I have a friend who lost a lover to AIDS. Nancy taught him to meditate. He finds as he goes back to the Catholic church, he can now interpret the ancient tradition—and see things as they are. Similarly, when I look at Yitz Greenberg's profound sense of Jewish integrity and social justice—so it's not just talking, but asking how can we manifest in the world what we believe in, I'm profoundly moved. I see why and how the Jewish tradition has preserved so much wisdom, because it has so much good stuff in it."

Many would find it confusing to combine practices of two religions, but for Lieberman, this has been mostly clarifying. He finds Judaism a complicated heritage to sort out. "I couldn't know which were the reliable voices to listen to. The glory of Judaism is that there is no single voice. There's no pope setting the key. So it's a vast musical library. People gravitate in Judaism to that which mirrors and reflects their own understanding of the world. Meir Kahane was just as Jewish as Yitz Greenberg, though Kahane was much more dominated by the demons of aggression and violence than Yitz. But they're both Jewish.

"The voice of clarity and wisdom, the voice that speaks to my heart, I'm only rediscovering now in Judaism because I have a much clearer experience of listening to my heart through meditation.

"At one point I realized Judaism was the most profound spiritual religion, because it said the stuff of spiritual life is getting a job, feeding kids, and going to sleep with bad breath: that the world is the stage of spirituality. I found it appealing that the Talmud is deeply fixated on the world as it is. At one level that's very Zen, very profound and true. At another level, Judaism seems among the most denying of all religions, because it doesn't equip people for stepping out into the ether. Judaism was never giving a path out of the world to see the world as it is."

I have observed Lieberman moving in both worlds, Buddhist and Jewish—planning a bar mitzvah for his son and for a Buddhist monastery in San Francisco—discomfiting himself and others, especially his Jewish friends and family, who need to know the name on his label.

Joseph Goldstein offered a good perspective. "The Buddha didn't teach Buddhism. He just taught dharma, how he understood the truth. Really, that's about love and compassion and wisdom. So as a way of relating to family—it's not necessary to take a stand on being a Buddhist. A woman came from a fundamentalist Christian family who hated that she was doing Buddhist practice. She wrote a letter to Ram Dass outlining the difficulties. She ended it by saying, 'My parents hate me when I'm a Buddhist and love me when I'm a Buddha.' We don't have to become anything. If we're more accepting and loving, less judgmental—that's the way to open contacts and connections."

Despite the difficulties and ambiguities, Marc Lieberman and some other JUBUs remain connected to their Jewishness. I found this as well in talking to David Rome, formerly the personal secretary of Chogyam Trungpa. At the time I interviewed him, in May 1992, he was living in Vajradhatu, a Tibetan Buddhist community in Halifax, Nova Scotia.

Rome graduated Harvard with a Boylston Prize in classics and served in the Peace Corps in Africa. As the heir to Schocken Books—the publishers of Kafka, Buber, and Scholem and at one time probably the world's most influential Jewish publishing house—he grew up in an intellectual household. "We were always surrounded by books, there was always a high caliber of discussion at the dinner table." He said his father, a Lithuanian Jew who was first in his class at Harvard, approached things "with great intellect and great curiosity."

Rome's family name is *notarikon,* or Hebrew acrostic, for Rosh Matifta, or "Head of the Yeshiva." "Supposedly we're descended from the Gaon of Vilna on my father's side." Elijah ben Solomon Zalman, the Gaon—or "eminence"—of Vilna was an oustanding eighteenth-century Lithuanian rabbi and one of the staunchest Orthodox opponents of the Hasidic movement. So David Rome could claim very serious *yichus*—Jewish lineage.

He was bar mitzvahed in White Plains, New York, and attended a Hebrew high school run by the Jewish Theological Seminary. But despite this rich Jewish background, he turned to Buddhism after college.

"I wasn't really looking. It just happened. Hitchhiking in Europe with an old friend from high school who had an interest in Eastern religions. He dragged me along to Samye-ling, the meditation center in Scotland that Trungpa Rinpoche had started. That was in 1971. There I experienced meditation for the first time."

Rome found in meditation "a sense that something was right—just very much intuition." Powerful too was "the quality of discipline in Buddhism," which gave "a way of working with yourself, a way of what Rinpoche called making friends with yourself. There was a path, which Buddhism talks about a great deal. You could actually have this commitment and work with it, work on it and progress, explore, go deeper, clarify.

"Though meditative practice survives in the Jewish tradition, the Buddhists are the world experts. Beyond that, Buddhism, being nontheistic and nondogmatic, manages to avoid a whole huge realm of problems of who's better than who, and who's got the truth and who doesn't have the truth, and all of those kind of issues. Jews on the whole do better than Christians in that regard, but there's still a fair amount of that in Judaism. And so in that sense the Buddhist sensibility is more ecumenical, more universal. That's precisely the appeal to Westerners. They're just not willing to go along any more with anybody who says, I am the best, I've got the answers."

Is he still a Jew? "I feel less and less the need or the accuracy of defining myself in any which way. I suppose I'm a Jewish Buddhist American Canadian at this point. Judaism is certainly a strong part of my identity, as is Buddhism. My practice is as a Buddhist, not as a Jew. But it's almost as if they represent different aspects of oneself. Judaism is my family, my background, and I feel very strongly for Jewish history," especially the Holocaust. "Buddhism is more of the spiritual side, the practice, of how do you experience life from moment to moment, how do you work with your mind and with other people."

David Rome felt Trungpa encouraged him to look at Judaism with respect. "Rinpoche said to me very early on that one of his hopes was that his own students would return to their traditions. At that time—it changed later on—he saw his work very much as dealing with a basic human wisdom from the East that was not very accessible in the West.

He did see bringing Westerners back to their own wisdom as part of his mission."

Rome began working as Trungpa's personal secretary in 1974. In 1983 his mother died and he returned to New York to take over the reins at Schocken Books. So it happened that an experienced Jewish Buddhist meditator headed the most influential Jewish publishing house when the late Rabbi Aryeh Kaplan's manuscript, *Jewish Meditation*, came across his desk.

"Bonnie Fetterman, the Judaica editor there, had the manuscript. She was a little befuddled by it. She knew Kaplan and respected him. He was a rabbi in a very Orthodox community. In fact, the series of talks that became the book were done somewhat on the sly. He met with a small group of students who were not part of his congregation.

"So she knew he was a good person and yet didn't know quite what to make of all this mystical stuff. She asked me to read it. Without necessarily presuming to completely understand it, I found that it all sounded familiar. He had obviously done some study of Eastern meditation. A lot of what he was describing had the quality of meditation, concentration, absorption practice, insight practice, and visualization. He also talked about the feminine principle, which is one of the things Bonnie didn't get and wanted to edit out. I said, 'No, you can't. That's really important.' I encouraged the publication strongly and helped with the editing. He had died, of course, abruptly and quite young, which is too bad." It proved to be one of the most successful books Schocken published in 1984.

Schocken is known for books about Jewish mysticism, most notably Buber's *Tales of the Hasidim* and Scholem's monumental *Major Trends in Jewish Mysticism*. But to Rome, Kaplan's book "was very different because an Orthodox rabbi and practitioner was saying, 'You can do this.' And that's certainly not what you get in Scholem. And in Buber you will only get a sense of inspiration and of a philosophical view or an ethical view, but not specific meditative exercises."

Rome found this interesting and exciting. He didn't try the meditations but "felt they corresponded with practices I had experienced in Buddhism." He was concerned, "especially since Rabbi Kaplan wasn't alive, what context this was happening in, what teacher principle or protection principle, what *sangha* or community is there."

By contrast, he felt that Buddhism's strong appeal to Westerners was having "teachers who are part of a continuous lineage, genuine masters who really understand how to be a spiritual guide for somebody pursuing a contemplative path." Also important was the sense of a "contemplative community," which is what he personally sought when he sold Schocken in 1987 and joined Vajradhatu in Halifax, though in the meantime, Trungpa had died. For several years Rome has served on the community's board of directors.

Yet these days David Rome finds himself with a de facto Jewish family—his wife, also a member of the *sangha*, is Jewish by birth, and he has a daughter of thirteen. Along with other Jewish Buddhists, they get together for Passover seders. Rome also celebrates Chanukah and other holidays. "I have wanted to give my daughter some access to the Jewish tradition so that if she feels inspired at some point to get into that more, at least she feels there's a doorway open for her. Other than that, I don't practice, I don't observe."

Yet he finds in Buddhism a continuity with his experience of growing up Jewish. Like Alex Berzin, he finds "a lot of respect for intellect" and scholarship in both traditions. "They've got just as much commentary and commentaries on commentaries going as the Jews do, maybe more." But the key attraction to Buddhism was that it provides a way of putting the intellect itself into perspective.

"At the heart, there's this notion of not becoming fixated in the conceptual realm." Buddhism teaches "how to be in touch with the ground before thought—or nonthought. Perhaps especially as a Jew, as somebody who grew up in a strong intellectual environment, I used my intellect a lot." In Buddhism he found something "true and profound and necessary in terms of how to balance the intellect for it not to become distorting."

Jews, by culture, training, and perhaps by genealogy, are highly oriented toward logic, intellect, reason. The delight in lively debate and argument, whether between two study partners in a yeshiva, or in a family argument over the kitchen table, is a marked feature of Jewish life. (I have noticed this more since living in the South where debate and vociferous public argument are viewed with fear and suspicion.)

The point is that, like David Rome, I have also sometimes felt a weariness with argument. Reading the Talmud one can marvel at the brilliance of intellect, but sometimes, at a certain point, one can also feel that all of this impassioned reasoning is too much of a good thing. I had those moments in Dharamsala during the debate over the prayer for the Dalai Lama.

If it is true, as the poet Eliot remarked, that only those who had personality could understand the desire to escape from it, likewise only those who've lived in intellect can know what it means to desire to escape from it. But escape where? *Shunyata*, as Trungpa taught, is not simply empty space, but open space. Another definition of *shunyata* that the Tibetans use is "dependent arising." Nothing arises of itself, all things are dependent one upon the other. The emphasis is not on absence or loss, but on the interrelatedness of all things. Through meditation practice, one not only comes to understand dependent arising as an idea or concept, but one experiences it. According to Buddhist practitioners, such meditation produces true wisdom.

Judaism, too, has its practices for balancing the intellect, as Zalman Schachter and Jonathan Omer-Man had made clear—namely, prayer and meditation. But I could understand why even a well-educated Jew like David Rome might have found the meditation techniques of Tibetan Buddhism more immediately accessible.

I thought it was a good sign of his own sense of balance that like Marc Lieberman, David Rome is more at ease than most JUBUs about belonging to the Jewish tribe. "I do feel special as a Jew," he told me, though he was quick to add, "At the same time I don't think any people are really more special than any other people." He added, "One of the really big challenges about what's going on in Israel, in becoming a nation among nations rather than God's people, is a danger of arrogance. It is not too much of a problem as long as you're being persecuted, but when you're not, then it's something you have to be very mindful about."

Rome observed the initial Tibetan-Jewish dialogue in New Jersey and came away impressed with how family practice has been key to Jewish survival. In his experience, that is something Jewish Buddhists are bringing to their Buddhist communities.

"The tendency has been for people to have their practice, which they do alone or in special group retreats. But it hasn't been so family oriented. Now many, many people have families and so we've been working with that for quite a few years. One of my friends, who comes out of a more observant Jewish background than I do, recently introduced the idea of a regular family-oriented gathering at the meditation center. It was designed like a Shabbat service."

Because he seemed more attuned to Jewish concerns than most Jewish Buddhists, I asked David Rome a question I knew many Jews felt strongly. It had been posed to me forcefully by Rabbi Shlomo Carlebach, who has made encouraging Jews to stay involved with Judaism his life's work.

"You know," Rabbi Carlebach said, "imagine, God forbid, our father's house burns down—and I'm moving into somebody else's house? No. I help my father to rebuild the house. After the six million we had nothing. No yeshivas, no spiritual leadership, no rebbes. All those people who hit it big in other religions, they could be rebbes. They have big *neshamas* [souls]. Sure it's easy to go away, it's hard to rebuild, but you can't permit them to do that. It shows a lack of character. What's going on? Why don't they ask God," What do you want me to be?'"

I asked David Rome how he would answer Shlomo Carlebach. "I'd say we're out learning some new skills so maybe later on we can come back and help rebuild the house. I appreciate where he's coming from, but more and more, as I get older, I find that my ethical responsibility, my responsibility altogether, is as a human being—although these days even that's not enough because it's to the ecosystem, too.

"But anyway, I have high ambiguity tolerance. I love to see people who are genuinely involved with Judaism. That's fantastic and there's even a bit of envy in that, but that's not what happened in my life. I have to be true to what happened in my life. If everybody is true to themselves and to the events of their own lives, then we will find a way to make it work out."

Rome felt "a teacher like Trungpa does appear as a rebbe. He's very powerful and can take you beyond your limitations. It's hard to find that from your average suburban rabbi, and it's very hard to do it on your own. The ghetto feeling of many Hasidic communities is something most modern people are not willing to put up with. The solutions may emerge over time. If you look at Buddhism and how it started up in Tibet and Japan, usually you see a generation that had to leave their country and spend twenty years in a foreign culture. But it takes only a generation and then it was planted. It may have to take a generation that goes elsewhere and comes back to Judaism. The next generation comes back."

That was an intriguing comparison, very much in the spirit of Zalman Schachter's circular dance. Over time Buddhism has adapted itself to many different cultures in the East, in China, Japan, India, Korea, Sri Lanka, and Vietnam. Historically, this has taken at least three hundred years to complete. By that measure, we are just beginning to see that process unfold in the West. It may well be that Buddhism will borrow a few dance steps from Judaism along the way.

Ram Dass, a close observer of the Buddhist scene, expressed delight when told how David Rome's community was adapting Shabbat. He commented that "the Eastern traditions are primarily monastic and as such they really give short shrift to family life. In terms of what we need at this moment in this culture—which is to respond to the alienation by a sense of community, by realizing we are interdependent with other people—Judaism, with its emphasis on the family and on spiritual living rather than on the other world, is a very vital and healthy vehicle." This, of course, was the same message we had tried to pass on to the Dalai Lama.

But the exchange goes in both directions. David Rome had been instrumental in publishing *Jewish Meditation*. Other experienced meditators have come all the way back to Judaism.

22

A Last Secret

At the 1991 P'nai Or Kallah, a biannual gathering of the Jewish renewal movement, I saw what happens when the energy of women, of Jewish meditation, and an active four worlds approach to davening are combined. Dynamic prayer services were led by women rabbis, spiritual leaders, and singers, including among them Hannah Tiferet Siegel, Rabbi Marcia Prager, and Shefa Gold. Siegel and Rabbi Prager introduced special gestures and dance movements to enhance prayer, and Shefa Gold rejuvenated a number of psalms with music that combined Hebrew words and fervent gospel rhythms. The total effect of such worship, especially at Shabbat, was overwhelming. Jewish prayer, especially in more liberal synagogues, can be a staid affair. These Jews were dancing, singing, shouting, and moving their bodies. They combined breath meditation with prayer and physical techniques such as tai chi and yoga, as well as traditional Jewish "yoga" of *shukeling*, praying while swaying the body. Was this very new or very, very old? One got the sense of renewing an ancient joyous energy, the dancing and singing in the days of the Temple, the harps and timbrels of the psalms.

According to Dr. Arthur Waskow, a leader of the Jewish renewal movement, "The whole rhythm in American Jewish history has been, from generation to generation, to dump the tradition more and more.

Ours is the first generation in American Jewish history that's drawn more on the tradition, rather than less. This is a return. But it's not a return to the old. The renewal response is to digest modernity, to absorb the truths that are in it. And they are: women are fully spiritual beings and their spirituality has to transform the traditions that have excluded them; other traditions do bear as much truth as our own, we have to honor and learn from them. Now on this small planet, we discover, God didn't speak at just one Sinai."

I asked Zalman Schachter, who has combined *vipassana* with the Yom Kippur service, why Jews might find meditation of increased interest now. In the past, he thought, Jews, Christians, and Muslims were mostly interested in recital. An elite of Jews, "less than a *minyan*," in Safed, Spain, and medieval Germany practiced meditation. "There was an explosion of spirituality after the Baal Shem Tov that was like fireworks. The Baal Shem went off and his disciples went off and within three generations, Poland, Galicia, and Lithuania were all dotted with Hasidic masters" practicing meditation.

The "demand for spirituality today" is "at the deepest level subjective, it's in the nominative, not in the accusative, the dative, the genitive. In shul, I'm there because it's genitive: my poppa belonged to the shul, I'm *of* it. I'm an accusative Jew because a *goy* calls me that way. Because I've been circumcised and I have this history, my dative says I'm a Jew. But unless it gets into the nominative, the first-person experience, I'm not a Jew. From that place, people become meditators."

Moshe Waldoks also feels Jews can learn from other meditative traditions. In fact, he does not think "there's a Jewish meditation or Buddhist meditation: there is meditation. There's a debate within the philosophy of religion about whether a mystical experience in one religion is the same as in another. It's a very academic argument." When he travels and teaches, he introduces meditation into the Jewish prayer experience with a presentation he calls CHAI Ch'ih. (*Chai* is the Jewish word for life.) He finds that all too often the synagogue service is modeled on the decorum of churches—the participants are not looking for personal transformation or a peak experience.

"My contention is very simple: that meditation and chanting and breathing, things we associate with the Eastern prayer mode, are in no way foreign to any of the Jewish services." That is why he thinks the

Jewish community could use the help of Jews who have experience of Eastern meditation.

Though Ram Dass is not yet ready to play this role, he has made a personal rapprochement with his Jewish background since I saw him last in that shul in Delhi.

As a Hindu and theist, Ram Dass had less trouble with God than many of the JUBUs to begin with. In a recent interview, he told me he found Allen Ginsberg's views of God as an external deity naive. He thought Judaism was "more interesting than that. Because you can't have something in which the basic mantra is, 'There is only one God, there is only one'—and then say there's one and also us. The one is the one, and that's what I understand from every tradition. You go back and get to one thing."

Still, he was not surprised by the negative attitudes of some Jewish Buddhists toward Judaism, because "usually the religion you grow up with, unless you were very fortunate and had a very deep connection, was often the last one in which you would find the living spirit once you were on the spiritual path. Because you have all the residuals. It's like staying very conscious around your family. The family is connected to you in a way that they know exactly where your buttons are to press. A lot of Catholics who went into Eastern religion come back to Catholicism only at the very end, because then they can see the beauty. Before, they are so busy reacting to the negative sides: insensitive nuns, authoritarian structures.

"The negativity I came away with from Judaism made me realize I had business to do there. But I kept saying I'd better wait to connect to some guide who isn't going to try to hustle me, proselytize me, or make me feel guilty, who's going to respect me and love me and let me come back in, in some way. I was just waiting for that because part of one's incarnation is to understand the uniqueness of one's predicament, and to honor it and come into harmony or relationship with it."

Ram Dass's Jewish predicament was spectacularly exoteric: his father, the president of the New York–New Haven Railroad, chaired the Joint Distribution Committee during World War II, rescuing Jewish children from the Holocaust. After the war, he was instrumental in founding Brandeis University and Albert Einstein Medical College. George Alpert was a *macher* with a capital *M*.

But religiously, the Judaism his son experienced had a "Holocaust redemption quality."

"I had never been connected with the spiritual aspects of Judaism at all. My whole connection was the sentimentality of the high holidays and the social political aspects of Dad's involvements. My father and mother grew up in Orthodox families, but we were liberal Conservatives—we only ate pork in Chinese restaurants."

In an article in *Conservative Judaism*, Nathan Katz commented pointedly on our encounter with Ram Dass in Delhi. After dinner, we had sung the *birkat hamazon*, the traditional after meal prayer. Ram Dass had asked, "What is that pretty tune?" Nathan's comment: with such a paltry background, no wonder he left.

When I quoted this to him, Ram Dass laughed and told me, "There was a very funny analogy. At one point we had a big summer place up in New Hampshire. When I came back from India in '68 or '69, people started to come to visit me until pretty soon there were two or three hundred people on a weekend. And my father let people camp up in the hills. He was wonderful. He didn't understand it at all. Once about 250 people in the barn were singing "Hare Krishna." He came up to me and he said, 'Who is this Harry Krishna guy?' And I said, 'Well, it's just another name of God.' And he said, 'It's a great tune, but why do they keep repeating the same thing over and over again?' So when I said to them, 'This is a great tune, what is it?' I realize I was my father to them, I was doing the same thing. It was like out of my own ignorance."

But just a year later Ram Dass was invited to lecture at the University of Judaism in Los Angeles, a stronghold of Conservative Judaism. Realizing the invitation was controversial, he retreated to a South Sea island and studied Jewish texts diligently, for the first time. He began with the Talmud. "It just struck me as very humorous that I would be reading these books about Orthodox practices while these women with bare breasts would be walking by. That was a wonderful juxtaposition. I thought, what a wonderful place—if I can find joy in Judaism here, I've got it made."

Evidently he was able to keep his eye on the page even under those conditions. "I said to myself, if I were an Orthodox Jew who loved God, how would I understand my religion? Then the halakhic laws fell into place, not as an authoritarian patriarchal or paternalistic law giving, but rather these incredible guides for how to remember God from moment to moment." He began to look at the beauty of Judaism, instead of judging it.

"Then I got into the Hasids, and people like Nachman and the Baal Shem Tov and other *tzaddiks*. And, of course, then I was meeting people that I recognized from Eastern traditions. I was meeting the saints, the mystics.

"Then I understood, when you were connected to God from that point of view, the laws were a joy to follow, not a heavy burden at all. I realized that when I first took psychedelics in the sixties, that had I been more on good terms with Judaism, emotionally, I probably would have turned toward kabbalah for a framework for understanding. As it was, I ended up through Aldous Huxley with the *Tibetan Book of the Dead*, which was a framework also. One that led me and a lot of others to the East."

In preparing for the lecture, he came to know Rabbi Omer-Man better. They talked about Judaism and he felt "very loving and connected" to Jonathan. The lecture itself was a popular success. Jonathan advised him that he might face hostility, but Ram Dass told him, "I'm going in loving everybody. We are fellow Jews and we're all trying to figure out what we are doing together." He spoke for three hours. "I just loved it. I was trying to share the joy I saw in Judaism."

To Jonathan Omer-Man, the lecture—attended by everyone from New Age Hindus to Jewish yuppies to bearded Hasids—was a remarkable event. Ram Dass "spoke beautifully as an outsider" of the Jewish experience. It was not so much a coming home to Judaism, as "acknowledging that home is a good place."

I liked talking to Ram Dass—he was a very pleasant man and very enthusiastic about Judaism—at least in theory. I was curious to know how far he would go with it—and where he would pull back. He told me that the summer after his speech, he'd spent time at Elat Chayim, a Jewish renewal summer camp affiliated with P'nai Or. He actively davened and celebrated Shabbat, practicing the Judaism he'd been contemplating in the abstract.

He told me, "In every religious tradition, what you invest is what return you get. And I'll tell you when we did the Shabbas and we did the *mikveh*, the whole idea that one day was going to be out of time, and one day was going to be the statement of what it was like after the Messiah came, and one day was the real wedding celebration—then I saw the Shabbas as something extremely profound and beautiful. I began to open to the use of time to go beyond time. I saw that the people who invested more were making Judaism into a living tradition they can grow from rather than simply honoring their own genetic history. Lighting the candles is a tiny taste.

"It's the same for me. I go to Burma and I spend two months in meditation. And the *bhikku* says to me, 'You know, don't leave, you're just beginning to get the sweetness. Spend two more years.' I say, 'I've got other business to do,' and he looks at me with pity. I understand his pity. I realize I'm a lousy Buddhist and I'm a lousy Hindu and I'm a lousy Jew and I'm a lousy Taoist and that's the way I am. That's my path. I don't distrust my own path. Yet I also understand that each one, as you go in deeper, you get more rewards from it. I don't mean to sound like this is all truth, but this is my experience.

"I don't think any longer that there's any one person in Judaism setting the rules. Because it's clear that you are a Jew for so many different reasons, that there are so many different ways that people can say with pride: I am a Jew. One way is to give to charity, or be a good community member, or a good member of a family. Others are deep into the study of Torah. I don't know that any of them are better Jews than anybody else—or should be arbitrating the laws of who should follow what."

I concluded that Ram Dass has gained a much clearer appreciation of Judaism as a spiritual path while basically continuing on his own merry and somewhat erratic way. But other Jews have danced all the way around the circle Zalman described to us in Dharamsala, from Judaism to Buddhism to Judaism.

Professor Nathan Katz is one. He tells how, on the lecture circuit, he frequently encounters Jewish parents concerned about their children's involvement with Buddhism and other Eastern religions. He advises them to be patient. His own life experience tells him that exploring meditation may be part of a process that brings people back to Judaism.

"I grew up in a traditional home, distanced myself in the sixties, but never severed ties. But I was not religious in any sense until my encounters with Buddhism." In the end, as he says, he came to Judaism through Buddhism.

During the period of his most intense involvement, from 1975 to 1977, he frequently met with Chogyam Trungpa for formal interviews. He felt a special bond to Trungpa and at the same time had met Zalman Schachter, who was also counseling him spiritually. It was a ping-pong effect. "Trungpa told me I should keep Shabbas as part of my practice. Zalman was telling me to do more meditation."

When Nathan saw Alex Berzin during our visit, he was very impressed by his spiritual development and a little envious. "I see meditation doing wonderful things for these people. Someone like Alex seems very close to enlightenment." But Nathan finds his fulfillment as a Jew—a commitment intensified by time spent living among Orthodox Jews in Cochin India. "You have to live the life to get committed to Judaism. When you go to synagogue constantly, you can really get someplace spiritually."

Another committed Jew with meditation experience is Rabbi David Blank, whom I met at the 1991 P'nai Or Kallah. We spoke on the campus of Bryn Mawr on a late summer afternoon, with sparrows providing counterpoint to the story of his spiritual circumnavigation, from Lubavitcher Hasid to Zen monk to the Aquarian Minyan. What interested me about his story is that, unlike many other JUBUs, he had been exposed to Jewish mysticism before encountering Buddhism.

David, in his early forties, has intense eyes and a very soft-spoken manner. He spoke with directness and humor. His background is mixed, his mother very Orthodox and his father not at all. She had sent him to Israel to absorb a more Orthodox influence. He arrived not long after the Six Day War. "People were crying, many had died and almost died. Yom Kippur was such a high there. They really lived it. Not like in Montreal where there was dry davening."

From the start Rabbi Blank was interested in a strongly devotional religious life. He found it at first in the Lubavitcher spiritual community, six years in Israel and six more in New York. Because he'd been "on the university track, not the yeshiva track"—he proved very useful in working with *baalei teshuva*—Jews new, or returning, to the Orthodox fold.

"I taught in the Lubavitcher yeshiva in New York to the beginners. In the early 1970s, they were coming from all kinds of different places. Macrobiotics. TM. They saw me as helping out with all these people because I could speak English and knew the idiom. If there was someone around from Hare Krishna they said, 'We'll send him around to David Blank, maybe he'll be able to find a language with him and bring him in.' I was successful. But then somebody thought, Maybe we can send David out to someone who hasn't even expressed an interest. So they made the mistake of asking me to rope in a person who was very happy in his path and wasn't interested in Judaism at all."

The intended target was David Radin, the roshi, or head, of the Zen Center in Ithaca.

"We had what he called a dharma war. We walked up and down this country road asking each other questions. I wanted him to come to a yeshiva and showed him there was quite high stuff in Judaism, very much on the level of Zen. He in turn showed me that Zen was very, very high. He also showed that through meditation one could attain these experiences.

"He started coming up with things. His father was a rabbi, and he'd studied kabbalah before he'd gotten into Zen. He said, 'I don't usually think about Torah, but since you've been coming here giving me all these Torah ideas, in the middle of my meditation I thought, on the verse *Shema yisrael adonai elohenu adonai ekhod*—why does it say *adonai* twice, you know?' Then he said, 'Because it's the lower level and the upper level. . . .'

"I said, 'I just read that in Schneur Zalman's work written in 1812. Did you learn that?' He said, 'No, I never learned that. I wasn't aware that in Judaism they had such stuff. If I were aware, maybe I never would have left.' So I said, 'Well, it's in Judaism, Schneur Zalman, 1812.'

"The next day, he brought me the *pusek* that says: On that day the Lord shall be One and His name shall be One. 'What does it mean—*ushmo ekhod*—His name is One? He's one, his name is one, what does it mean?' And he gave his *drash* on it.

"I said, 'I think Azusha was reported as having said something similar in the 1700s. Have you read these works?' 'No, again,' he said, 'I wasn't aware of there being anything like this in Judaism.'

"'Well, you should,' I said, 'Azusha wrote them in 1799.'

"This was the last time we had together. So finally I said to him, 'You see—it's all in Judaism. You can find it there. Doesn't it make sense for you to come and learn what else is in Judaism?' Which I thought was a terrific argument. But he wiped me out by saying, 'I'm getting it from my Zen meditation. I really haven't studied these works; I'm getting these insights from meditation alone.'"

Radin challenged David Blank to study Zen, saying, "Doesn't it make sense for you, who know what Azusha and Schneur Zalman and all these guys *say*, to come and learn how to get this out of your own experience? That's how I'm getting it. You're just reporting this from other people."

That's how the roper-in was roped in himself. David Blank told me that his marriage broke up at about the same time that he declared himself a Zen Buddhist. He had grown disenchanted with the atmosphere in Crown Heights, the emphasis on spreading the word to large numbers of people. "I needed intensity of spirituality. I saw it in Zen."

"I went to sit in the Zen Center in meditation for a year. And it got progressively more and more serious." A Japanese teacher was brought in. But Blank encountered a reservation.

"I didn't want to sit in the temple because they have a Buddha they all bow to and I thought it was pretty primitive. I told the roshi that and he said, 'Come with me,' and we went into the Zendo.

"He said, 'Do you think we really bow to this thing?'

"'Well,' I told him, 'It looks bad. How do I know you don't?' He took it by the head, turned it upside down, and opened the storage room, and flung it, very disrespectfully, bounced it into the wood storage room and slammed the door. He said, 'If we were going to bow to it, do you think I would do that?'

"People came in and saw there was no Buddha and they bowed to the emptiness. So I had no trouble after that, sitting in the Zendo where the Zen teacher could do that."

But after a year, "I started pulling away from it, asking questions: When did this idea come up? At what age did these ideas develop? The roshi said, 'Those are very rabbinic questions. Before you know it you'll be a scholar, that is not what Zen is about.' My intellect was starting up again because my heart was dropping out.

"So my Zen teacher said, 'It would probably be more of a Zen thing for you to leave the temple and hitchhike around America because you are hiding here like you were in the yeshiva because they taught you the *goyim* are going to kill you with pitchforks as soon as you expose yourself to them. So I suggest that perhaps you go hitchhiking around America, preferably don't take any money with you, throw yourself on the mercy of the *goyim* and see what happens. If you die, you die.'

"And I did quite well. The *goyim* were very nice to me, and it was a big change. I hitchhiked out to California eventually. I walked into a Shavuous done by the Aquarian Minyan, they were very warm, light, loving, and affectionate. They were influenced by Zalman Schachter. It was a way of reconnecting to Judaism with tai chi in it and meditation and expanded consciousness. I thought I could bring the Zen and the Hasidism together—they were both accepted in this place."

Such stories make Nathan Katz's notion of previous contact between Judaism and Buddhism far more plausible to the imagination. They suggest how such exchanges might have occurred on the personal level. There have always been Sarmads and Ram Dasses, Alex Berzins and Chodrons, Marc Liebermans and David Blanks, passing through other traditions and sometimes coming back. A Jewish student with a Buddhist teacher, a Buddhist student with a Jewish teacher, a Jewish Buddhist, a Buddhist Jew—it could have happened in the ancient world as it is happening today. We know that in the third century B.C., the Indian emperor Ashoka, a committed Buddhist, made a determined missionary effort. He sent emissaries to Syria and Egypt to teach dharma. Is it possible that these Buddhist teachers brought with them the whole idea of monasticism? The monastic idea never gained a strong foothold in Judaism, but it did flourish beginning in the second century B.C.E. in both Israel and Egypt among the Essenes and the Therapeutae. Where did the pattern come from? It's conceivable that Jewish and Christian monasteries owe their origin to Buddhism.

Other scholars have speculated that Buddhist concepts infiltrated Jewish Gnostic circles in the first century. Alexandria is a possible locale for such interactions. This highly cosmopolitan port had separate quarters for Greeks, Jews, Egyptians, and a settlement of resident Hindus. There was a constant stream of merchants from western India—and Buddhists were merchants par excellence. Moreover, the city was full of philosophers who wrote books and lectured in lecture halls. It is not hard to imagine Buddhist and Jewish merchants, sitting around a table in cosmopolitan first-century Alexandria, at the time of Philo, exchanging merchandise, but also ideas and religious concepts, such as rebirth. Jewish Gnosticism is one acknowledged source for the later developments of kabbalah.

All of this is highly speculative, but thanks to the dialogue, I have a vivid sense of how it might have been. For instance, one afternoon at Kashmir Cottage I noticed Chodron and Jonathan Omer-Man sitting quietly together. "Jonathan had asked someone to come and teach him meditation," Chodron told me. "So I met with him on a few occasions, not as teacher and student, but as spiritual friends.

"I started explaining breathing meditation and he was saying he does that same thing, saying the name of God as you breathe in and out, trying to calm the mind down. It was very similar to what we do in Buddhism."

Jonathan learned from the experience that "the Buddhist approach to meditation is much more disciplined and structured than ours is. Nevertheless, there is a wonderful parallel, and even almost identical techniques. She gave me a very powerful meditation, a moment of wonderful joy and recognition and laughter."

Marc Lieberman offered a biological metaphor for such exchanges. "I don't know how Judaism assimilated stuff from other cultures, how, for instance, Aristotelian thought so thoroughly infiltrated the Jewish mind in the Middle Ages that rabbis since then have been obsessed with logic. Or how the gnostic experience in the Second Temple era was so profound that Judaism could no longer be a sacrificial religion, because Jews realized there were universal principles of cosmic wisdom. I don't know how the interface of Judaism and the world around it works. But it's like a cell wall. It's not simple diffusion. There are active pumps deciding whether this stuff is toxic or not.

"Some part of me says that this interface with Buddhism, dharma, meditation, maybe there's some very profound osmotic gradient, reminding lots of Jewish people that our picture of Judaism is just that, one picture in time. There are other materials to work with if we are spiritually hungry, the warehouse is a lot bigger than the room we are playing in."

Similarly, to Rabbi David Blank "Judaism is like a big archaeological heap of shofars and Torahs and good ideas. It's up to us to forge a coherency in the spiritual path so it does speak in one voice to us at the layer that we are on and we can choose whatever we want from the heap of treasures and half broken things that we don't understand.

"It's important for us to do that, and I don't think the work has been done yet. We need a coherent spiritual path in Judaism. There is none. We are in between right now. We need a great teacher to come to show us a new way to do it."

For now, there are only hints of what this coherent spiritual path would look like. Certainly Zalman Schachter and the tiny Jewish renewal movement represent part of the change. But whether they will be able to significantly influence the mainstream of Judaism remains to be seen. The cell wall of Judaism that Dr. Lieberman describes can get quite rigid when it comes to assimilating new ideas. Indeed, some in Jewish renewal, such as Rabbi Omer-Man, retain a certain caution. He explained, "One can find a commonality with other traditions and the commonality is extremely valuable. Yet in every esoteric tradition that I know of, there is an insistence that you must come through the exoteric, Sufis through Islam, Christians through Christianity, Jews through Judaism, to reach the esoteric."

Still, the common ground we discovered between the Jewish and Buddhist esoteric left me fascinated. At the 1991 P'nai Or Kallah, I asked Zalman Schachter what he felt when we saw so many points of likeness with Buddhism, such as doctrines of rebirth and systems of meditation.

"That's what I see as the no frills stuff," he answered. "It's the generic religion behind the whole business. You know . . . "—he closed his eyes to come up with the phrase, and a big smile lit up his face—"those are the ACTIVE INGREDIENTS. The rest of it is food coloring, packaging. The active ingredients is what works, you know?"

I knew. I had felt what works in Judaism many times during our trip to India, and never more so than during our last moments together in Judah Hyam Synagogue. Certainly, as I remember Ram Dass there, and Marc Lieberman behind him, and Joy and Blu and Yitz davening, and Isaac Malecar and his daughter, it seems that for a moment, all the elements of our journey had come together in one place, and all the Jewish secrets of survival we'd brought to the Dalai Lama were represented. Ironically, while Rabbi Greenberg felt obliged to stand apart when Joy

Levitt led the davening in Dharamsala, in Delhi he had an Orthodox *minyan,* with Ram Dass the tenth Jew. That was something to contemplate. My midrash: to be complete, Jews need to be more inclusive.

That evening in Delhi, a Jewish Hindu and a Hindu Jew joined the entire circle of those who have stayed within Judaism, and all those who might return if, as Rabbi David Blank put it, the right teacher—and the coherent teaching—can be found.

We were one already, at least in voice. Even after the formal service, we kept singing, really into the spirit of the thing, knowing these were our last moments together, not wanting to let go. As we sang "Etz Chayim," a tree of life, Paul Mendes-Flohr filled glasses of wine on a silver tray.

Then with Isaac Malecar's coaching, his daughter launched into a very hearty "Shalom Aleikhem," the traditional welcome to the angels who accompany worshipers home to the Shabbat table. I remembered again the Angel of Tibet and the Angel of the Jews.

Isaac asked his daughter to sing one more song. I couldn't help but think of my own daughters, to hear the familiar melody so far away from home, quavering in the air, tenuous and fragile, like Jewish survival, which always rests, as Blu had told the Dalai Lama, with our children.

"Lekha Dodi" was one last secret of Jewish survival. I heard in the song her father's pride and his efforts to sustain the last notes of a tradition in India that goes back thousands of years. I heard tradition and joy, family and the feminine, the lore of the Shekhinah and a hint of the esoteric, the legacy of Safed. Was I hearing the voice of an angel? I listened as a young girl welcomed the Shabbat Bride to the last shul in Delhi.

23

In a Pool of Nectar

Two years later, one effect of Jewish dialogue with the Dalai Lama has become clear. He now consistently describes the Tibetan tragedy as "cultural genocide" and a "Buddhist Holocaust."

Affirming his connection to Jewish history, on *Yom Hashoah* 1993, Holocaust Memorial Day (April 26), he became the first official visitor to the Holocaust Museum in Washington, entering it moments before the doors were thrown open to the general public. According to one account, he moved through three floors of exhibits, "his monk's robes lightly touching the floor, his head occasionally shaking in what appeared to be dismay. In the Hall of Remembrance, a chamber reserved for solace, he stood for four minutes in silence, his hands clasped to his chin in meditation." I wonder if he recalled there Rabbi Greenberg's lesson, "Always remind." In Dharamsala, Rabbi Greenberg had urged him to combine Buddhism with a more "this-worldly" consciousness. And at a tribute to Tibet that followed his visit to the Holocaust Museum, Elie Wiesel—his fellow Nobel Peace Prize winner—was even more blunt than Yitz had been. Wiesel said he respected Tibet as a place that "believes in prayer. But now Tibetans better learn the facts of life that the twentieth century has taught us: Prayers alone are not sufficient."

There is evidence that this very vigorous Jewish message has struck home. This is a real change. In Dharamsala, the religious leadership distinguished saving Tibet from saving Buddhism. Karma Gelek told us, "Because of the success of establishing monasteries, we don't worry about the disappearance of our culture from the surface of the earth."

Today the Dalai Lama does worry about it. This is clear from his statement to American Buddhists at the Tibetan Buddhist Learning Center later distributed in the spring of 1993. Although he noted with satisfaction the present spread of Tibetan Buddhism in the West, with "some one thousand centers around the world with over two hundred fifty in the United States alone," he argued against a "fatalism" among Western Buddhists "about the history and problem of Tibet; 'Well, it had to happen that way—otherwise Tibetans would not have come out of isolation into the world.'"

Instead, "in the midst of what can accurately be called 'the Buddhist holocaust' of the twentieth century," the Dalai Lama suggested that "as Buddhist practitioners, you should understand the necessity of preserving Tibetan Buddhism. For this the land, the physical country of Tibet, is crucial. It is very unlikely that [the sacred land of Tibet] can survive as a cultural and spiritual entity if its physical reality is smothered under Chinese occupation. Clearly, in this light, active support for the Tibetan cause is not just a matter of politics. It is the work of dharma." He seems to have become a dharma Zionist—with Tibet as the spiritual homeland of dharma.

Some other practical results followed our dialogue. Several major Jewish organizations have now gone on record in support of the Tibetan people in their struggle for freedom. In the summer of 1992, a promise was kept when Blu Greenberg arranged for two principals from Tibetan schools in India, Phuntsok Namgyal and Tenzin Sangpo, to visit Jewish day camps in the Catskills, Berkshires, and Dutchess County.

The Jewish-Buddhist dialogue also continues at the religious level. In the summer of 1992, the Naropa Institute sponsored a course taught by a rabbi and a JUBU Zen Buddhist abbot, Bernard Glassman. (Glassman had observed the first Jewish-Buddhist dialogue in New Jersey.) Elat Chayim, a Jewish spiritual camp affiliated with Zalman Schachter's group, P'nai Or, held a session on Torah dharma with Ram Dass. Later that fall, the Barre Center for Buddhist Studies sponsored a weekend retreat on Jewish Buddhist issues, led by Joseph Goldstein, with participation by Marc Lieberman and Moshe Waldoks. In the summer of 1993, similar programs were offered at Elat Chayim and once again at Naropa.

Rabbi Omer-Man's school of Jewish meditation in Los Angeles has taken the name Metivta. It has proven remarkably popular and has already served more than six hundred students. Marc Lieberman and Nancy Garfield are working on establishing a Buddhist vihara in San Francisco, and in fall 1992 Marc's son was bar mitzvahed. Blu Greenberg has been rallying women's groups in support of Tibetan women who are being sterilized by the Chinese. Rabbi Greenberg was roundly criticized by the Orthodox rabbinical assembly and almost expelled, but he continues his tireless efforts on behalf of *clal yisrael,* the community of Israel. Nathan Katz has edited an issue of the *Tibet Journal* on Tibetan-Jewish dialogue and published a book on Jews in India. Rabbi Zalman Schachter's group, P'nai Or, has reorganized itself as ALEPH, an alliance for Jewish renewal with a network of groups across the country. He also continues dialogue and teaching with a number of Buddhists, both Tibetans and Westerners.

Every participant from the Jewish side felt transformed by the dialogue experience. Rabbi Omer-Man, for instance, described the encounter with Tibetan Buddhism as the most important spiritual experience of his life, one that has empowered him in his Jewish work ever since.

My image of the encounter goes back to the moment we first saw the Dalai Lama in Dharamsala, at Tsuglakhang, the main temple. We were sitting in a row on metal folding chairs. I overheard Richard Gere explaining to Zalman Schachter some of the many *thangka*s hung about the temple, painted on silk in the bright primary colors Tibetans delight in. One behind the Dalai Lama depicted a layer cake of Buddhas, rising up in rows.

Zalman asked about the pool of water where they meditated. "Actually," Richard Gere said, "that pool of water is really a pool of nectar."

I couldn't have described our encounter with the Dalai Lama any better. He provided us a pool of nectar to look into, sweeter than a mirror, so that we Jews could see ourselves, not necessarily as we are, but as we might be.

This is what I saw: Judaism, stripped away of all its historical baggage, the long history of anti-Semitism and the defenses it has aroused. Judaism with its own joys and sweetness, and its own deep wisdom. The Dalai Lama gave each of us a glimpse of that, a glimpse so powerful it changed every one of us who experienced it.

Seeing Judaism in the light of Tibetan Buddhism, I realized that the religion of my birth is not just an ethnicity or an identity, but a way of life, and a spiritual path, as profound as any other. That path has three parts: prayer, study, and acts of loving-kindness.

I learned too that Jewish prayer in depth has more in common with Eastern meditation than I had realized. From my own experience at Beth Kangra—our outdoor synagogue in Dharamsala—I felt that davening is not just empty recital but can be a way of attunement, of becoming aware of relations between body, feelings, mind, and spirit. I learned too the power of "blessing," of finding the words to fit the occasion, seeking to make blessings and thereby making worldly experience holy.

As for study, I learned that Torah is not just a historical record, but truly a tree of life to those who hold fast to it. It is a source of wisdom that can comment on our lives, that can and must continually be made new. Our task as Jews is not simply to take it as it is, but to renew it through our study, through the creativity of our own commentary, our own midrash.

Finally, for deeds of loving-kindness: I have always known that Judaism demands we take action and enhance life. When I see Jews reaching out to the Tibetans, I know that aspect of our spiritual life continues to create blessings.

There is no reason for Jews to feel superior to any other people, nor must we separate ourselves to avoid contamination. We live in a pluralistic society and I think we are ready to take our place in it, as Jews. Our being Jewish is not an inheritance to waste, nor can we rest on our laurels. We have a constant challenge to live up to our ideals and traditions, and to let our actions speak louder than our words.

Altogether then, I came away with a deeper picture of Judaism and a message of Jewish renewal. As Rabbi Joy Levitt said, there's plenty of wisdom in the Jewish tradition, but what we need is a way to teach it.

Doors need to be opened for the many Jews who do not have access to the richness of Jewish spiritual wisdom.

What are the possibilities for Jewish renewal? First we need to understand clearly our religious history in America, how we got where we are today.

When Rabbi Greenberg presented the Dalai Lama with the power of Jewish memory, he was speaking from an Orthodox position. He was certainly correct about the modalities of Jewish life, the prayers and customs that keep Jewish memory alive—but only as once lived in Europe and by the Orthodox and ultra-Orthodox in America. One could make a counterargument: that the thousands of Jews who fled religion in the old country and assimilated in America also greatly ensured Jewish survival—and that their slogan, far from being "always remind," was really "always forget."

Though the Jews who came here in massive numbers around the turn of the century were nominally Orthodox, their degree of observance was never as great as Yitz described. For instance, in the 1960s it was estimated that fewer than 4 percent of all who considered themselves Orthodox Jews actually observed the Shabbat.

This trend also applies to the earlier wave of German Jewish immigration. The first rabbi of my own hometown synagogue, Baltimore Hebrew, was Abraham Rice. He was also the first yeshiva-trained Orthodox rabbi in America. His tenure met with despair and failure. His congregants refused to observe the Sabbath and very quickly fired him when he tried to keep Shabbas breakers from having *aliyot,* that is, reading publicly from the Torah. In a sad letter home, Rabbi Abraham Rice described the Jews in America as Moses described the dancers around the golden calf, as "a people broken loose."

The whole history of Judaism in America has been a jettisoning of most of Jewish memory. And the criterion for what to discard has been social, not spiritual. American Jews dropped whatever would distinguish them greatly from their Gentile neighbors or would keep them from competing in the secular world. This included keeping kosher and observing Shabbat.

In a stunning, if gently phrased challenge, the Dalai Lama asked Yitz Greenberg if our diaspora observances have changed as a result of now having a state of Israel. Our general laughter was telling. The Buddhist leader was posing the core choice most American Jews now face: give up our Diaspora traditions as irrelevant, or make aliyah. Most American Jews know they will do neither. Instead, we have created, de facto, the space for a third possibility, if only by our refusal to choose the other two.

The result has been a highly exoteric religion, conditioned by political causes such as support for Israel, and social and familial pressures. The pressing issues in American Jewish life today—intermarriage, Israel, anti-Semitism—are either social or political.

The Jews who are turned off to all spirituality, and the JUBUs and other Jews who have left the burnt house of Judaism for other traditions, are responding, then, to a real crisis. The materialism of much of Jewish life today, the lack of spirituality in our synagogue life, and the failure to communicate Judaism as a spiritual path have led, and will lead, many Jews to look elsewhere.

The house of Judaism in North America has not been satisfactorily built—it does not have a spiritual dimension for many Jews. Too many Jews are like me: our Jewishness has been an inchoate mixture of nostalgia, family feeling, group identification, a smattering of Hebrew, concern for Israel, and so forth. Yet we feel we are Jews, very strongly, and sense that somehow none of the current denominations really speak to our needs. As the state of Israel develops its own very different culture, it's clear that America will increasingly be on its own, as the Jewish historian Arthur Hertzberg argues convincingly. The vicarious relationship to Israel as a cause will not sustain Jewish affiliation in the long term—any more than devotion to other Jewish causes, such as civil rights, social equality, and combating anti-Semitism. There just isn't enough juice cheerleading for Israel to sustain Jews as a people in America, much less as a religion. Nor under current conditions, and despite the deep fund of world anti-Semitism, can we Jews derive our Jewishness solely by reacting to those who hate us.

Is there any hope for North American Judaism to emerge as a distinctly Jewish religion? Or will American Jews continue on the current path of staying loyal to a tradition that is not answering their needs? That is the question the Dalai Lama left us with—warning that if a tradition does not benefit people, in the long run they will not adhere to it.

If only Jews could see themselves as sweetly as the Dalai Lama saw us. Then we would see Judaism renewed. We need to work past the divisions among denominations to recognize what we have in common as Jews, promoting more tolerance among ourselves and greater self-respect. The terrible split between Orthodoxy and other Jews has damaged both sides. Most American Jews who are not Orthodox tend to feel that the Orthodox are the real Jews. In effect such Jews condemn themselves as inauthentic. This schizophrenia is unhealthy.

Creative Judaisms have emerged again and again in Diaspora—from Babylon to Spain to medieval Germany. I'd like to argue that we American Jews have always considered our situation different from the start, even if we didn't fully articulate it. Movements like Reform Judaism, Conservative Judaism, Reconstructionism, Modern Orthodoxy, and now the *chavurah* and Jewish renewal movements have all tried to come to grips with the unique opportunities and difficulties of American Jewish life.

The *chavurah* movement in which Zalman Schachter and Moshe Waldoks have been active is now twenty-five years old and its members are mostly middle-aged. New *chavurot* are being formed, and there are perhaps fifteen hundred families in *chavurot* nationwide. It remains to be seen whether a new generation will continue the movement or whether it was a response to the unique situation in the 1960s.

Nevertheless, certain thinkers and theologians have been conceptualizing what serious Jewish renewal might mean. Arthur Waskow moved from radical politics in the late 1960s to Jewish renewal. Since then, he's explored creative midrash in *Godwrestling* and the Jewish holiday cycle in *Seasons of Our Joy*. Judith Plaskow is a theologian who has carefully formulated the groundwork for a feminist Judaism in her book *Standing Again at Sinai*. Another important figure is Rabbi Arthur Green, who participated in the first encounter with the Dalai Lama in Washington, New Jersey. He founded the pioneer *chavurah*, Chavurat Shalom, and is a scholar of Jewish mysticism who until recently headed the Reconstructionist Rabbinical College. Rabbi Green has articulated a Jewish renewal theology in many articles and books, most recently in *Seek My Face, Speak My Name*. Speaking at a Jewish Buddhist conference in Barre, Massachusetts, in October 1993, he said, "As a Jewish theologian I've been told, 'You know you're really a Buddhist.' There's a little bit of truth in that. But my path has been entirely Jewish. I've felt that the spiritual life calls me to simplicity, calls me to sameness, a regular discipline. I'm a Jew for whom prayer is the central act."

Later, a participant at the conference echoed Ram Dass's insight that Jews know how to come together as a community. He said, "Jews have their *sangha* down." Green replied that "Judaism's dharma is less accessible than its *sangha* because Judaism's language is a hard language. Our dharma is harder to get to, takes a lot of patience to work on."

He told an anecdote of a "Holy Man Jam" in which he participated with Bro. David Stendl-Rast, a Catholic monk. He and Bro. David patiently explained the role of holy days in their respective traditions. By contrast, the Hindu priest who followed simply chanted and the Buddhist monk led a silent meditation. Afterwards, Green asked Bro. David, "Why couldn't we do that? Why did our practice have to be teaching our symbolic language, which is the way the West guards its spiritual treasures?"

In fact, Green argues, "Mysticism doesn't have to be esoteric, doesn't have to be a secret, and yet Judaism kept it a secret." He speculates about the reason for this. Perhaps it is because if everything is God (as Chabad mysticism teaches), then "what's the difference between Jews and *goyim*—why [eat] lambs and not pigs? If everything is God, then all the drama of distinction is hard to defend. And this threatens sanity, it threatens the order of life."

Perhaps, too, one could argue that insofar as European Jews perceived themselves as under threat of destruction from the other—from *goyim*—the need to keep such distinctions was an element of survival.

For Rabbi Green, the trauma of the Holocaust cut off the possibility of what he sees as a "natural progression from Hasidism to the modern world." For instance, within a circle of Jewish mystics in prewar Poland there was a generation of Hasidic thinkers coming to terms with modernity. "But then three-fourths of the teachers were killed and the rest were freaked out of their minds, running away from the universal, saying, We were wrong to trust the *goyim*. The Holocaust deeply poisoned Judaism in a xenophobic way."

But today, Green feels, Jews must get beyond the Holocaust poisoning and pick up the thread of that more universal Judaism suggested by Hasidic thought. Jews face the problem of creating a spiritual life. He thinks it is necessary to "be the spiritual Jew you are in a public and accessible way, to create a study group or *minyan* that's open and accessible to people. Make the spiritual reality of the tradition available. The only salvation for the Jewish *sangha* will be a spiritual path."

At the organizational level, there is currently a network of thirty Jewish renewal *chavurot* connected with P'nai Or as well as a large national network of *chavurot* under the National Havurah Committee based in Philadelphia. Since many participants also belong to synagogues, Jewish renewal attitudes are influencing many of the established denominations and will continue to do so. So it is also possible that some form of Jewish renewal will emerge from within the denominations. It will be interesting to see what happens as a generation of Jews raised in Orthodox and ultra-Orthodox settings in America confront the contemporary world. If separation continues to work for them, they will stay within the fold. But if it doesn't, they may contribute to the development of Jewish renewal as they seek new forms of expressing Jewish life in America today.

I cannot predict the future or know how—or even if—Jewish renewal will take place. But I have some notions of what it might look like if it does. Jewish renewal will recognize the power of what is holy in our lives today. Just as Rabbi Greenberg could see the call to pluralism as part of God's will, so Jewish renewal can recognize the power in the movement toward full equality for women, in granting full dignity to gays and lesbians, and in the search for a livable environment.

At the same time, Jewish renewal will be much more respectful of tradition than Reform Judaism historically has been, seeking, in Zalman Schachter's words, "a maximum of Jewish expression." Intense davening, *mikvehs*, or ritual baths, and other customs and expressions associated with Orthodox Judaism will also be found in renewal. Orthodox rites formerly practiced only by men will also be practiced by women, who will infuse old traditions with new energy and joy.

Jewish renewal will be pluralistic, open to dialogue with other Jews and with other religions. Just as Jews tried to be a blessing for Tibetans, so Jews in America have proven already to be a model of a successful religious minority. In that sense we can relate to burgeoning minorities of American Muslims and Asian Buddhists. Very soon, in the U.S., practicing Muslims will outnumber Jews, and they are increasingly reaching out to us. The day may well come when Muslims, Jews, and Buddhists will share a similar agenda—in America.

Here again, the pluralism in American Jewish life gives Jews a safe context to appreciate our own history more richly and variously. This contrasts with the more defended Orthodox separatism. A Judaism that is pluralistic and respectful of the wisdom of other groups will be highly consonant with American life.

A renewed Judaism will be more porous—more willing to acknowledge that Judaism has borrowed from other cultures in the past, and more willing to borrow techniques and practices from other religions today, reassimilating them into a Jewish context. Sufi *dhikr* and Buddhist meditation on the breath are influences from the Eastern prayer mode that can be easily absorbed by Jews.

A renewed Judaism will certainly be more aware of its own mystical tradition, seeking through specific practices of prayer and meditation to increase *kavvanah*, and to realize in everyday life the spiritual values of the Hasidim.

This brings me to practice, and none of these changes will be meaningful without a deepening of Jewish practice. But that deepening can no longer be seen as an all-or-nothing proposition. We Jews must become more flexible and welcoming to those who are sincere about exploring our spiritual richness. We could again learn from Buddhist teaching—and the Lubavitchers—by offering a few practices at a time.

Just as Shabbat and keeping kosher were the first practices to be discarded by many American Jews in their quest for assimilation, so they may be the place to begin again. Interestingly, as increasing numbers of Americans become vegetarians, keeping kosher via keeping vegetarian will no longer separate Jews from others. It will therefore be easier to commit to vegetarian kosher as a matter of health, environmentalism, and spiritual practice. As for Shabbat, it is essential that Jews learn to taste the sweetness of this core secret of Jewish life.

It's interesting to observe in the nontraditional Western Buddhist community, how its practitioners are grappling with the same problem Jews faced in coming to America: how to combine spiritual practice with daily life. Since most Buddhist practitioners hold jobs and many have families, the monastic model is not an option. Instead they have opted for a temporary monasticism in the form of weekend, weeklong, and monthlong retreats to Buddhist meditation centers. They move in and out of the spiritual and material world, and the big question they are facing is how to handle the transitions, how to move between the purity of a meditative life to the demands of the samsaric world.

Obviously, since most American Jews have dumped the Sabbath, it's difficult to say that it's a real model for Western Buddhists. But Shabbat, when done right, does create a very carefully planned retreat from the world in the context of family life.

What Jews might learn from Buddhists is how to deepen Shabbat, heighten its meditative content. A rabbi once declared to me her experience of a Buddhist monastery, "It's Shabbat all the time!" What Buddhists might learn from Jews are the forms or shell of the Shabbat, the rituals such as the *mikveh,* the candle lighting, and the blessings, which enable Jews to make a transition from a worldly to a spiritual realm and back again.

Deepening the prayer experience is essential to Jewish renewal. When the Jewish spirit was renewed in eighteenth-century Eastern Europe, the Hasidim turned away from an emphasis on studying Talmud, because the community in the small towns and *shtetls* of Podolia was poor and poorly educated. Instead, the Hasidic masters opened wide the door of prayer. I'd like to suggest that an emphasis on prayer would also be the best door for Jewish renewal in America today. Because we too are poor—in spirit—and poorly educated, in Jewish techniques of inner transformation.

In effect, I'm calling for a kind of neo-Hasidism, because without an infusion of Jewish spiritual fervor in prayer and blessings and observances, the reason to stay Jewish, the juice, will be lost.

I can only offer this brief sketch of Jewish renewal. Others have been working hard to fill in the outlines—theologians, activists, rabbis, and leaders, and of course the Jewish women and men in *chavurot* and Jewish renewal communities. Even if their numbers are relatively small, their work is important. If, as Yitz Greenberg asserted, Judaism is now facing a crisis as great as the first century, then, too, like the first-century rabbis, we must renew to preserve.

The dialogue with Tibetans has heightened my awareness of the precious value and fragility of all of our world's ancient spiritual traditions.

The Chinese attack on Tibet's religion is a particularly virulent example of the global destruction of the religious ecosystem by materialists who uproot religious environments along with natural ones in their quest for productivity and profits. It is an attack predicated on scientism—the belief that the objectivity of the laboratory is the only model for knowing truth.

I confess that before I encountered the spirituality of Buddhism—and Judaism—in Dharamsala, I was more inclined to the scientific, if not scientistic, viewpoint. I was a materialist and a skeptic, at least when it came to defining reality. The transformation in my own life tells me that the subtlety of consciousness—the quiet mind—that a Dalai Lama develops cannot be denied. It is as real as anything—it is as real as any *thing*. And far more precious.

Our ancient sources of wisdom call on human beings to rise to their highest capacity and behave in extraordinarily open and generous ways to one another, under difficult circumstances to transcend differences and create understanding across all barriers of convention and fear. This wisdom is fragile as our environment is fragile, threatened by an overwhelming material culture. I believe in a spiritual ecology. In today's world, Judaism and Tibetan Buddhism and other wisdom traditions are endangered species.

Like the Dalai Lama and Rabbi Greenberg, I worry in particular that Tibetan Buddhism will not survive. Not just for the Tibetans' sake, but for the world's sake. As the Dalai Lama has stated, "Tibetan culture belongs to all humanity, and its extinction would not just affect Tibetans, but all humanity."

I worry too about my own people. I am grateful we have an Israel and that some remnants of the great Talmudic and Hasidic traditions have survived the Holocaust and propagate themselves in America. Perhaps it is true that the only Judaism to survive in the long run will be among these separationists, these preservationists. Or perhaps in the future there will only be two types of Jews: totally assimilated and Israelis. I am hoping for a third alternative. I am hoping Judaism will survive and renew itself, because it has something vital to offer the world.

In comparing Judaism to Buddhism, I have come to value the Jewish emphasis on adding a sacred dimension to daily life, especially through the Shabbat, which brings families together and allows every Jew to taste the sweetness of a spiritual life without retreating utterly from the world. As Jews we do not have to choose between family life and the monastery—we have a blueprint for combining both, if only we will follow it.

The Holocaust and its aftershocks, and the politics of Zionism, have both been key issues for American Jews. But the sadness and pain of our memories—and the tensions of political struggles, both internal and external—have often obscured our inner joy.

Jonathan Omer-Man described to the Dalai Lama "a path of joy." "People are very much into bringing more fun into Judaism," he told me, "but fun is not joy. Joy is ecstatic knowledge with all parts of one's being, an integrated way of knowing. It's truly a quest."

It is time now to continue that quest—and essential to Jewish survival.

Notes and References

INTRODUCTION

p. 1 *I studied the modern history of Tibet.* The best single source is John Avedon, *In Exile from the Land of Snows* (New York: Vintage, 1986.) The International Campaign for Tibet, 1518 K Street, NW, Suite 410, Washington, DC 20005 publishes *Tibet Press Watch* and other sources of information on events in contemporary Tibet.

CHAPTER 1 SPARKS

p. 19 *the kabbalah teaches that the Jewish soul is composed of many brilliant sparks* The *nitzatzot ha-neshamot* or "sparks of the soul" is a development of the Lurianic kabbalah. For a brief account, see Gershom Scholem, *Kabbalah* (New York: Meridian, 1978), pp. 347–48. For a beautiful account of kabbalistic teaching in general, as seen by a practitioner, see Aryeh Kaplan, *Inner Space* (Brooklyn: Moznaim, 1990).

p. 27 *The history of the spread of Buddhism to the West* I am indebted to Rick Fields's *How the Swans Came to the Lake* (Boulder: Shambhala, 1981), a very readable history.

Charles Prebish's book is *American Buddhism* (Duxbury Press, 1979).

p. 11 *A Torah scroll was unwrapped* See *New York Times*, September 26, 1989. Baltimore *Jewish Times*, October 13, 1989.

CHAPTER 2   FLAMES

p. 18 *Lieberman had sent each of us* **The Dhammapada** The text was *The Dhammapada: The Path of Truth,* trans. Ven. Balangoda Maitreya, revised by Ruth Kramer (Novato, CA: Lotsawa, 1988).

p. 21 *The historian Arthur Hertzberg* See Hertzberg's excellent account, *The Jews in America, Four Centuries of an Uneasy Encounter: A History* (New York: Simon and Schuster, 1989).

See also Charles Liebman, "Orthodoxy in American Jewish Life," *American Jewish Year Book,* 1965 (66) (Philadelphia: Jewish Publication Society, 1965), pp. 21–27.

CHAPTER 4   HEIGHTS

p. 42 *the Torah portion* The portion was *Lekh Lekha.*

p. 45 *active at the inception of the chavurah movement* See Richard Siegel, Michael Strassfeld, Sharon Strassfeld, *The First Jewish Catalog* (Philadelphia: The Jewish Publication Society, 1973) pp. 296–318. Zalman Schachter's article, "A First Step: A Devotional Guide," is an excellent introduction to Jewish renewal spirituality.

p. 48 *Rabbi Joseph Soloveitchik* Rabbi Soloveitchik died in 1993. His major works are: *Halakhic Man,* trans. Lawrence Kaplan (Philadelphia: Jewish Publication Society, 1983), and *The Lonely Man of Faith* (New York: Doubleday, 1992).

CHAPTER 5   BLESSINGS

p. 61 *the long history of Jewish blessings* See Hayim Donin, *To Pray As a Jew* (New York: Basic Books, 1980).

p. 63 *Yitz felt the Dalai Lama himself had removed such claims in his latest autobiography* Tenzin Gyatso, Dalai Lama XIV, *Freedom in Exile: The Autobiography of the Dalai Lama* (New York: HarperCollins, 1990), p. xiii.

CHAPTER 6   CONTACT

p. 65 *how the rebbe tied his shoes* Attributed to a disciple of Dov Baer, the great Maggid of Mezhirech. See Martin Buber, *Tales of the Hasidim: Early Masters* (New York: Shocken, 1961), p. 107.

p. 68 *Katz believed that Judaism and Buddhism had contact in the past* For a fuller account and references, see Nathan Katz, "Contacts between Jewish and Indo-Tibetan Civilizations through the Ages: Some Explorations," *The Tibet Journal* 16, no. 4 (1991): 90–109. The Jataka tale Katz cites is found in the *Mahoshadha Jataka,* which he compares to the judgment tale of King Solomon (1 Kings 3:16–28).

CHAPTER 7   THE ANGEL OF TIBET
AND THE ANGEL OF THE JEWS

p. 72 **Kavvanah** *is an important element of Hasidic devotional practice* The term is used in the Talmud (*Eruv,* 95b) but developed to its height by Rabbi Isaac

Luria and his followers in Safed, from whom it passed to the Hasidim. See Gershom Scholem, *Major Trends in Jewish Mysticism* (New York: Shocken, 1973), pp. 275–78.

p. 75 **The deep way is the way of kabbalah** Major scholarly works on kabbalah include the following texts: Gershom Scholem, *Major Trends in Jewish Mysticism;* Gershom Scholem, *Kabbalah* (New York: Meridian, 1978); Gershom Scholem, *On the Kabbalah and Its Symbolism* (New York: Schocken Books, 1965); Moshe Idel, *Kabbalah: New Perspectives* (New Haven: Yale University Press, 1988). For books on kabbalah from the point of view of a practitioner, see: Aryeh Kaplan, *Inner Space* (Brooklyn: Moznaim, 1990); Aryeh Kaplan, *Meditation and Kabbalah* (York Beach, ME: Samuel Weiser, 1989).

p. 76 **In Tibetan Buddhist teaching** An excellent popular introduction can be found in Nancy Ross, *Buddhism: A Way of Life and Thought* (New York: Vintage, 1981), pp. 101–140.

p. 76 **The four supernal worlds** These are known as the *olamot,* or universes. See Kaplan, *Inner Space,* p. 137

p. 77 **The four worlds cosmology comes straight out of the Lurianic kabbalah** For a brief scholarly discussion of this history, see Scholem, *Major Trends,* p. 272.

p. 77 **Rabbi Schachter's update** A recently published account of four worlds davening can be found in *Worlds of Jewish Prayer,* ed. Shohama Wiener and Jonathan Omer-Man (Northvale, NJ: Jason Aronson, 1993). See also Zalman Schachter's introduction to the *Or Chadash* siddur published by the P'nai Or Religious Fellowship, 7318 Germantown Avenue, Philadelphia, PA 19119; and by the same publisher, *Gates to the Heart.*

p. 85 **Shunyata *is also called by the Tibetans "dependent arising"*** See the *Prajnaparamita-hridaya,* or Heart Sutra. The topic was developed in the writings of the Indian Buddhist Nagarjuna. For two contemporary discussions by Tibetan Buddhist practitioners, see Chogyam Trungpa, *Cutting Through Spiritual Materialism* (Berkeley: Shambhala, 1973), and Thubten Chodron, *Open Heart, Clear Mind* (Ithaca, N.Y.: Snow Lion, 1990). For the Dalai Lama's own account of *shunyata,* see *The Dalai Lama at Harvard* (Ithaca, N.Y.: Snow Lion, 1989). See also The Dalai Lama, "Dependent Arising," *Cho Yang: The Voice of Tibetan Religion and Culture.* (Dharamsala) 3, 1990.

CHAPTER 8 ALWAYS REMIND

p. 93 **As Jewish sociologist Arnold Eisen has noted** In an article published in the *American Jewish Year Book* 1991 (91) (Philadelphia: Jewish Publication Society), pp. 3–33.

Rabbi Greenberg's book on the covenant is *The Voluntary Covenant* (New York: National Jewish Resource Center, 1982).

p. 97 **"Each of the holy days was reinterpreted"** For an excellent account of how this works in practice, see Rabbi Greenberg's *The Jewish Way: Living the Holidays*

(New York: Summit, 1988). See also Arthur Waskow, *Seasons of Our Joy* (Boston: Beacon, 1982).

p. 98 **memory theaters of ancient Roman rhetoric** See Francis Yates, *The Art of Memory* (Chicago: Univ. of Chicago Press, 1966).

CHAPTER 9   DEBATING MONKS AND ANGELS

p. 111 **Rav Kook, the great chief rabbi of Israel** Rabbi Abraham Isaac Kook (1865–1935) was the chief rabbi of Palestine. See *Abraham Isaac Kook—The Lights of Penitence, Lights of Holiness, The Moral Principles, Essays, Letters and Poems*, trans. Ben Zion Bokser (New York: Paulist Press, 1978).

p. 114 **The monks were debating** For the Dalai Lama's account of his own training in debate, see *Freedom in Exile*, pp. 25–26.

CHAPTER 10   SHABBAT SHALOM AND TASHE DELEK

p. 119 **training of young tulkus** The *tulku* is a unique development of Tibetan Buddhism not shared by other forms of Buddhism. For a sympathetic discussion of the institution, see Ross, *Buddhism: A Way of Life*, pp. 107–110. John Avedon's account of how the Dalai Lama was discovered makes fascinating reading and can be found in chapter 1, *In Exile from the Land of Snows.*

p. 124 **Vipassana [insight meditation]** There are many excellent guides to insight meditation. Among them are Thich Nhat Hanh, *The Miracle of Mindfulness* (Boston: Beacon Press, 1987); Nyanaponikia Thera, *The Heart of Buddhist Meditation* (London: Rider, 1983); Joseph Goldstein and Jack Kornfield, *Seeking the Heart of Wisdom* (Boston: Shambhala, 1987).

p. 125 **The geshes described their training** For an account of training at the Namgyal Monastery both in Tibet and now in exile, see Kalden Lodro and Jeremy Russel, "Namgyal Monastery," *Cho Yang* 3 (Dharamsala, 1990).

CHAPTER 11   JEWISH BUDDHISTS, BUDDHIST JEWS

p. 140 **In the Mishneh Torah** See Isadore Twersky, ed., *A Maimonides Reader* 140 (New York: Behrman House, 1972), p. 54.

CHAPTER 13   TIBETAN INTELLECTUALS, TIBETAN ORPHANS

p. 158 **A more militant path** Lhasang Tsering was interviewed in Nepal in 1993 by R. W. Ankerson, Jr., of the *Independent*. He stated his opposition clearly: "I think the Tibetan people should come to certain ground realities, that in the foreign policy of governments there is no place for love, compassion, and kindness—it's all a question of self-interest." See *The Independent*, Kathmandu, Nepal, February 3, 1993.

CHAPTER 14   AN INTERVIEW WITH THE ORACLE

p. 173 **visualization practice** For a description of visualization practices, see Part Five of Kathleen McDonald, *How to Meditate: A Practical Guide* (Boston: Wisdom Books, 1990).

p. 174 **maaseh merkavah** See Scholem, *Major Trends,* pp. 40–79.

p. 175 *This same Joseph Karo had regular communications with a* maggid See Louis Jacobs, *Jewish Mystical Testimonies* (New York: Schocken, 1976), pp. 98–122. Jacobs has compiled fascinating accounts of Jewish mystical experiences throughout the ages.

CHAPTER 15 SECRET DOORS

p. 188 *the four levels of interpretation* Interested readers may explore the Torah commentaries of Rashi and Nachmanides. The classic rabbinic midrash are compiled in several volumes for each of the five books of Moses, as *Genesis Rabbah, Exodus Rabbah,* etc. For examples of contemporary midrash, see Arthur Waskow, *Godwrestling* (New York: Schocken, 1978) and Lawrence Kushner, *The River of Light* (San Francisco: Harper & Row, 1981).

p. 192 *chanting the name of God, but using different vowel sounds* Similar techniques are described in greater detail in Aryeh Kaplan, *Meditation and Kabbalah* (York Beach, ME: Samuel Weiser, 1982), pp. 87–92. This passage is based on texts of the Spanish kabbalist Abraham Abulafia. There are other developments of this in the Lurianic *kavvanot.*

p. 194 *much of the work of inner clarification we do in dialogue with a teacher* See Zalman Schachter-Shalomi, *Spiritual Intimacy: A Study of Counseling in Hasidism* (Northvale, NJ: Jason Aronson, 1991).

p. 195 *going alone to a place and shouting and crying to God* This seems to be a description of *hitbodedut* meditation as practiced by Rabbi Nachman of Bratzlav. See Kaplan, *Meditation and Kabbalah,* pp. 309–13. Kaplan quotes from Rabbi Nachman's *Hishtapkhut HaNefesh* (Outpouring of the soul).

CHAPTER 16 TANTRA AND KABBALAH

p. 201 *through that visualization you bring the practice of method and wisdom together* The Dalai Lama is outlining *tantrayana,* or Buddhist tantric meditation practices. For more detailed descriptions see Daniel Cozort, *Highest Yoga Tantra* (Ithaca, N.Y.: Snow Lion, 1986), and David Snellgrove, *Indo-Tibetan Buddhism* (London: Serindia, 1987). For an insightful and provocative account of the relationship between female sexuality and tantric practices, see Rita Gross, "Yeshe Tsogyel: Enlightened Consort, Great Teacher, Female Role Model" in Janice Willis, ed., *Feminine Ground: Essays on Women and Tibet* (Ithaca, N.Y.: Snow Lion, 1989).

p. 205 *As described in Rabbi Aryeh Kaplan's* Jewish Meditation See ch. 17, pp. 154–61.

p. 205 *the entire mystical Shabbat was organized in anticipation of the sexual union* This is explored in detail in Elliot Ginsburg's selection from *Tolaat Yakov,* a sixteenth-century kabbalistic work by Meir ibn Gabbai. See Ginsburg, *Sod Ha-Shabbat (The mystery of the Sabbath)* (Albany: SUNY Press, 1989).

CHAPTER 17 SURVIVAL STRATEGIES

p. 221 *That indeed is what the* Zohar *makes explicit* See Sperling, Simon, Levertoff, trans., *The Zohar (III)* (New York: Soncino, 1984), p. 253. "Said R. Abba:

'When the smoke came out of Mount Sinai a fire ascended enveloped therein, so that its flames were of a blue color. They flared high and dwindled again, and the smoke emitted all the aromas of Paradise. . . . It was the *Shekinah* who manifested Herself thus at the giving of the Law in the wilderness on Mount Sinai. . . .'"

p. 218 *The Tibetan nuns needed special support* For an excellent account of the life and the joys and difficulties of Tibetan *anis*, see Janice Willis, "Tibetan *Anis*: The Nun's Life in Tibet" in Willis, *Feminine Ground: Essays on Women and Tibet* (Ithaca, N.Y.: Snow Lion, 1989).

CHAPTER 19   A BUDDHIST JEW—THE ALLEN GINSBERG STORY

p. 240 *Back in 1962, the Tibetan dzog chen master, Dudjom Rinpoche, had advised Ginsberg* Interestingly, Ginsberg did not mention his meeting with Dudjom Rinpoche in his 1965 *Paris Review* interview with Tom Clark. He did mention a visit with the Dalai Lama during this same journey.

CHAPTER 20   A SYNAGOGUE IN DELHI

p. 249 *The scholar Walter Fishel notes* See Walter Fishel, "Jews and Judaism at the Court of the Moghul Emperors in Medieval India," *Islamic Culture* 25:105–31. See also Nathan Katz, "Sarmad 'the Everlasting': An Eccentric Jewish Sufi of Mughal India," *Journal of the Society of Rabbis in Academia* 2, no. 1 (January 1992): 13–17.

p. 249 *When I looked at the text* For the text of the Dabistan see Shea and Troyer, trans., *The Dabistan, or School of Manners* (Paris: Oriental Translation Fund, 1843).

p. 251 *As Sarmad has written* For excerpts from Sarmad's poetry and a brief biography see B. Hashimi "Sarmad: His Life and Quatrains," *Islamic Culture* (1933, 1934), pp. 663–72 and 92–104.

CHAPTER 22   A LAST SECRET

p. 273 *Other scholars have speculated* Earlier writers on Gnosticism associated the movement with Christianity, but Gershom Scholem argued for a Jewish origin to the teachings. Many scholars have seen a Buddhist influence on Gnostic teachings. An early article is J. Kennedy's "Buddhist Gnosticism: the System of Basilides," *J.R.A.S.*, 377ff. The Buddhist scholar Edward Conze writes, "It seems to me remarkable that during the same period of time—i.e., from ca. 200 B.C. onwards—two distinct civilizations, one in the Mediterranean, the other in India, should have constructed a closely analogous set of ideas concerning 'Wisdom,' each one apparently independently from its own cultural antecedents." He notes several similarities between "Chochma and Sophia on the one side and the Prajnaparamita on the other." See Conze, *Buddhist Studies: 1934–1972* (San Francisco: Wheelwright Press, 1972), p. 20.

Gershom Scholem notes the similarities between the tzaddik and the bodhisattva, though he finds the two systems historically unconnected. See Scholem, *On the*

Mystical Shape of the Godhead (New York: Schocken, 1991), p. 212. However, in the same essay, he writes of "vestiges of an early Jewish Gnostic tradition" reaching kabbalists in medieval Jewish Europe "from the Orient." If Gnosticism could be proven to have been influenced by Buddhism, this would establish a link. Moshe Idel, commenting on similarities between mandalas used in Hindu meditation and the diagrams of *sefirot*, writes that "one cannot underrate the possibility that Hindu traditions infiltrated into Kabbalah, perhaps via the intermediacy of Sufi material." See Idel, *Kabbalah: New Perspectives*, p. 108.

CHAPTER 23 IN A POOL OF NECTAR

p. 277 *his monks robes lightly touching the floor* See Arthur Magida, "A Museum for Americans," Baltimore *Jewish Times*, April 30, 1993.

Glossary

A Note on Spelling

For Hebrew words, I've followed the convention of spelling the Hebrew letter *koof* with a *k* (kabbalah), and *khof* with *kh* (Shekhinah, halakhah). The *kh* sound does not appear in English. It should be pronounced like the *ch* in the Scottish *loch*.

I've reserved *ch* to represent the Hebrew letter *ḥet,* hence Chanukah, Chavurah.

For Tibetan words, I have followed the simplified spellings. Many consonants have been left out. For instance, the simplified spelling of the Dalai Lama's name is Tenzin Gyatso, whereas the more accurate transliteration is Bstan-'dzin-rgya-mtsho.

HEBREW AND YIDDISH

Adam Kadmon The first Adam, a fifth kabbalistic realm conceived as the mystical body of the original Adam.

ain sof lit., without bound. The impersonal aspect of God about which nothing can be, properly, thought or said.

aleinu lit., "it is incumbent upon us." Prayer of divine sovereignty.

aliyah, pl. *aliyot* lit., going up. 1. One who is called to read from the Torah. 2. One who ascends by returning to live in Israel.

assiyah lit., action, doing. One of four kabbalistic realms.

atziluth lit., nearness. One of four kabbalistic *olamim* (realms or worlds).

ayin Nothing.

Baal Shem Tov lit., Master of the Good Name. Rabbi Israel Baal Shem Tov was the founder of Hasidism.

baalei teshuvah lit., those who return. Jews returning to religious observance.

bar mitzvah lit., son of the commandment. Male who has passed a Jewish literacy test by reading from the Torah and haftarah.

barkhu The call to prayer, from the Hebrew *berekh*, or knee. Recited with bowed head and bent knee.

bat mitzvah lit., daughter of the commandment. Female, same as bar mitzvah.

beriah lit., creation. One of four kabbalistic worlds.

binah lit., understanding. One of the ten sefirot.

birkat hamazon Prayer after the meal.

boychik (Yiddish) Boy or son, affectionate.

brakha, pl. *brakhot* Blessing.

bsar vdam Flesh and blood.

chavurah, pl. *chavurot* lit., a fellowship. A small informal Jewish prayer group.

chazzan Cantor.

chesed lit., loving-kindness, mercy. One of the ten sefirot.

chokham, hokham A wise person, and specifically a Torah scholar.

chokhmah, hokhmah Wisdom. Also, one of the ten sefirot.

chutzpah (Yiddish) Nerve.

clal yisrael (also, *klal yisrael*) The community of Israel.

daven (Yiddish) To pray.

drash, also *drush* A midrash.

Etz Chaim lit., tree of life. Hymn in praise of the Torah, from passage in Proverbs.

galut Exile.

gevurah lit., strength, power. One of the ten sefirot.

gilgul Reincarnation.

glatt lit., smooth. Very stringent standard of kashrut.

gornisht (Yiddish) Nothing.

goyim Gentiles.

haimish (Yiddish) "Home-like," friendly and familiar, comfortable.

halakhah The body of Jewish law.

Hallel Group of psalms chanted in praise of God.

Hallelujah Praise God.

hasid pl. *hasidim* A pious person, and in Talmudic texts, a saint.

Hasid, pl. *Hasidim* Member of a religious and mystical spiritual revival movement, beginning in the eighteenth century in the Ukraine and Poland.

hitbodedut lit., self-isolation. A form of Jewish meditation taught by Rabbi Nachman of Bratzlav, involving an individual's calling out to God.

hitbonenut lit., self-understanding. A form of Jewish meditation taught in the Lubavitch tradition, involving a contemplation of all things in relation to God.

hod lit., glory or majesty. One of the ten sefirot.

kabbalah lit., tradition. Body of Jewish esoteric doctrine and lore.

Kaddish An ancient Aramaic prayer in praise of God's powers, recited as prayers for the dead and at other points in the prayer service.

kappoteh (Yiddish) Liturgical robe or caftan.

kavvanah, pl. *kavvanot* intention. Meditation prior to prayer or holy act.

keter lit., crown. One of the ten sefirot.

keter malkhut lit., crown of sovereignty. A Jewish mystical path.

kiddush Blessing over wine, recited at the Sabbath and holidays.

kippah Skullcap.

kreplach Delicious Jewish wonton.

l'chaim To life. Traditional Jewish toast.

Lekha Dodi lit., Welcome to the Bride. Sixteenth-century mystical Sabbath hymn, composed by Solomon Alkabez, in Safed.

Lubavitcher Member of a particular sect of Hasidim founded by Rabbi Shneur Zalman of Lyady (1745–1813).

maariv Evening prayers.

macher (Yiddish) Influential person. Big cheese.

malkhut lit., kingdom. One of the ten sefirot.

matzah Unleavened bread used at Passover.

mensch (Yiddish) A decent human being.

menschlichkeit (Yiddish) Behavior of a decent human being.

midrash Imaginative Torah commentary.

mikveh Pool of water for ritual immersion.

minyan Prayer quorum, traditionally ten men.

mishegos (Yiddish) Craziness.

mitzvah Commandment; good deed.

mohel Ritual circumciser.

naarishkeit (Yiddish) Foolishness.

netzach lit., reverberation or endurance. One of the ten sefirot.

Oneg Shabbat lit., rejoicing in the sabbath. A festive meal following a Shabbat prayer service.

ophan Wheel angel.

parasha Portion of Torah read, according to the calendar.

payos, payot Sidelocks.

pilpul lit., pepper. A Talmudic quibble.

pogrom Deliberate large-scale murder of Jews, encouraged by the Czarist state.

pusek A passage from the Torah.

reb Rabbi. Affectionate title.

rebbe (Yiddish) Rabbi. Affectionate title for Hasidic rabbi.

seder Ritual Passover meal.

sefer Book, often a holy book.

Sefer Yetzirah Book of Formation. Earliest kabbalistic work, attributed to Rabbi Akiva.

sefirah, pl. *sefirot* lit., numbers. The supernal lights, divine grades, aspects, attributes of God. The names for the seven lower sefirot are derived from 1 Chron. 29:11.

Sephardi, Sephardic Referring to one of two main divisions of Jews, the Sephardim. Sepharad (Obad. 9:20) was identified with Spain. The Jews of Spain, North Africa, and the Middle East.

Shabbas, Shabbos, Shabbat Jewish Sabbath.

shakharit Morning prayer service.

shaliakh tzibbur Prayer leader.

shalom aleikhem Peace unto you. Greeting. Also a Shabbat hymn sung to the angels that accompany worshipers.

shammas Synagogue caretaker.

Shekhinah God's indwelling presence, conceived as female.

Shema 1. Prayer affirming unity of God (Deut. 6:4). 2. Three Bible passages read in morning and evening prayers (Deut. 6:4–9, 11:13–21; Num. 15:37–41).

shlep (Yiddish) To haul, carry.

shokhet Kosher meat slaughterer.

shpilkes lit., pins. Nervousness

shtiebl (Yiddish) lit., a little house. Small room for prayer gatherings.

shul (Yiddish) Synagogue.

Shulkhan Arukh lit., the Set Table. A concise guide to Jewish law, compiled by Rabbi Joseph Karo.

Simchat Torah lit., Rejoicing in the Torah. Holiday celebrating completion of yearly cycle of Torah reading.

streiml (Yiddish) Fur hat worn by some Hasidim.

tallit, tallis; pl. *tallisim* Fringed prayer shawl.

Talmud Compendium of rabbinic law, stories, and wisdom, composed and compiled from 200 B.C.E. to 500 C.E.

tefillin Phylacteries. Prayer amulets bound by leather straps to the forehead and the left arm.

tiferet lit., beauty. One of the ten sefirot.

tikkun lit., repair. In Lurianic kabbalah, an act of devotion designed to raise sparks to a higher level.

tikkun olam Repair of the world, whether manifested in the social realms as concrete acts of goodness or as a mystical process of restoring the sparks to their proper place.

Torah The five books of Moses, and by extension, all of Jewish tradition and teaching.

tzuris (Yiddish) Troubles, pain.

urim and *thummim* Lots used for divination by the high priest.

yarmulke (Yiddish) Skullcap.

yeshiva School for rabbinic study.

yesod lit., foundation. One of the ten sefirot.

yetzirah lit., formation. One of four kabbalistic worlds. See *olamot*.

Zohar The Book of Splendor, kabbalistic masterpiece from thirteenth century Spain.

TIBETAN AND SANSKRIT

ani lit., auntie. A Buddhist nun.

anicca Impermanence.

Avalokiteshvara The Bodhisattva of Compassion. Tibetan Buddhists consider the Dalai Lama to be a manifestation of Avalokiteshvara.

bhikku, bhikshu Monk.

bodhichitta Good heart, altruism.

bodhisattva One who forswears the achievement of nirvana to aid others. "The Bodhisattva ideal is the aspiration to practise infinite compassion with infinite wisdom" (XIV Dalai Lama).

Buddha lit., the awakened one. The historic Buddha, Gautama. Mahayana Buddhism contemplates many incarnations and manifestations of the Buddha.

chakra lit., wheel. Energy center in the body.

chuba Tibetan wool tunic.

dakini lit.; "She who goes in the sky." In Tibetan Buddhist practice, a goddess, and, in the largest sense, a symbol of *shunyata*.

Dalai Lama lit., Ocean Teacher. Honorific for the temporal and spiritual leader of Tibet.

deity yoga Form of meditation in which practitioner visualizes self as a deity.

deva Deity.

dharma The teachings of the Buddha and more generally, Buddhist wisdom.

dukkha Usually translated, suffering. Discomfort, unsatisfactoriness.

dzog chen A Tibetan form of Chan Buddhism with methods of rapid enlightenment.

gelukpa Tibetan Buddhist sect headed by the Dalai Lama.

geshe One who has completed advanced study in Tibetan Buddhist teachings.

harijan A member of the untouchable caste.

jataka tales Stories of the Buddha's lives in previous incarnations.

kagyu Sect of Tibetan Buddhism.

Kalachakra Tantric teachings about the cycles of time.

kar sevak Hindu fundamentalist.

Kashag The Tibetan cabinet in exile.

katak A white silk scarf used ceremonially.

kuten lit., physical basis. The medium of the Tibetan oracle.

lam rim Graduated path. Teachings leading to enlightenment.

lama A Tibetan Buddhist sage.

lingkhor Holy walk. A circumambulation path for pilgrims.

Mahayana lit., greater vehicle. Buddhism which emphasizes that nirvana is not to be sought for individual alone. The Buddhism of Tibet is Mahayana.

mala Meditation beads.

mandala A sacred diagram, used in visualization and meditation.

mantra Verbal formula repeated as form of meditation, e.g., Om Mani Padme Hum.

mo-mo Delicious Tibetan pancake.

nadi Energy channel in the body.

nirvana Extinction of desire; freedom from rebirth.

Om Mani Padme Hum A Sanskrit mantra. According to the Dalai Lama, "this is almost our national mantra." The meaning is, "The Jewel in the Lotus." Jewel = thought of enlightenment, Lotus = mind.

Potala The Dalai Lama's winter palace in Lhasa.

prayer wheel A device for mechanically producing a mantra. May take the form of a large cylinder in a temple, or a small handheld cylinder with a handle that is whirled.

rinpoche lit., precious one. Tibetan teacher or master. Often used for tulkus, or reincarnates.

roshi In Zen Buddhism, the head of a monastery.

sakya Sect of Tibetan Buddhism.

samsara World of delusion, i.e., this world.

sangha The community of Buddhist practitioners.

shunyata Emptiness. Important doctrine in Tibetan Buddhism brought over from the teachings of Nagarjuna.

stupa A repository for relics.

tantra, tantras 1. Collection of Hindu texts brought over to Tibet. 2. Practices associated with tantrayana.

tantrayana Esoteric Tibetan Buddhism, advanced meditation teachings, including deity yoga, said to promise speedy enlightenment. Same as vajrayana.

tashe delek Peace unto you. Tibetan greeting.

thangka Tibetan devotional painting on silk scroll.

Thekchen Choeling lit., Island of Mahayana Teaching. Compound in Dharamsala including Dalai Lama's residence, Tsuglakhang, and Institute of Buddhist Dialectics.

Theravada, Theravadan lit., way of the elders. Form of Buddhism practiced in Sri Lanka, Thailand. Emphasizes individual nirvana and focused more on the teachings of the historical Buddha.

tsampa Barley flour.

Tsuglakhang In Lhasa, now in Dharamsala, the Tibetan "central cathedral."

tulku A reincarnate. A highly realized master has the ability to be reborn in whatever body will most help suffering sentient beings.

Tum-mo lit., inner heat. Advanced tantric meditation practice involving control of autonomic processes of the body.

tujaychay Thank you.

Vajradhatu lit., realm of the diamond. Chogyam Trungpa's Tibetan Buddhist community in Boulder, later Halifax.

vajrayana Way of the Vajra, or diamond truth, in Tibetan Buddhism. The same as tantrayana.

vihara A Buddhist monastery in the Theravadan tradition.

vipassana Insight meditation.

yidam A deity visualized in deity yoga.

Plus:

An Afterword
by Rodger Kamenetz
New Orleans, 2007   306

Plus:

AFTERWORD

I wrote *The Jew in the Lotus* to bear witness to a real event, though looking back on it now it sometimes feels like a dream. Dharamsala is a magical place with snow-topped peaks and huge green vistas, Hindu soldiers in khaki and monks in maroon and saffron robes. Against a backdrop of golden Buddhas, I saw a rabbi with a white beard and a Buddhist master with shaved head and bare arms, sharing divine conversation of angels and devas. Was it a dream? Yet Zalman Schachter and Tenzin Gyatso (His Holiness, the Dalai Lama) were also actual persons at an extraordinary intersection of two ancient religions meeting for the first time in recorded history.

The Jew in the Lotus is a spiritual travelogue of an implausible event. The story was received with a great deal of affection and hope. If Jews and Buddhists could overcome their obvious differences and come to a deeper understanding, could this not model other ethnic and religious dialogues? So over time the true story acquired a mythic aura and joined the late '90s zeitgeist. It had the scent of miraculous events to come: the peaceful collapse of the Soviet Union, the liberation of South Africa, and the famous handshake between Arafat and Rabin on the White House lawn. The rise of the Internet, globalization of trade and exchange, and increasing environmental awareness all indicated a new way of thinking and feeling. Old boundaries were being taken down, old enmities resolved, and we looked forward to realizing the highest dreams of humanity as we moved together into a new millennium.

We all know what happened next.

The first American war with Iraq, which loomed as we met in Dharamsala, was followed by a second American war with Iraq, which, at this writing, is still going on. Rabin was assassinated, a new war erupted between Israelis and Palestinians, and the handshake was forgotten. 9/11 happened, motivated by religious extremism. Globalization of communication and trade is inspiring, but globalization of fear and terror is traumatizing. After his first session of dialogue, as we strolled together outside the Dalai Lama's temple,[1] Rabbi Greenberg expressed the concern that "all religion might go down the tubes" if it began to be seen as the cause of violence and war. Now we are seeing it, for in the wake of violent fundamentalism abroad and narrow-minded religious-based politics at home, there is a growing loss of faith in faith itself. In this darker moment, the very beautiful and profound Jewish-Buddhist dialogue may seem to some a charming relic of a lost era.

Yet the story of the Jewish-Buddhist dialogue lives on, because, I think, people can read their own dreams into it. For some it is a magical tale like *The Wizard of Oz;* for

---

1. See Chapter 9, page 110.

Plus: Insights, Interviews, and More

others an all-too-realistic portrait of the Jewish world in miniature, with all its fireworks and seams. For some it is all about the Dalai Lama and Tibetan Buddhism; for others it's a discovery of the hidden treasures of kabbalah or the joys of Jewish renewal. I simply tried to tell the story as I experienced it, very personally, with feelings intact. I had no thought of writing a dispassionate account—because the place where such a dialogue registers most deeply is not in the intellect, but in the heart.

The Tibetan struggle with China was at the forefront of our hearts and minds in 1990 as the Dalai Lama asked the delegation for "the secret of Jewish spiritual survival in exile." The hope the Dalai Lama shared with them, of his own return to the land of Tibet, has been continuously disappointed. The Chinese government has proven tenacious and unyielding, and sometimes it feels as if the Dalai Lama's approach of dialogue and nonviolence has produced few tangible political results. After all, he still lives in exile along with 131,000[2] Tibetans, and Tibet is still not free.

In its homeland, Tibetan religion endures under grave threat. Government forces have a strangle hold on monastic life. John Ackerly, president of the International Campaign for Tibet, reports that the religious oppression in Tibet is "invisible" to many tourists. The

2. See www.savetibet.org/campaigns/refugees/facts.php for more information.

Chinese government has rebuilt the huge monasteries that in the past they destroyed, but every monk is required to forswear allegiance to the Dalai Lama—and must undergo periodic political "education." Any monastic who steps out of line endangers not only himself or herself, but beloved senior teachers. Crimes include publishing a newsletter, peaceful demonstrations, or even praising the Dalai Lama. According to the U.S. State Department report of 2006, "Overall, the level of repression in Tibetan areas remained high and the Government's record of respect for religious freedom remained poor.... Dozens of monks and nuns continued to serve prison terms for their resistance to 'patriotic' or political education." In early October 2005, a twenty-eight-year-old monk was found dead in his room at Drepung Monastery near Lhasa, following "a heated dispute with the monastery's 'work team' over his refusal to denounce the Dalai Lama." Government officials claimed this young man's death was due to natural causes.

The highest level religious figure in captivity is the Panchen Lama, Gendun Chokyi Nyima. After the Dalai Lama recognized him in 1995, the six-year-old boy was put under house arrest in Beijing, making him the world's youngest political prisoner. The Panchen Lama's traditional role is to ratify the next Dalai Lama. But now there are two Panchen Lamas, for the government has chosen their own. It's clear the Chinese are maneuvering to create the next Dalai Lama.

Nonetheless, the Dalai Lama has continued his extraordinary worldwide diplomacy based on religious and intellectual dialogue and has received broad recognition as one of the most inspiring spiritual leaders on the planet. But he is shadowed wherever goes by Chinese diplomats who strenuously protest any hint of official recognition from a foreign government. However, there has been a diplomatic breakthrough. Since 2002 Lodi Gyari, the Dalai Lama's special envoy, has met with Chinese officials four times, most recently in February 2006; he has traveled to Beijing, Lhasa, Shanghai, and Tibetan areas of Yunnan Province. Unfortunately, the pace of the discussion has been agonizing and as of the summer of 2007, there are no new talks scheduled.

In the end, the survival of Tibetan Buddhism cannot depend solely on what goes on at the highest levels of the political and religious hierarchy, but it must also depend on the courage and resourcefulness of the people on the ground in Tibet. Here Rabbi Greenberg's discussion with the Dalai Lama seems entirely relevant. Greenberg emphasized the importance of democratizing religion as one Jewish "secret of spiritual survival." He told the Dalai Lama that after the destruction of the Temple 2000 years ago, the rabbinic sages retired to the hinterlands, raised many students, and gave more responsibility to individuals and householders. In today's Tibet, something similar has been going on.

In eastern Tibet, near Serthar,[3] a highly respected teacher, Jigme Phuntsok—known by his title, "Khenpo" or abbot,—created a less formal teaching institution that for a time escaped the scrutiny of the government.

At Larung Gar—"gar" means "encampment"—instead of only focusing on producing a few teachers at the highest levels, as in traditional monasteries, "Khenpo" trained a large group of paraprofessional monks in the essentials of Tibetan Buddhism and then sent them back to their villages to teach. Founded in 1980 with fewer than one hundred students, by 2002 Larung Gar had over 8,000, including several thousand Chinese Buddhists.

After a visit to the Dalai Lama in 1990, Khenpo came under increasing attack. A charismatic teacher, his travel privileges were revoked in 1994, and in 1998 he was interrogated three times by the Central Government's Religious Bureau.

Alarmed by his popularity with both Tibetans and Chinese, in the summer and autumn of 2001, government "work teams" forcibly expelled 7,000 students, including 3,000 nuns. After Khenpo's death in 2004, access to Larung Gar was limited, and in 2006, eighty-three homes built around the encampment were destroyed.

---

3. Serthar is in western Sichuan Province, outside the TAR (Tibetan Autonomous Region) as defined by the Chinese government. However, the Tibetan exile community considers it part of the traditional Tibetan province of Kham.

The story of Larung Gar has a gloomy ending, but if there's a silver lining, it's the indication of a growing Chinese interest in Buddhism. According to John Ackerly, thousands of Chinese Buddhists head to Tibet each year, and thousands already live and study Buddhism in Tibet. "It does offer some hope. It's actually quite extensive, including some communist party members, sons and daughters of influential leaders who are Tibetan Buddhist."

When young Chinese tourists flock to the rebuilt monasteries in and near Lhasa, they may not be seeing the real thing, but their thirst for spiritual values is evident. Buddhism is historically the most important connection between Tibet and the people of China and may bring the two parties closer in the future.

In the meantime, those who wish the Dalai Lama well can continue to support the Tibetan cause financially and politically. We can play a very positive part as the negotiations between China and the Dalai Lama's representatives continue. We can contribute to the International Campaign for Tibet (www.savetibet.org), and remind our representatives in Washington of our support for the Tibetan hopes in their dialogue with the Chinese government.

These days "tikkun olam" ("repair of the world") is a pragmatic Jewish response to injustice or need. Almost immediately on her return from Dharamsala, Blu Greenberg practiced tikkun by fostering a visit of Tibetan educators to Jewish summer camps, and in another program, to Jewish day schools. Both visits proved helpful. The educators were very impressed by the warm informal relationships between teachers and students, as contrasted with the traditional formality of religious instruction conducted by Tibetans.

As word of the dialogue spread, the Dalai Lama was warmly received by major Jewish organizations across the spectrum of denominations, who also called openly for political support of the Tibetan cause. For instance, the Religious Action Committee of Reform Judaism, headed by Rabbi David Saperstein in Washington, D.C., hosted a special seder for Tibet in the spring of 1997. I'd borrowed the idea from the Tibetan seder proposed by Rabbi Schachter on the way to Dharamsala. The event was attended by members of Congress, Supreme Court Justice Stephen Breyer, and other dignitaries, as well as Adam Yauch of the Beastie Boys.

At the seder, I sat beside His Holiness, who wore a black yarmulke and expressed real zest for matzah. As the four questions were recited by several kids, we called to mind the captive Panchen Lama, who that week was celebrating his eighth birthday in an unknown location. My daughter Kezia read from the diary of Anne Frank, and we listened to a recording smuggled out of Tibet of a song of freedom. We heard the quavering voice of Phuntsok Nyidron, a brave Buddhist nun first imprisoned in 1989 at the age of nineteen. Because of this smuggled recording, her sentence was extended. In addition to singing a song of freedom, her other "crime" was chanting, "Long live the Dalai Lama." She was only released in 2004, having undergone brutal torture. Since that first seder in Washington, seders for Tibet have been celebrated in Hillels and synagogues across the country. In the seder Jews remember their own struggle for freedom. By joining that memory of the past with the current struggles for religious freedom in Tibet, I believe we honor the tradition and strengthen the bonds between Jews and Tibetans.[4]

One of the Dalai Lama's hopes in meeting with Jews in India was to foster a trip to Israel. In Dharamsala, Paul Mendes-Flohr was approached by several Tibetan officials to see what could be arranged, and when he returned to Israel, he helped found Israeli Friends of the Tibetan people (Yativ), an organization that has facilitated the visit of Tibetans to Israel to study in educational institutions, mostly in the fields of technology and agriculture. (See www.tibet.org.il/)

Since March 1994, His Holiness has visited Israel three times. He has drawn large, enthusiastic crowds, and according to Professor Mendes-Flohr, Buddhist studies have become extremely popular in Israeli universities. (Dharamsala is also frequented

---

4. A full account of the seder with the Dalai Lama, and also an earlier seder I helped lead in Dharamsala can be found in Chapter 26 and the Afterword of my book, *Stalking Elijah*.

by Israeli travelers now, so much so there are street signs in Hebrew.) Before the dialogue in 1990, Yitz and Blu Greenberg were roundly criticized by some in the Orthodox community for meeting with an "idolator." So when Yitz joked with His Holiness about appointing him "Chief Rabbi of Israel," he probably could not have imagined that in February 2006, the Dalai Lama would be personally received in Jerusalem by both the Ashkenazia and Sephardi Chief Rabbis. At that meeting the Ashkenazi Chief Rabbi, Yona Metzger, called for the establishment of "a religious United Nations" representing the religious leaders of all the countries in the world— with the Dalai Lama at its head.

The dialogue was also noticed widely in the Asian world, Professor Nathan Katz reminded me recently. Katz is now professor of religious studies at Florida International University and directs the new Center for Spirituality there. Since Dharamsala, he cofounded and co-edits the Journal of Indo-Judaic Studies and has published a book on the Jews of India. From Katz's perspective, the dialogue with the Dalai Lama anticipated a much wider trend, which he characterized as a "reorientation." "Jews are realizing their religion is Asian; Israel is realizing it's Asian." He cited as one recent development, a visit by the same Chief Rabbi Metzger to India for a conference with Hindu swamis. That's not a development we might have dreamed on the way to Dharamsala, but Dharamsala clearly made it possible.

The story of the dialogue with the Dalai Lama has had a very large and lasting effect on the spiritual life of the Jewish community, especially in North America. It led Jews to reassess their religion in a new way, and to try to find Jewish answers to the very profound Buddhist questions the Tibetan master was asking. His interest in Jewish techniques for "overcoming afflictive states of mind," and his affirmation of the esoteric, helped inspire an explosion of interest in Jewish meditation and kabbalah and Jewish renewal. The Dalai Lama's advice that Jews should make their esoteric traditions more widely available was taken deeply to heart. Kabbalah and meditation, which were once seen as highly esoteric matters, have been embraced by the mainstream, and have even become commonplace. Rabbi Jonathan Omer-Man, who seemed like a lonely advocate for meditation in 1990, says now that "fifteen years ago, I was ten years ahead of my time." He has retired from Metivta, but praises new organizations and teachers devoted to teaching Jewish meditation, among them Chochmat Halev in Berkeley. Rabbi Rachel Cowan heads up the Institute for Jewish Spirituality, which sponsors meditation training and retreats for rabbis and cantors. Rabbi Joy Levitt was moved by her personal experiences with meditation to create Makom, a Jewish meditation center housed in the Manhattan JCC, the institution she now serves as executive director. Another who has discovered the value of sitting quietly is the ebullient Moshe Wal-doks, who is, in fact, now Rabbi Moshe Waldoks of Temple Beth Zion in Brookline. On his return trip from Dharamsala, during a long conversation with Zalman Schachter, he first committed himself to being a rabbi after years as a vagabond scholar. "The discussion gave me the courage to come out as someone not affiliated with any one denomination. Our trip demonstrated the possibility of the denominations melting away into something much more organic and real."

Jewish Renewal, which I found to be a meaningful response to the call to bring the esoteric to life within the heart of Jewish practice, is now extremely well organized as "Aleph" (www.aleph.org). Its active training programs are raising up a new generation of renewal rabbis and leaders, all under the watchful eye of Rabbi Zalman Schachter-Shalomi, whose amazing energy and mystical erudition continue to inspire. After moving to Boulder in 1995 to assume the Wisdom Chair at the Naropa Institute (America's only Buddhist university), Reb Zalman retired in 2004, but is still very ac-tive at age eighty-three. The spirit of Jewish Renewal has energized Judaism from one end of the spectrum to the other.

Blu Greenberg remains at the forefront of the movement to reconcile feminism and Orthodox Judaism, and in 1997 cofounded and served as first president of JOFA, the Jewish Orthodox Feminist Alliance. Rabbi Irving Greenberg is currently president of the Jewish Life Network, well known in Jewish circles for its "birthright Israel" program. From 2000–2002, Greenberg served as chairman of the United States Holocaust Memorial Council. He continues to write and think about dialogue especially between Jews and Christians.

The most extensive new commitment to aid Tibetans has come from the chief organizer of the dialogue, my old friend, Dr. Marc Lieberman. In 1995 he created the Tibet Vision Project, with the main purpose of bringing advanced sight-saving eye care to rural Tibet, where it was sadly lacking. As he personally told the Dalai Lama shortly after the project began, "When you do return to Tibet—I want the Tibetans to be able to see you."

The problem was great: large numbers of Tibetans living in rural areas suffer blindness due to cataracts. It's a problem exacerbated by high altitude exposure to ultraviolet radiation. Rural Tibet lacked facilities, equipment, or surgeons trained in modern techniques. With his usual energy and fervor, Lieberman has visited Tibet twice a year for the past twelve years. He found doctors and nurses to train and hospitals in which to work, and raised funds to supply modern medical instruments and supplies. Operating under difficult conditions, he and his team have performed miracles—in one three-day stretch his Tibetan surgeons reached the magic Buddhist number of 108 operations. His lasting contribution to Tibet has been to raise up from scratch a team of highly skilled native Tibetan eye surgeons. Their work, and the doctors they will train in the future, ensures that Lieberman's project will be a perpetual gift to Tibet.

Lieberman sees the Tibet Vision Project as the best answer to his old puzzle about Jewish roots and Buddhist wings. After the dialogue in Dharamsala, he says, "I no longer felt the need to resolve a conflict of identities. I just needed to integrate who I was. His Holiness inspires the comprehension that one can be engaged in the world but not of the world, and that is where my heart wanted to go."

Call what he's doing tikkun olam or Buddhist compassion: either way, the results can be seen (at www.tibetvision.org) on the smiling faces of Tibetan men and women who experience "the indescribable joy of seeing once again." Equally moving to me are the words of an old peasant, blind for decades, who had his sight restored. After the bandages were removed, he told Lieberman, simply, "Now I can see the road ahead of me."

As for my own road, I can say the dialogue also opened my eyes and lifted my horizons. I remain deeply impressed by the power of Tibetan Buddhist practice for transformation, so evident in the many Buddhist practitioners I've met and in the person and teachings of the Dalai Lama, whom Lieberman calls aptly this "great four-dimensional mensch." But I did not become a Buddhist. I was led to ask, what is there in Judaism like this? I explored long lost Jewish meditative practices from leading teachers in the U.S. in

Stalking Elijah, which received the National Jewish Book Award in 1997. Two years later, Laurel Chiten's documentary film *The Jew in the Lotus* was broadcast on PBS, spreading the word of the dialogue even further.

Simple sitting meditation for me was a great beginning, but in time I became even more fascinated with the way Tibetans used images for inner transformation. At first this seemed one area where Judaism and Tibetan Buddhism had little in common, but a remark Reb Zalman made[5] in the Library of Tibetan Works and Archives planted a seed. As we looked at a three-dimensional display of a complex Buddhist visualization, he likened it to the visionary journey of the *merkavah* mystics, also known as the chariot riders. Could some remnant of ancient Jewish visualization practice have survived? I found the first clue in Jerusalem in the summer of 1995, working with Madame Colette, a teacher of healing imagery with family roots in the old kabbalah of Gerona. From visualization, I was led to dreams: in 2000, I met a suave Tibetan master of dream yoga in Copenhagen, Tarab Tulku. Then nearer to home, I found Marc Bregman, a crusty, wholly American dream teacher living in northern Vermont.

For the past six years I've been exploring with him the oldest spiritual technology on the planet, the dream. It's a technology cultivated in a different way by Tibetans. But I think with the heritage of Jacob's lad-

---

5. See Chapter 14, page 173.

der, Jews can also claim to be a people of the dream. For me it's a return to the simple roots of all religious experience, and to the stories of dreamers in Genesis.

It is not an entirely easy path, but its power and simplicity move me deeply. The encounter with Tibetan Buddhism, with its rich imagery, helped me see what had been missing. Religions of the world need imagination and soul, and dreams nourish them both. But that's a story for another day, another book, *The History of Last Night's Dream.*

These days, the dialogue feels like a dream that was also real. I remember still that beautiful Friday night on a mountain slope in Dharamsala, an evening shared with exiled monks and lamas of Tibet.[6] Rabbi Joy Levitt led us in the psalm of Shabbat. It was the psalm Rabbi Greenberg had mentioned the day before. The Dalai Lama remarked, "So, it's a visualization." So it was. After we sang softly, "When God returned us to Zion from exile, we thought we were dreaming," the monks answered us with a dedication prayer. Our Hebrew kissed their Tibetan as we said farewell.

Shabbat Shalom. Tashe Delek.

Was it all a dream, or was it real?

The answer is, yes.

—New Orleans, 2007

---

6. See Chapter 10, page 126.

RODGER KAMENETZ is the author of the National Jewish Book Award-winning *Stalking Elijah* and *A History of Last Night's Dream*. He has written five books of poetry, including *The Lowercase Jew*, and he has been called "the most formidable of the Jewish-American poets." His memoir, *Terra Infirma*, has been described as "the most beautiful book ever written about a mother and son."

Kamenetz is professor in the department of English and in the department of philosophy and religious studies at Louisiana State University in Baton Rouge. He is the founding director of the MFA program in Creative Writing, and also the founding director of the Jewish Studies Program. He holds a B.A. from Yale College and graduate degrees from Johns Hopkins and Stanford Universities.